After Jackie

**Fifteen Pioneers Who Helped
Change the Face of Baseball**

After Jackie

Fifteen Pioneers Who Helped Change the Face of Baseball

by

Jeffrey S. Copeland

Paragon House

First Edition 2022
Published in the United States by
Paragon House
www.ParagonHouse.com

Jackie Robinson cover photo used courtesy of Mile High Auction Company and Ben Gassaway, Auction Coordinator.

Cover Design by Brock Swarbrick

Library of Congress Cataloging-in-Publication Data

Names: Copeland, Jeffrey S. (Jeffrey Scott), 1953- author.
Title: After Jackie : fifteen pioneers who helped change the face of
   baseball / by Jeffrey S. Copeland.
Description: First edition | Saint Paul, MN : Paragon House, 2021. |
   Includes bibliographical references. | Summary: "Most people know the
   story of Jackie Robinson and his courage and struggles when breaking the
   color barrier in Major League Baseball. However, Jackie was the pioneer
   for only one of the sixteen teams in Major League Baseball at the time.
   What about the "other fifteen" pioneers? These are their accounts. While
   they faced many of the same hurdles and roadblocks as Jackie, each had
   individual twists and turns in his journey pioneering great change in
   race relations in baseball and American society. Mr. Robinson took the
   field for the Brooklyn Dodgers in April of 1947, but it wasn't until
   twelve years later that the last team added a person of color (Pumpsie
   Green, in 1959, for the Boston Red Sox)"-- Provided by publisher.
Identifiers: LCCN 2021015048 (print) | LCCN 2021015049 (ebook) | ISBN
   9781557789488 (paperback) | ISBN 9781610831291 (ebook)
Subjects: LCSH: African American baseball players--Biography. |
   Discrimination in sports--United States.
Classification: LCC GV865.A1 C655 2021 (print) | LCC GV865.A1 (ebook) |
   DDC 796.357092/2 [B]--dc23
LC record available at https://lccn.loc.gov/2021015048
LC ebook record available at https://lccn.loc.gov/2021015049

Manufactured in the United States of America   10 9 8 7 6 5 4 3 2 1

For my dad,
who took me to Sportsman's Park in St. Louis where
I fell in love with baseball,
and for my Uncle Doug,
who introduced me to the joy of sitting in the bleachers
at old Busch Stadium

Contents

Foreword

I BECAME A BASEBALL FAN, more specifically a St. Louis Cardinals fan, in the mid-1960s. It was the perfect time for a young baseball fan in St. Louis to fall in love with the game. The Cardinals appeared in three World Series that decade, winning twice, including a Series victory over the Yankees in 1964. By then, every major league team had been integrated. My Cardinal heroes were Bob Gibson and Lou Brock, both Hall of Famers. There was also Bill White, who went on to become President of the National League, and Curt Flood, whose legal battle against baseball led to free agency. Gibson, Brock, White, and Flood were a pretty impressive group. One Cardinal that I wasn't familiar with until long after his playing days was Tom Alston, the first Black Cardinals player. Several years ago, as a TV reporter in St Louis, I was assigned to do a story on Alston, which included a trip to the St. Louis Cardinals Hall of Fame. I was born in 1954, the year Alston became the franchise's first African American player. As you'll learn in this book, all of the "firsts" had to put up with difficult experiences because of the racial climate of the time. In Alston's case, there was even more to overcome: mental illness. Alston heard voices and was constantly fatigued, affecting his ability to play ball. Alston set a church on fire for no reason. He attempted suicide. As a Cardinals fan, I couldn't believe that I had never heard his story. When you read Jeff Copeland's book, you may have the same reaction, over and over, as you hear the stories behind these pioneers.

Art Holliday
TV and Radio Broadcaster
St. Louis, Missouri and Nationally

Author Note

FROM LARRY DOBY TO PUMPSIE GREEN, the men in this book all contributed in special and individual ways as they built upon the changes initiated by Jackie Robinson's groundbreaking work. This was a multiple-front struggle, spanning everywhere from baseball to society at large; therefore, change came very slowly. To complicate matters, motivations for helping with the changes weren't always the same. In the Dodger organization, individuals believed knocking down the color barrier was the right thing to do. Other organizations, like the St. Louis Browns, had financial motivations and thought adding persons of color would help them stay solvent. Still others—like Boston, Detroit, and the Philadelphia Athletics—faced strong pressure and threats of boycotts from multiple groups if they didn't take action. Whatever the reasons each team had at the time, all eventually realized these were just first steps.

It was twelve years from the time Jackie took the field for the Dodgers before Pumpsie did the same for the Boston Red Sox. *Twelve years.* However, Mr. Green's appearance in 1959 wasn't an act of closure. It didn't mean the struggle ended. To the contrary, the pioneering work of these men built the foundations, but it would still take extraordinary acts and resolve to right injustices and make baseball, and the world, more inclusive.

As the national pastime, baseball has a special responsibility to provide leadership and *example through action* to help continue the fight for respect and equality. One manner of demonstrating baseball's resolve takes place every year on April 15, a date which has now been designated as "Jackie Robinson Day" throughout Major League Baseball. This day commemorates the date in 1947 when Jackie took the field for the Brooklyn Dodgers and changed baseball and the world forever. On this special day, members of all teams across baseball wear Jackie's "42" uniform number to honor the memory of his accomplishments and legacy.

At the same time, organizations in and around baseball recognize the milestone work done by the "other fifteen" and are spotlighting their contributions in special ways. The Chicago White Sox have added a statue of Minnie Minoso in a place of honor at their ballpark. The Cincinnati Reds recently added a statue of Chuck Harmon just outside the entrance of their Urban Youth Academy. Larry Doby's statue greets visitors at the main entrance of Cleveland's home stadium. The Chicago Cubs placed a statue of Ernie Banks just outside Wrigley Field. The St. Louis Cardinals have placed a commemorative plaque honoring Tom Alston in the walkway near the west entrance of Busch Stadium III, right next to the iconic statue of Stan Musial. Other memorials have been dedicated, or are currently in the works, to commemorate the accomplishments and contributions of the "other fifteen" to help keep their legacies alive.

The men and their achievements included here are not intended in any way to discount or discredit the important contributions made much earlier by such individuals as Moses Fleetwood Walker, credited by many as the first African American to play in Major League Baseball in the late 19th Century and Luis Castro, who played for the Philadelphia Athletics in 1902—and others who played such a vital, early role in setting the stage for change. Rather, the focus here is kept on the pioneering accomplishments of players from baseball's modern era. Hopefully, additional studies will be made of the lives and careers of those who played and paved the way for others in earlier days.

Finally, the chapters that follow are structured as they are by design—each one in three segments—in order to provide a more detailed representation of the lives and careers of these pioneers.

Each chapter begins with a section describing the individual's early life and his path to the Major Leagues. This is followed by an account of a scene (or scenes) representative of a milestone moment in his career to help the reader understand the complexity of his journey. Each of these scenes is based on details gathered from interviews, oral histories, biographical/autobiographical accounts, and box scores and news reports in order to keep them as close to the actual events as possible. Finally, I present a summary of the player's life after baseball. All three sections blend together to present the challenges and the groundbreaking work of the "other fifteen" men who stepped forward to help change not just a sport, but a nation. Their legacies continue to inspire us.

— JSC

Introduction: "The Other Fifteen"

On Tuesday, April 15, 1947, Jackie Roosevelt Robinson stepped onto Ebbets Field, the home park for the Brooklyn Dodgers of the National League, and forever changed baseball. The first person of color to play in a Major League Baseball game in the modern era, Jackie faced discrimination and challenges that have been well-documented through the years. By some estimates, no fewer than a thousand books and scholarly/historical pieces—and everything from comic books to plays to movies—have been written about his milestone journey as he helped tear down the color barrier. Jackie's accomplishments have become part of the very fabric not just of baseball, but of our society at large as he continues to represent just how powerful the contributions of one person can be in changing the world.

However, Jackie was the pioneer for only *one* of the sixteen teams in Major League Baseball at the time, eight each in the National and American Leagues. What about the other fifteen? Far fewer pieces have been written about the groundbreakers for the other fifteen teams, and much of what has been written about them has typically been statistical and chronological descriptions and accounts of their careers. While they faced many of the same hurdles and roadblocks placed in front of Jackie, each also had individual twists and turns in his unique journey.

What most had in common were very specific expectations. *All* were expected to be in most ways, and especially on the ball field, *exactly like* Jackie Robinson. Fans, sportswriters, members of team ownership, and even teammates thought they'd be welcoming players of extraordinary talent who would change the nature of their teams and the level of play. However, there was only one Jackie Robinson, so when many of the "other fifteen" showed up in the dugout, disappointment greeted them when their skills didn't match Jackie's. Some were outstanding players in their own right and did improve their teams, both on the field and in intangible ways. However, unfulfilled expectations led even the great Hall of Fame manager Casey Stengel to say to reporters after Elston Howard joined his team and broke the color barrier for the Yankees, "I finally get [one], and he can't run." Stengel no doubt made his comments because Jackie ran the bases with wild abandon, driving other teams to distraction and often altering the course of a game with his raw speed alone. How many players could measure up to that and Jackie's other skills? The "shadow of Jackie Robinson" was cast upon most of the "other fifteen," a shadow that was, at times, both a blessing and a curse. In walking through the door Jackie opened, these men faced comparisons and pressures in an already complicated, and often volatile, situation.

On and off the field, these pioneers faced many of same discriminatory practices and roadblocks that had been placed in front of Jackie. In just one such example, Jackie was not allowed to stay with the rest of his Dodger teammates in the Chase Park Plaza Hotel in St. Louis, Missouri, when they were in town to play the St. Louis Cardinals. The "other fifteen" discovered the same state and local laws and special ordinances restricted them while on road trips with their teams. Sometimes, lodging would be found for them in hotels in other parts of town where persons of color were welcome. Other times, "host families" were found in African American neighborhoods. No matter what arrangements were made, the individuals found themselves isolated from the team "community." Even when they joined their teams, with few exceptions, they were not assigned roommates during the alternate living arrangements.

Separate lodging arrangements were only the beginning of the discrimination these men had in common with Jackie. Whether on the road or in the towns where they played, they were often refused admittance to restaurants where their teammates were dining. This prevented them from participating in the camaraderie and team building being fostered on such occasions. The same exclusion held true in many movie theaters and other entertainment venues. They were literally alone—and often experienced boredom, loneliness, and bitterness at a time when they were asked to jump into games and immediately show what they could bring to the field. This added another layer of difficulty to the challenges they faced.

In short, their baseball worlds were a microcosm of the discrimination found throughout society at large, and change in these areas would be slow to come. Some teams did fight to end these practices, at least as much as they could within their own circumstances. For instance, the New York Yankees started refusing to stay at hotels where Elston Howard could not be given lodging with the rest of the team. Members of the Boston Red Sox team once walked out of a restaurant *en masse* when Pumpsie Green was refused service. However, actions such as these were isolated.

During those times when the "other fifteen" *were* with their teammates, many, like Jackie, did not receive warm welcomes. In a typical example, when Hank Thompson showed up to the St. Louis Brown's dugout, breaking the color barrier for that franchise in July of 1947, several on the team turned their backs to him and refused to shake his hand. One teammate even refused to play on the same field as Thompson and, while cursing loudly, left the stadium that day in protest. However, some players went out of their way to welcome their new teammates. For instance, Pee Wee Reese stood up for Jackie Robinson at a time when support was badly needed. Ted Williams was among the first to welcome Pumpsie Green to the Red Sox and help him get involved with the team. Stan Musial immediately befriended Tom Alston when he joined the St. Louis Cardinals and helped him acclimate to the Major Leagues, both on and off the field. However, such kindness and mentoring were more often the exception rather than the rule.

Many faced other complications right from the start, making their own journeys even more difficult. For players like Minnie Minoso and Carlos Paula, the language barrier caused one complication after another often leading to even greater discrimination and challenges. In the case of Carlos Paula, sportswriters chose to mock his lack of proficiency with English, quoting him through exaggerated, phonetic representations of his responses to their questions. This made him come across as cartoonish and the worst of stereotypes. Minnie Minoso faced much of the same, often having his words distorted to fit agendas of writers, causing him to appear stupid to fans, which couldn't have been further from the truth. For these players and others who had come to the United States from other countries to play baseball, not only did they face discrimination, they had to do so while not knowing how to communicate well with their managers, teammates, and the press. Misunderstandings and miscommunications abounded, severely hampering their ability to advance their careers. At the same time, because of the international tie-ins and bridges created through these men—everywhere from Cuba to the Dominican Republic to Puerto Rico and other points of the globe—many other opportunities opened for those who followed them. Thus, they were important pioneers in this regard as well.

It should also be mentioned that some of these men were *reluctant* pioneers who at first didn't want to be brought up to the Major Leagues. Ernie Banks was one such player. When the Chicago Cubs organization purchased his contract, he was playing for the Kansas City Monarchs of the Negro Leagues and enjoying his time there alongside future Major Leaguers Gene Baker and Elston Howard and being taught the intricacies of the game by Negro League legend

Buck O'Neil. Ernie was initially not at all happy he had to move on. Pumpsie Green grew up on the West Coast before Major League Baseball expanded that direction, so he knew very little about the teams and players in the National and American Leagues. While growing up, he followed the Oakland Oaks of the Pacific Coast League and said many times he'd have been perfectly happy remaining in California and building a career with that team. After being promoted to Washington's big club, Carlos Paula almost immediately missed the way the game was played in Cuba where he had grown up and he had many problems adjusting to the different style of play in the States. Bob Trice, while playing for the Philadelphia Athletics, never did fully adjust to the pace and style of play in the Major Leagues and eventually asked to be sent back to the minors. Many of these groundbreakers were building outstanding careers in leagues other than the Major Leagues when their contracts were purchased, and then suddenly found themselves in a different system entirely. For these men, the change was dramatic and emotional. Some adjusted and rose quickly through the new ranks. Others found the transition difficult if not insurmountable.

Each chapter that follows tells the story of the first person of color who played for each of the Major League Baseball teams—an integration that spanned a period of twelve years. In the end, while Jackie and the "other fifteen" had many experiences and challenges in common, most of these men came from very different backgrounds, traveled different paths, and had to learn for themselves individual ways to navigate the hurdles before them. Like Jackie Robinson, they are pioneers who helped change not just baseball, but the world at large. What follows are their stories, some poignant, some humorous, some full of drama and conflict but, in the end, all are historical accounts that inspire and inform us as we continue to build upon their legacies.

Larry Doby

Cleveland Indians

Larry Doby with his 1947 Cleveland Indians teammates
(Larry middle row, 2nd from right).

Larry Doby was born in Camden, South Carolina, but spent his formative years in Peterson, New Jersey, where he excelled as a three-sport, All-State athlete. Basketball was his first love, but when he was seventeen a scout for the Newark Eagles of the Negro National League saw him star in several high school games and coaxed him into signing his first professional contract. At the end of his second season with the Eagles, he was drafted into the U.S. Navy and served in the Pacific Theater during World War II. Following his discharge, Larry returned to the Eagles for three seasons, developing his skills and earning a reputation as an outstanding fielder and powerful hitter who was especially tough and competitive in tight game situations. Word of his prowess on the diamond spread, and three months after Jackie Robinson stepped on the field for the Brooklyn Dodgers, Larry Doby, at age twenty-three, became the second player to break the color barrier in modern Major League Baseball history. When he took the field for the Cleveland Indians the evening of July 5, 1947, he became the first player to move right from the Negro Leagues to the Majors and the first to play in the American League.

However, events before and during that first game also foreshadowed the challenges that were ahead for him. As his manager, Lou Boudreau, introduced him to his teammates before the game, three refused to shake his hand and several others turned their backs as he made his way to his locker. When it was time for pre-game warm-ups, nobody stepped forward to play catch with him. In the top of the seventh inning when he finally got into the game as a pinch hitter, he tried too hard to make an impression, striking out on a ball thrown nearly over his head. Bill Veeck, the Indians owner, invited Larry into his office after the game, asked him to sit down, visited with him for over an hour, and told him he was there to stay. And stay he did, building a career that was beyond his wildest dreams.

….. ….. …..

April 21, 1948
Little Rock, Arkansas

"Land sakes, Mister! Ain't you never been on a horse before?" asked Jimmy Davis, the twelve-year-old son of the host family Larry Doby had spent the late afternoon and night with the day before. "You gotta give him a little kick to get 'em goin'. Don't you know nothin'?"

Larry stared down at the boy, grimacing. "First time. And if I have my way, it'll be the last. Just get me going." He gripped the reins tightly. "But first, tell me something. How do you steer one of these things?"

Larry was a sight to behold—sitting stiffly upright in the saddle and in full uniform, with "Indians" emblazoned in bold, red script across his chest.

"Ain't like no Indian I ever seen in the pictures. That for sure," Jimmy laughed.

Before Larry could respond, Jimmy smacked the ancient, sway-backed plow horse on the rump, and it slowly started clomping down the uneven gravel road. "Hold on, Mister! And don't fall off!"

Larry clutched the reins tighter and shouted, "Now what do I do?"

Jimmy laughed again and yelled back, "You might try prayin'!" The young boy leaned against an oak tree and watched as Larry squirmed and lightly flicked the reins against the horse's mane. "He's called Zeus! Likes it if you talk 'em up!"

Larry turned back one last time and asked, "How long will it take me to get back to town this way?"

Jimmy just waved. "'Bout a week," he said to himself.

....

The day before, on the journey back home from Cleveland's spring training camp in Tucson, Arizona, the team pulled into Little Rock, Arkansas, for a quick stopover to play an exhibition game against a local semi-pro team. The club set up these games as "goodwill" endeavors, but the players hated them. They longed for the regular season to start and couldn't wait to get back and settled into their homes, rooming houses, or hotels where they would live in Cleveland during the season. Still, the exhibitions did provide one last opportunity for game-speed practice and shaking off the winter rust before the team stepped onto the field for games that counted. So, understanding why they were needed, players tolerated these games.

That afternoon, just after the bus dropped the team off at the Albert Pike hotel in the heart of downtown Little Rock, Larry Doby's manager, Lou Boudreau, called him off to the side as the players made their way to the front entrance.

When they were out of earshot of the others, Lou stopped, looked down, kicked at the well-manicured grass just off the main sidewalk, and said, almost in a whisper, "Look, Doby, um, it's like this. I don't like it myself, but there's laws in this town that say you can't stay here with us." He finally looked Doby in the eye. "Listen, Jackie Robinson does this all the time when Brooklyn's on the road."

Larry stared at him, blankly at first, but then the full meaning of Lou's words hit him. He shook his head. "Doesn't make it right."

"I know that . . . but, this is cracker country and . . .." Lou's voice trailed off. "The mayor here stepped in when Lankford, our new traveling secretary, made the reservations. Mayor said we have to play by their rules. We're not the home team here, if you know what I mean."

"I know *exactly* what you mean," Larry said, staring briefly at the hotel.

"There isn't anything I can do about it."

Larry felt he had gotten to know his manager quite well and appreciated the support he had shown right from the start. The night of his first game in his rookie season, and for weeks after, nobody would play catch with Larry in pre-game warm-ups. Lou finally noticed this before Larry's third game, grabbed an old glove the equipment man had stored away, motioned Larry out to the field, and started playing long-toss with him. He continued that before every game from then on until Joe Gordon, their regular second baseman, stepped in one night and said he'd take over. Lou even made the time to visit with Larry immediately after games, whether they won or lost, whether Larry had done well or had a rough day, so he wouldn't have to sit by himself in front of his locker while the others showered. His teammates had made it clear he wasn't welcome in there until the last of them toweled off. Lou had always been there when times got rough—but the problems, the insults, just kept coming.

"Lankford has it all set up for you. He found a host family who'll take you in. Out in the country north of town. Lots of fresh air. I'm sure you'll be eating better than we will." He waved his arms. "And you won't have all this noise of the city to wake you up while you're in the sack."

"Don't mind the noise, Skip," Larry responded.

A long, uncomfortable silence followed. Both men fidgeted, Lou looking repeatedly at his watch, and Larry bending down to tie his right shoe lace over and over. Lou finally broke the silence when he saw the traveling secretary walking back to the bus.

"Lankford!" Lou called out. When Ralph Lankford turned around, Lou motioned for him to come over.

When Ralph got to them and before he could speak, Lou said, "I've just been telling Larry about the arrangements, but I'm a little fuzzy about the details. Look, Larry can't go inside the hotel, so I want you to explain everything to him."

Ralph looked at Larry only briefly before turning to face Lou. "It's like I said. He'll be driven out to the Davis place. It's only seven or eight miles out. I hear it's a wonderful family. Wife supposedly a good cook. Sounds fine to me." He looked at this watch and asked, "What's the problem?"

Lou cleared his throat and pointed at the hotel. "You sure there's no way to get Larry inside?"

"Positive. Can't do it," Ralph said, a little too loudly, his voice clipped.

Larry finally spoke. "Don't like it."

Ralph cut him off. "See that taxi stand on the corner. Let's go over there. I'll give him the address and tell him the team will pay the fare. Nothing to worry about. We'll keep your suitcase. Take your uniform with you and change tomorrow before coming to the park. Apparently, they have other rules about the park, too."

"Guess it has to be done. I'm sorry," said Lou, giving Larry a quick pat on the shoulder.

Larry picked up his small suitcase, handed it to Lankford and, without looking back, started walking slowly to the corner.

"Make sure he gets there, Ralph. This is bad enough already." Lou didn't try to hide his frustration.

Ralph Lankford shielded his eyes from the sun and said, defensiveness in his tone, "I'll do my job." He turned and followed Larry to the taxi stand.

….. ….. ……

Mrs. Davis' home cooking and the warmth and hospitality of the Davis family did much to lighten Larry's mood, but he still felt the sting of being separated from his team. After a restless night's sleep, Larry woke to a new dilemma. Although Lankford truly had found a fine host family for Larry, he had also forgotten one small detail: making the arrangements to get Larry back to town to rejoin the team.

So, now here he was, riding a horse, trying to make it on time to an exhibition game in which he was to start in center field. Manager Boudreau seldom lost his temper, but he had rules that were not to be broken. The foremost of these, the one he spent the most time dwelling upon, was not to be late for team meetings or games. For nearly a mile, Larry had these thoughts in his head as he tried everything to get Zeus to move faster—flicking the reins harder, kicking his feet back against the horse's rump, and even slapping him on the neck. Nothing got his message across. Zeus plodded along, never more than ten feet or so in a straight line, so Larry had to keep urging him back and forth. No cars passed, and he hadn't seen a single farm anywhere on the horizon. Shaking his head, he muttered, "Now I know where 'The Middle of Nowhere' is."

As Zeus slowly crested a small rise in the road, Larry noticed up ahead a car parked just off the shoulder of the rough road. As he made his way closer, he could see a Black family of six, all standing by the car in the shade of a large tree. The father was wearing a clerical collar.

The youngest child, a boy Larry guessed to be about five or six, called out, "Hi, there! We need help!" The mother, a tall, slim woman who looked to be in her late thirties, appeared embarrassed and quickly pulled her son behind her.

"What is it? What's the matter?" Larry yelled back. Zeus wasn't going to speed up, so Larry yanked his foot from the stirrup, swung his leg over the saddle, and tried dismounting while Zeus ambled ahead. As his feet touched the uneven gravel, Larry lost his balance and down he went, a loud rip up the left side of his uniform pants following.

The man ran over and helped Larry back to his feet. "Young man—are you OK? That was quite a fall!"

Larry dusted himself off. "I'm fine, Sir. My pride hurt is all— and I guess these pants." He pointed to the rip, which ran from his waist down to his knee. "I'm not used to horses."

At that moment, he looked up and saw Zeus continuing his march down the road. He started to call out, but the man yelled to his oldest boy, "Samuel—go get him. Now!" Turning to Larry, he extended his hand and said, "I'm Reverend Jackson. Joshua

Jackson. This is my family—my wife, my two boys, and our twin girls." They all waved as Reverend Jackson pointed to the back of the car, his voice mirrored his frustration, "Another flat. Third one this week. Seems like it happens every time we drive now."

Larry shook his hand firmly before stepping to the side to look at the tire. "Have a spare?"

"I do—but don't know how good it'll be. It went flat couple of days ago. I patched it but don't know how long it will hold up."

"I'll help you. Might as well give it a try. By the way, name's Larry Doby. It's nice to meet all of you."

Samuel, who had returned with Zeus, stepped forward and said, excitedly, "You play for the Cleveland baseball club, don't you? Saw in the paper you were going to be here."

Larry took off his cap, "Yes—yes I do. We have a game today. You coming to watch us? You a fan of baseball?"

Samuel lowered his head and replied, "Can't. Can't go to the park."

From the tone of his voice, Larry knew immediately what he meant. "Don't worry, Samuel. We'll clobber the local team. You won't be missing much of a game."

Reverend Jackson asked, "Then what are you doing out here? You're a *long* way from town."

"Well, they said they didn't need me at the hotel or want me going early to the park, so they sent me out here to stay with a wonderful family, the Davises. Know them?"

"Sure! They're members of our congregation. Good people. But I'm sorry you had   to—"

Quickly changing the subject, Larry said, "Let's get at that tire. And then, would it be too much trouble to drive me to town—too much out of your way? Honestly, I'm lost. I have no idea where I'm going."

"It will be an honor. And, thank you for your assistance. I'm not much good at these mechanical tasks. Samuel, let's get out the spare and help Mr. Doby."

For the next several minutes, the two men set up the tire jack and prepared to remove the flat tire. Because the shoulder of the road was muddy from the recent storms that had blown through, Larry had to reposition the jack's small base several times before he felt it would securely hold the weight of the car. While Larry ratcheted the jack's arm higher and higher as the bumper rose, Reverend Jackson urged him on, "Looks good! Looks good!"

When the bottom of the tire finally cleared the ground, Larry started to move toward the spare tire so he could roll it over and have it ready for the switch. However, the cleats of his left shoe caught on a tree root poking through the ground, and he went down, hard, face first. It happened so fast he didn't have a chance to put up his arms to cushion his fall. As his chest and chin crashed against the jagged gravel, the wind was knocked out of him.

"My goodness!" Mrs. Jackson shouted as she ran over and knelt down next to Larry. "You're hurt! You're bleeding!" She dabbed at his chin with her handkerchief, dabbing away a steady stream of blood that oozed from just below his lower lip. "You just stay still. Don't try to move yet."

Larry slowly sat up, took a few quick breaths, and said, "I'm fine, Ma'am. Just couldn't breathe for a minute. All happened so sudden. Give me a minute. I'll be fine."

"Well, you don't *look* fine," Samuel said, laughing and pointing at Larry's uniform, now caked with so much mud the name stitched on his shirt said only, "DIANS."

"That'll be enough of that, young man!" his father scolded, but even he couldn't help but smile once he saw Larry was going to be fine.

"That bad?" Larry asked, looking down. A large drop of blood had dotted the "I" in the team name, and when he started to stand, he became aware of just how bad the rip was in his uniform pants.

"I'm afraid you do look a sight," Mrs. Jackson said as all started laughing, even Larry, who threw up his hands and said, "Well, might as well get at that tire. After all, what could possibly happen next?"

The answer to his question came swiftly enough. The spare hissed loudly and went flat as soon as the weight of the car came in contact with the ground. They all just stood there a few moments, no one saying a word.

Reverend Jackson started to speak, but it was at that moment Larry realized Zeus had wandered off and was now nowhere to be seen. "Where's Zeus?" Larry called out. "Couldn't have gone far. Moves like a snail."

"Probably over that rise and halfway home by now," Samuel said, pointing the direction back toward the Davis' home. "Want me to run after him?"

Larry didn't respond right away. Instead, he looked up and down the road both directions, looked up at the sun to try to gauge the time, and finally said, "No. No time for that. I'm probably missing the morning workout, so to limber up I might as well start joggin' toward town. You all just stay here. I'll find somebody down the way and see if I can get a ride. Then, I'll try to get someone to come back here with a tire. Town's that way, right? I've got to get back fast as I can. If I don't, my manager will really let me have it. And probably fine me, too."

Reverend Jackson sighed heavily. "I'm so sorry we can't drive you. Guess that's best to do, given the circumstances. We'll just wait here, but I'll also send Samuel back there to the Edwards' place to see if maybe there's a tire there somewhere. Appears that's all we can do now."

Larry shook his hand, nodded toward Mrs. Jackson, waved to the children, and said, as he started jogging away, "Was nice meeting you. And, don't worry. I'll get somebody back to you—somehow."

He was soon alternately looking down at the gravel to make sure he wasn't stepping into holes and scanning the road ahead. There were no people or cars to be seen anywhere.

….. ….. …..

"What're you doin' here?" the officer asked gruffly as he stepped out of his car. A younger officer also swung open his door and stepped from the passenger side, quickly moving behind Larry so that Larry was sandwiched between the two.

"Speak up!" the older officer barked. Seeing Larry's uniform, he added, "This better be good. Don't look like no Indian I ever seen."

Larry drew in a breath loudly, shook his head, and said, "I've heard that already today."

"You lippin' me, boy?" The older officer moved closer.

"No, Sir. I'm just lost is all. Can you please tell me the way to the baseball stadium?"

"No, but I can sure as heck tell you the way to the county line," the officer sneered. "Want a ride?"

Just then another patrol car pulled up. Captain Clark Lewis of the Little Rock Police Department stepped from the car, walked over, and asked, "What's the problem here? What's going on?"

"No problem, Cap. Was just going to give this, this *Indian* a ride out of the county. Don't need his kind here, do we?"

The younger officer laughed. Larry remained silent and stood absolutely still, staring right at Captain Lewis, who finally broke into a wide smile and said, "Been looking all over for you. You're Doby, right? Where've you been?"

"He's not under arrest, is he?" Larry's teammates taking the field stopped in their tracks and turned around to hear the response.

"No," Captain Lewis replied, laughing. He turned and nodded at Larry before continuing, his voice becoming serious. "He's late because he helped me save some lives. A bad car wreck—out on Highway 3. He helped me tend to them and get them to the hospital. That's what kept us."

Larry jumped in, "Thanks, Officer, but Skip, you see, it was really this way. I had to ride this horse, and then it got away from me—"

"Oh, shut up!" Lou barked, a smile betraying him. "I've heard some cock-and-bull in my day, but this . . .. Just get a glove and go in for Kennedy. And try not to have that uniform come completely off. They've made this a Lady's Day, too, for heaven sakes!"

Larry turned and shook Captain Lewis' hand, firmly. "Thank you," he said, before ducking into the dugout.

"Geez—Doby, you're holding up the game. Get a move on!" Lou called after him as he stepped onto the field.

The minute he did so, the crowd grew absolutely silent.

....

When Larry Doby signed with the Cleveland Indians, Bill Veeck, owner of the club, said, "You are doing something that will be history someday. There are thousands of Black youngsters awaiting your footsteps." Larry did, indeed, pave the way for so many. His Major League career spanned thirteen seasons, during which he played in over fifteen hundred games and compiled a .283 average. He also slugged 253 home runs and drove in 970 runs. While building this record of accomplishment, he achieved many milestones. In Game 4 of the 1948 World Series, he became the first African American to hit a home run in the Fall Classic. In 1952, Larry ended the season as the first African American to lead either league in home runs. He became a seven-time All-Star, six of those years in succession (1949-1954). After his playing days drew to a close, he became the second African American manager in Major League Baseball, taking over the reins of the Chicago White Sox in 1978. He served a stint as "Special Assistant" to the President of the American League, Gene Budig, and was also a member of an ownership group that operated several minor-league clubs. Larry's "firsts" and other career accomplishments were extraordinary by any measure, and they culminated in his induction to the Baseball Hall of Fame in 1998.

Following Larry's death in 2003 at age 79, MLB Commissioner Bud Selig echoed Veeck when he released the following statement: "Like Jackie, he [Doby] endured the pain of being a pioneer with grace, dignity, and determination and eased the way for all who followed."

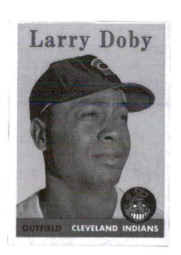

1958 Topps #424, Larry Doby
Courtesy of The Topps Company, Inc.

2

Hank Thompson

St. Louis Browns

Hank Thompson (left) and Williard Brown as members of the 1947 St. Louis Browns. They were never photographed with the rest of the team.

During his playing career, when sportswriters asked Henry (Hank) Thompson what his childhood had been like, he most often told of a wonderful time with a loving family and a large group of close friends. Nothing could have been further from the truth. His early life and path to the Major Leagues were marked by conflict and turmoil at nearly every turn.

Hank was born December 8, 1925, in Muskogee, Oklahoma and grew up in North Dallas, Texas. His father, a strict disciplinarian, often beat him for the slightest infraction. His mother, the major breadwinner for the family, was seldom home because she worked several jobs to make ends meet. His father's drinking and abuse of his children and his wife finally led to divorce just before Hank turned seven. Because his mother could spend very little time at home, he was raised by an older sister and brothers. Constantly in trouble in and away from school, Hank ended up in reform school at age eleven.

When he was released, he tried his best to turn his life around and devoted as much time as he could to his one true passion in life: baseball. The game offered him an escape, at least momentarily, from the unsettled world around him. Several years later, a scout for the Kansas City Monarchs of the Negro American League saw him play in several games around Dallas and thought Hank had real potential. After a game during which Hank banged out several hits and made a couple spectacular plays in the field, the scout asked him if he'd like to try out for the Monarchs. He did, and the Monarchs liked what they saw. Soon he was playing right field and hitting for both power and average.

The following year, 1944, Hank was drafted for military service and became part of a growing group of ballplayers who joined the war effort. He would not return to the Monarchs until 1946, but when he did, he picked up right where he left off. The future looked bright. Then, in less than a year, an opportunity presented itself that would change his life forever.

….. ….. ….

July 13, 1947
Kansas City, Missouri

"Brownie! Quick—get up!" Hank Thompson shouted as he threw his ball glove at his summer roomie, Willard Brown, who was napping on the tattered divan in their small flat. "We got to make a plan. This could be the day we both make it!"

"Make it where?" Willard asked as he rolled over, steadied himself on his elbow, and rubbed his neck. "What in the great world are you talkin' about?"

"Just our futures is all," Hank shot back. "We can't waste this. No, sir, let's talk this out. We need a fool-proof plan." He rubbed his hands together and started clapping softly as he walked back and forth in the small room.

"What? You up to one of your schemes again?" Willard squinted and shook his head. "Last time you had that look you had a *sure thing* at the track, and what happened then? I ended up with nothin' but lint balls in my pockets, and we almost got evicted because our rent money went up in smoke. You remember?"

"Never mind that. Listen up a minute. This'll make you forget all your worries. Guess who just showed up to the park? Fordy, who's pitchin' today, was the one who pointed him out. The main scout for the St. Louis Browns—that's who's here! When I found out, I started a catch with Fordy, so I could get close enough to hear what he was saying to Dunc. Guess what? Scout's come to look at Taborn. The Browns need a catcher, and fast, so he's supposed to check him out six ways from Sunday. If he likes what he sees, Taborn goes back with him."

"So, where do *we* fit in? What's this have to do with *us*? If he wants a catcher—"

Hank didn't give Willard a chance to finish his thought. "Well, he might be looking for a catcher, but *we* are going to be the stars tonight. If I have anything to say about it, he'll forget all about Taborn. No, what he wants—he just doesn't know it yet—is a slick fielding shortstop who can hit, too, and a centerfielder who rips the seams right off the ball. We've got to make him want us so bad he'll be knocking down Dunc's door after the game to sign us."

"And how do we do that?" Willard asked, standing and placing his hands on his hips. "Just what do you have in that mind of yours? You gonna hold a gun to that scout's head?"

Hank smiled. "If I have to. If it comes to that."

"But this is Taborn's day," Willard said. "We talked about this before. If we know someone's being looked at, we'll all do everything we can to make him look good. Lots of pats on the back. Cheer extra loud when he hits or makes a play. Spotlight him best we can. We took an oath. We promised!"

"*You* promised. I didn't. Besides, that's dumb. It's every man for himself in this life. Always has been. Always will be. No, it's *our* day today. That's the way I see it, and we're going to shine. Get your glove and spikes. Let's go. Hurry up!"

"That's pretty rotten, Hank. I don't know about this."

Hank walked over and stood right in front of him. "Look, you're gettin' old. Don't have much time left if you want a shot. You know it's true. You say you're, what, thirty-four? Who you trying to kid? You're at forty if you're a day."

"Thirty-four!" Willard shouted, moving closer. "And age don't matter anyway. I'm still on the sunny side of my game."

"Whatever you are, you're still old in ball years," Hank said, stepping back slightly. "Didn't mean anything by it. Just saying what's true. They want youngsters these days. Hey, I'm twenty-two, and I need to make time while I can. I'm ready, *now*. I know it. I don't care if it's rotten. I can live with that."

"I believe you could," Willard said, shaking his head. "I'll tag along, but I don't like this much."

"You won't say so when we're eatin' steak and gettin' some of that Major League money. You'll see. Now, shut up and get ready. We got to get to the park."

…..   …..   …..

The Kansas City Monarchs were set to open a two-game series at Blues Stadium with the visiting Birmingham Barons with second place at stake. Kansas City was just a game behind the Barons in the standings, so the games took on an extra special significance, especially because the two teams didn't like each other. Earlier in the season, games had been marked by beanballs, high spikes on the base paths during slides, and even bench-clearing brawls. In their last game, Tom Cooper, Kansas City's regular right fielder, had his throwing arm broken when someone stepped on him in the pile that formed during one skirmish, and he was now out at least a month, possibly longer.

Kansas City's manager, Frank Duncan, thought about this as he finished making out his lineup card. He wanted Willard Brown in center and batting cleanup not just because he could hit, but also because of his imposing physical presence out on the field. He stood almost 6'4" and was a tight two hundred and fifteen pounds, so few wanted to tangle with him when tempers flared. Thus, the number four slot was easy to mark.

Frank looked out into the stands—already filling nicely—as he crossed out the name of Jimmy Charles, a youngster they just signed out of high school and whom he wanted to take a look at on the field as soon as he could. However, he didn't want to throw him into the fire too quickly and especially not against the Barons. Instead, he slowly penciled in Hank Thompson at shortstop and batting second. Hank was the regular shortstop and was having a fine year, batting nearly .340. However, while his batting and fielding skills were among the best on the team, his temperament while on the diamond had initially caused Frank to leave him off the lineup card. The bad blood between the teams would already be simmering as the players took the field, and Hank could make it boil over in short order. He had gained a pretty good reputation as an instigator, a gamesman—one who could get under the skin of an opposing team. He was good at that, and he enjoyed it.

However, even his own teammates were growing weary of his antics, which often came back to haunt them as well. Just two weeks before, he had found a dead skunk down the street from the stadium, put it in a cloth sack, snuck it into the visitor's locker room, and hung it from a light fixture high in the ceiling. With a temperature that day right at a ninety, the smell hung in the air so thick the players were soon coughing, gagging, and rubbing burning eyes. The stench grew so bad the other team moved into a small area under the stands to change into their uniforms and get ready for the game. Hank's teammates laughed—until they realized he had gotten the smell on his own shoes and clothes and brought it into their clubhouse, which caused them to seek refuge elsewhere, too. They tried throwing Hank into the showers, but he broke free and ran out onto the field, laughing at them the whole time.

Duncan knew the scout was there to see Taborn and knew how important this game was not just for him, but for the whole team. The more players went up, the faster others would be able to follow. So, he started to scratch out Hank's name again, but stopped and said to himself, "We need this game. Got to take a chance."

He put down his pencil, stared at the card, and blew out a breath as he walked out of the dugout and into the locker room.

....

The crowd at Blues Stadium, estimated by the stadium announcer as 3,297, stood and cheered the hometown team as they came to bat in the bottom of the fourth, leading 6-1. Fans had already seen quite a game with a little bit of everything: home runs, a bench-clearing brawl at third base, hit batsmen, four fielding errors, and a fan near first base hit by a foul ball and needing to be carried out of the stadium on a stretcher. On top of all this, they had seen the "Thompson and Brown" show. Hank was two for two with three RBI's. His first hit was a line-drive home run with one on in the first that cleared the right field wall and bounced across the street. He also tripled with a runner on in the second, a rocket off the right field fence. Even though it was clear he was easily going to be safe, he very dramatically slid, spikes up, slicing a nice gash in the third baseman's leg in the process. When the Barons' third baseman, Johnny Britton, came after Hank, both benches emptied immediately. Hank wrestled Johnny to the ground, grinding him down with a tight headlock. Player after player joined the pile until it was difficult to see who was fighting whom. The umpires finally started yanking players away, two at a time, and separated everyone. Hank was the last to stand up, and when he did, he raised his fists and shook them, as if saying, "We won this one!" The crowd cheered and rose to their feet.

Hank's show didn't stop with his hitting and fighting. In the top of the second, Baron's right fielder, Ed Steele, hit a high pop-up between short and left field. Running as fast as he could toward the outfield while yelling, "I've got it!" Hank dove, extending himself almost completely parallel to the ground, and made a spectacular one-handed catch.

Immediately after holding up the ball to show he had caught it, he rolled over to his back and appeared to pass out. His teammates quickly gathered around him to see how badly he was hurt. Herb Souell, the Monarch's third baseman, leaned over him and asked, "Is he dead? Doesn't look good at all." As Herb shook his head and stepped back, Hank moaned softly and tossed his head side to side.

Duncan knelt beside him, leaned down, and patted his cheek repeatedly, trying to revive him. The first base umpire tapped Duncan on the shoulder and asked, "Dunc—your man going to be OK? Should I send for a doc? An ambulance?"

The crowd grew tense as a low rumble spread through the stands, and several along the third base line could be heard praying for his swift recovery. Hank moaned again, turned his head toward his manager, slowly opened his right eye—and winked at him, a thin smile forming across his lips. Before Duncan could say anything, Hank sat up, brushed himself off, then slowly stood up while waving to the crowd. Cheers erupted as he gathered up his cap and glove, pounded his fist in the pocket, and shouted so that everyone around could hear, "What are you looking at? We're here to give every-thing we got on every play. Just the way the game is supposed to be played. Let's get at it." As the crowd roared even louder, clapping and stomping their feet, Hank waved toward his teammates, "Back to positions! Let's go!"

The Brown's scout had moved down several rows, placed his notebook on the top of the Brown's dugout, and jotted notes as fast as his pencil would scratch. Hank, glancing to his left, noticed this, smiled deeply, and turned toward Willard, who was backing out toward center field. Willard shook his head and looked up to the sky.

A batter later, right before the Monarch's pitcher, Ford Smith, started his windup, Hank suddenly yelled as loud as he could, "Time! Ump—time!" He ran over to the mound, pulled his glove up to his mouth so that only Ford could hear him, and whispered, "Nice pitchin', Fordy. You look good today." With that, Hank ran back to his shortstop position as Ford looked after him, wondering why he had so dramatically come to the mound. On the next pitch, Birmingham's powerful star centerfielder, Piper Davis, topped a changeup weakly toward Hank, who easily threw him out. As soon as he had done so, Hank shouted so all could hear, "Told you so! Way to go, Fordy!" The rest of the infield just stared at Hank, dum-founded. However, out of the corner of his eye, Hank, seeing the scout again scribbling furiously on his notepad, put his glove up to his lips and smiled broadly.

Willard had also put on a demonstration of his own skills. He was two for two with three RBI's. He had doubled to deep left-center with a man on first and followed that up in the bottom of the second with a towering home run with a runner on. The instant the ball had hit his bat, the sweet click told everyone in the stadium a home run would follow. The only question was how far it would travel. Willard wasn't called "Home Run" Brown for nothing. Several of his blasts earlier in the season had cleared the left field bleachers and bounced against the tailor shop across the street. This shot did the same, drawing *oohs and aahs* not just from the fans, but from the players. Hank and Willard had six RBI's between them—and the hearts of the fans. It was no wonder that the fans rose to their feet and cheered when the Monarchs started the bottom half of the fourth.

First up was Chico Renfro, the Monarch's second-sacker, who walked on four pitches, none of them close to the strike zone. Then Hank slowly strolled toward the plate, taking violent practice swings while doing so. The crowd roared and called his name, so he stepped out of the batter's box, doffed his cap, and pointed his bat at a group of youngsters hanging over the railing down the first base line, smiling and nodding to them. Then, digging his left foot deep in the box, he stared out at Nat Pollard, the Barons' pitcher. Just as Pollard was getting ready to begin his windup, Hank suddenly called time, which was granted by the home plate umpire. He backed out, lifted his right hand to shield his eyes, and appeared to be staring out at the right-center field bleachers. The cheering rose again, reaching a crescendo as Hank stepped back in, tapped his bat on home plate, and readied himself for the pitch.

Pollard double pumped his windup, kicked his left leg high, and let loose with a fastball that caught too much of the lower inside portion of the strike zone. The second the ball left his hand he knew he had missed his mark. Hank knew it, too, and gauging his timing perfectly, caught the ball just below the trademark on his bat. The crack that followed sent everyone in the stands to their feet. The ball rocketed toward the right-field bleachers, seeming to rise higher and higher as it flew. Both the right and centerfielders never moved. They knew it was gone.

The rest of the game was anticlimax as the Monarchs went on to win 12-1, with the only Barons' run coming on a passed ball by Taborn in the top of the ninth. It was a fitting end to his game; his box score line read four strikeouts, an error, and two passed balls. He wanted to make an impression on the scout, and he most certainly had done that—only it wasn't the one he hoped for.

As the team left the field, the scout called Duncan over to the stands while the team went to the clubhouse. As soon as they were all inside, Buck O'Neil, elder statesman on the club and father figure to most of the younger players, grabbed Hank by the front of his uniform and slammed him to the wall next to his locker.

"Just what the blazes was that?" Buck screamed, shaking Hank and pushing him back against the locker. "I can't think of what to call you now. You make me sick."

Buck turned to face Willard. "I half expected it from him, but I thought you were better than that. Why? Why'd you do it?"

Earl Taborn slowly and quietly walked over, stuck his right arm between Buck and Hank, and said, quietly, "Let him alone. I'm the one to blame. Wouldn't have mattered what anyone did if I hadn't been so pitiful. *Four* strikeouts. I haven't had four yet this year until today. *Four*. And I dropped that easy popup in front of the plate. Treated it like a grenade."

Here he lowered his voice even more, and said, "I wouldn't sign me up to watch over a kid's game." He threw his glove high against the wall at the clock, missing it a foot to the right. "Figures." He turned and walked into the shower area, his uniform still on, turned on a spigot, and stood right underneath, the water cascading all around him.

Buck eased his grip on Hank and said, disgust punctuating his words, "You won't be able to wash off what you did that easy." Buck dramatically wiped his hands on his pants, shook his head, and walked to his locker. Nobody else said a word. Instead, players quickly moved to their lockers and started undressing.

Just then Duncan stepped into the locker room, pointed to Hank and Willard, and said, loudly, "You two. My office. Right now."

Duncan was already seated behind his desk when Hank and Willard came in. "Don't say a word," he barked sternly. "I hope you're proud of yourselves." He looked each man in the eye then cleared his throat before going on. "Scout's interested in your contracts. Thinks you could help the Browns. Wants to see you, outside. Wants to see what kind of *men* you are." He paused. "Don't worry. I didn't tell him what I think of you. I don't stick knives in backs, like some I know around—"

Hank interrupted him and shouted, "I knew it!" Turning to Willard, he said, "Pack your bags, Brownie. This is it!"

Willard looked at his manager and said, "Skip, I'm sorry. I didn't mean to—"

"Maybe you didn't." Duncan looked down at some papers on his desk. "But you fell right in line with him, didn't you?" Abruptly slamming his fist on his desk, he looked sharply at Hank, and said, "Get out of here. Don't keep him waiting. I guess I wish you luck, but I'll be damned if I know why. Out! Both of you!"

On their way out of the clubhouse, Hank turned to Willard and said, "I told you today would be our day. I knew it!" He slapped Willard on the shoulder. "Let me do all the talkin'. I'll take care of this. You'll see. Our next stop'll be St. Louis!"

Willard smiled weakly and nodded. "It better be. Don't want to go back in that clubhouse now—that's for sure."

"Forget them." Hank waved his hand before him. "That's the past. We got our futures right here. Right now. You watch. This is it."

When they were finally outside, the scout walked over and introduced himself. Hank talked nonstop for the next five minutes.

....

Hank Thompson's debut with the St. Louis Browns came on July 17, 1947. He went on to play nine seasons and nearly a thousand games in his Major League Baseball career. He finished with a solid .267 batting average and three 20-HR seasons. He played in two World Series and was part of the 1954 World Champion New York Giants team. He was also part of many "firsts," including the following:

* First person of color to play for teams in both the American and National Leagues.
* First African American to play on the same team, in the same game, with another African American player (Willard Brown).
* First African American batter to face an African American pitcher (Don Newcombe).
* Member of the first "All Black Outfield," along with Willie Mays and Monte Irvin.

After his playing days, Hank was offered a job scouting for several teams, but he turned down these opportunities. Instead, turmoil and strife again took center stage in his life. He was arrested over half a dozen times for infractions ranging from petty theft to the armed robbery of a liquor store in 1963. The latter resulted in a ten-year prison sentence, of which he served just over four years before being paroled. Trying to get his life turned around, he moved to Fresno, California, and became a playground director. In that role, he devoted his time to helping youngsters stay out of trouble and away from the sorts of situations he had gotten himself into earlier in life. Sadly, on September 30, 1969, the years of hard living caught up with him, and he passed away. He was forty-three years old. Through the peaks and valleys of his life, Hank Thompson left an unsettled legacy for future generations.

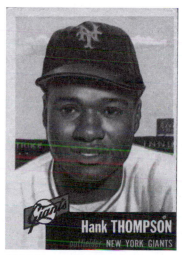

1953 Topps #20, Hank Thompson
Courtesy of The Topps Company, Inc.

3

Monte Irvin

New York Giants

Monte Irvin with his 1949 NY Giants teammates (Monte top row, 5th from the left; Hank Thompson bottom row, 3rd from right).

Monte Irvin was born February 25, 1919 in Halebury, Alabama. When he was very young, his family moved to Orange, New Jersey, where he spent most of his childhood and attended public school. A natural athlete, he became a star player in high school on the baseball, football, basketball, and track teams. His performance on the football field was so good Lincoln University in Oxford, Pennsylvania gave him a scholarship to play football. His initial dream was to become a dentist, but the rigorous football practice schedule didn't allow him to study as much as he wished, which led to constant disagreements with his football coaches over how much time should be devoted to each area. He finally decided to drop from the team, which meant the loss of his scholarship, and the bills soon mounted.

However, ever since high school, he had been playing semi-pro ball—occasionally for the Newark Eagles of the Negro National League—to make a few extra dollars. He did so under an assumed name to protect his amateur status. To help earn enough money to stay in school, he started playing baseball again, and it wasn't long before the Newark Eagles offered him, at age nineteen, a contract to play full time. It was a tough decision to leave school, but Monte had always dreamed of playing professionally. He played for Newark from 1938 until 1942. After he and the Newark ownership couldn't agree on a salary for 1942, Monte signed on with Veracruz of the Mexican league and played so well that season he won the Triple Crown, which attracted attention from scouts everywhere. However, Monte decided, as many ballplayers had done, to put his baseball career on hold so he could join the war effort. He joined the Army and served in the Corps of Engineers until his discharge in 1945.

When Branch Rickey, General Manager of the Brooklyn Dodgers, made up his mind in 1945 to be the first to sign an African American ballplayer to a professional Major League contract, Jackie Robinson was one of several players he felt would be excellent for this pioneering role. Mr. Rickey, and many of his advisors, at first thought Monte Irvin might be the best choice. Monte, a veteran of several seasons of outstanding performance in the Negro Leagues, had the type of disposition Mr. Rickey was looking for. All scouting reports indicated he was a beloved teammate everywhere he played, he was friendly to all, he mentored younger players, and his kindness and likability made him someone everyone wanted to be around. At the same time, when he stepped on the diamond, he was a fierce competitor who led by example and knew what it took to win games.

Mr. Rickey felt he was an excellent choice, but there was a problem: the timing. When Monte completed his military service, he was, by his own account, terribly out of baseball playing shape. On top of that, he had a lingering ear infection that affected his balance. So, when Mr. Rickey signed Jackie Robinson, he also attempted to sign Monte, who declined. Monte decided it was in his best interest to go back to the Puerto Rican Winter League, where he'd had great success in the past, and work himself back into shape. It turned out that was a good choice. He won the Triple Crown and was named league Most Valuable Player. The next season he returned to the Newark Eagles, led the league in hitting, and helped lead the team to the pennant. The New York Giants took notice and purchased his contract, assigning him to their AAA affiliate in Jersey City. He also excelled at that level, and on July 8, 1949 was finally called up to join the big club, starting his Major League career and becoming the first person of color to play for the New York Giants organization.

....

May 23, 1942
Veracruz, Mexico

The game between the 4th place Veracruz Blues and the 6th place Monterrey Industrial team had been, from the start, a wild, see-saw affair. Monterrey scored five runs in the first inning, largely the result of two throwing errors, both times with the bases loaded. The Veracruz fans booed loudly after the final out of the inning but, before the crowd could become too restless, Veracruz responded with four runs of their own in the bottom of the inning, courtesy of a two-run homer by Monte Irvin and a double off the left center field wall with two runners on by Ernesto Bianco, the Blues shortstop, which drove in two more. The Blues took the lead in the second on another two-run shot. Monterrey promptly went ahead in the fourth after a triple with two runners aboard. After that, each team scored single runs in the next four innings, with the Blues finally coming to bat in the bottom of the 9th down 11-10. The Veracruz faithful, with what little energy they had left after the ebb and flow of the emotionally draining contest, stood and cheered as their team opened the home half of the frame.

Shouts of encouragement and support erupted as the first batter of the inning, Angel Abreu, the Blues second baseman, drew a base on balls, putting the tying run on base. However, the next batter, Alfonso Nieto, their right fielder, struck out while attempting to sacrifice the runner to second, drawing jeers from the fans. Fernando Barradas, Blues first baseman, was up next. The count quickly went to three balls and no strikes, bringing many in the stands to their feet in anticipation of the go-ahead run getting aboard. Given the green light to swing away rather than take a pitch, Fernando took a vicious cut and lined a scorcher right at the shortstop. Two outs. The fans booed, this time not because their own player had made an out, but because the opposing shortstop, Alberto Leal, had positioned himself perfectly on the play. Alberto smiled because he knew the boos really signaled a show of respect for his skills.

Down to their last out and the tying run still on first, Monte Irvin, the Blues left fielder and cleanup hitter, strolled slowly toward the batter's box as the fans stood and cheered. Monte was leading the league in batting average and home runs, and at this point in the season had already earned the respect and admiration of not just his own fans but of players and fans across the league. Everyone in the stadium knew that if the outcome of the game was going to come down to the performance of one player in one at-bat, Monte Irvin was who they wanted at the plate. As Monte approached the batter's box, Monterrey's catcher and his dear friend, Roy Campanella, asked the home plate umpire to dust off the plate so he could have a few words with Monte.

The evening before, Roy and Monte had supper together at Monte's small apartment. The two had become fast friends while playing in the Negro Leagues in the States, and now each served as a connection for the other to a shared past and their beginnings in professional ball. About halfway through their meal, Roy had put down his fork, pushed his plate toward the center of the table, and said, "If you come up in a situation tomorrow where you can beat us, I'll order the pitcher to drill you in the back. I just want to make that clear. Our friendship won't stop that. We're in 6th but only two games behind you. I want at least that third-place money if that's the highest we climb this season. I need it."

They were close enough friends that Monte didn't need to reply. Instead, he nodded and pushed Roy's plate back toward him, urging him to take seconds. There was no more talk about the upcoming game.

Now, as Roy stalled and directed the umpire to get the last of the dirt off home plate, he turned to his friend and said, "You're lucky, Mister. Manager just signaled we're going to pitch to you. You've already had three hits today. You're hot, and he knows it. He's also afraid of putting you on because you could end up with the winning run. No fastball in the back today. Yeah, you really dodged it this time."

Monte smiled. "It's killing you, isn't it?"

"It is, but you ain't getting nothing but that sweeping curve of his," Roy said. He knew full well they'd feed him nothing but fast-balls fired by Daniel Rios, the Industrial's flamethrower, but tried to plant a seed of doubt and confusion in Monte. "You'll never put wood on it. I'm not worried."

As Monte stepped in the box and started digging in, a loud commotion just behind the Blues' dugout drew everyone's attention.

Veracruz's owner, Jorge Pasquel, was shouting and waving wildly at the home plate umpire, asking for time to be called so Monte could come over to the stands. This wasn't that unusual. Mr. Pasquel interrupted games all the time. He was a tall, loud, cigar-chomping, gregarious man who felt because he was paying the salaries and keeping the stadium in good playing shape, he had the right to do as he pleased while attending games. Therefore, the umpire backed up, pointed to Monte, and told him he could go—but to make it fast.

"Here we go again," Campanella stood and said disgustedly as Monte trotted over to the low rail separating the box seats from the field.

"Monte," Mr. Pasquel said, urging him to lean forward so he could put his hand on his shoulder and draw him closer. "You *must* hit a home run. Now!"

"What?" Monte asked, not sure he had heard Mr. Pasquel correctly because of the increasing crowd noise.

"I mean it," he replied. "Over the wall. I want this game over. My heart can't take any more of this. All of you are killing me with this back and forth."

"But, Mr. Pasquel—" was all Monte could get out before he was abruptly cut off.

"I'm ordering you to hit a home run. Right now. Of course, there will be compensation for you. Five hundred American dollars for you to put into your pocket. I know you are friends with their catcher. Give him two-fifty, if you need to, to get him to call a pitch for you. Just get it done. I don't care how."

Monte knew Mr. Pasquel was used to getting his way, and the look in his eyes showed he was dead serious about this. "Mr. Pasquel, all I can guarantee is I'll try every way I can to keep the inning going—to move the runner along. I just can't promise a home run. I can't."

Mr. Pasquel pointed toward home plate. "A home run!" he said strongly, sitting down and folding his arms.

There was nothing else for Monte to say, so he turned and headed back. When he got to the plate, Roy asked him, "What was that all about? What's he up to now?"

"He says I have to hit a home run," Monte replied. "That was all."

Roy laughed, stood up again, took off his mask, and said, "Not going to happen. Oh, it isn't that you couldn't hit one. It's just that with that kind of pressure, you'll be lucky to look good striking out."

By this time, the umpire had had it with everyone and ordered play to resume. As Monte dug in, Roy laughed again and said, "Well, Slugger, let's see what you can do. Here comes a curveball."

Monte knew he was being played, so he was ready for the fastball that came in chest high. His swing was timed perfectly, but he got just under the ball and fouled it up and back into the stands. "That's strike one," Roy chided. "Probably the best swing you'll have. Get ready—here comes another curve."

The next pitch was also a fastball, but this time Monte thought Roy would switch up on him, so his swing was late. The loud pop of the ball hitting Roy's glove punctuated strike two. The fans *oooohed* and called out his name, urging him to bear down. "Swinging like an old garden gate now. You're in trouble, Slugger. I got one more curve for you. You ready for it?"

Monte backed out of the box and looked over at Mr. Pasquel, who was now standing with nearly everyone in the stadium. The stomping feet and applause made the old stadium feel like an earthquake was starting up. Monte wiped his hands on his pants, adjusted his cap, took two quick practice swings, and dug back into the box, this time inching back a little. He figured fastball, and he was right.

The minute the ball hit the bat Monte knew it had a chance. As he started running toward first, he heard Roy shout, "I don't believe it!" Monte watched the left fielder running back toward the wall and for an instant thought it was going to be caught. The left fielder leapt, planting his right foot on the wall as he tried to climb even higher. When he was at full extension, the ball just ticked the top of his glove—and continued its flight into the stands. The game was over.

Before Monte had reached second base, fans were already pouring onto the field. He had to alternate darting left and right as he continued his way around the bases in order to avoid running over anyone. Dozens slapped him on the back or rump as he rounded third and headed for home, where Roy and the umpire were waiting to make sure he touched the plate. As soon as he did, he was mobbed by his teammates, who raised him on their shoulders and started carrying him around the bases again to the roar of the crowd that fell in line and followed. When Monte looked to his right, only Mr. Pasquel was still in that section of the stands. He was puffing his cigar, clapping, and nodding his head.

When they reached home plate again, Monte's teammates eased him to the ground, this time shaking his hand and offering their congratulations. Roy elbowed his way through the group and shouted to his friend, "You are the luckiest dog I've ever known! Couldn't do that again in a million years!" Smiling, he added, "I hate you, Irvin."

Monte moved over to him and said, "You're pretty lucky, too. Mr. Pasquel said he'd give me five hundred to hit that—and I should give you two-fifty for calling my pitch. You sort of did that, so I'm going to give you half. Make you feel any better?"

Roy slapped him on the back. "You're my man, Irvin! My man!" Both men laughed heartily and headed to their dugouts, where a celebration awaited in one and a good chewing out in the other.

The news reports the next day said Monte's home run was the first "game ender" ever hit by a foreign-born player in the history of the Veracruz Blues and possibly the first of that type ever hit by an

American in modern Mexican League history. That wouldn't be the last "first" by Monte Irvin. Not by a long shot.

....

October 4, 1951
Yankee Stadium, New York City

Monte Irvin and Hank Thompson sat quietly at their lockers, each lost in thought in the visiting clubhouse at Yankee Stadium. They were the first of their team to arrive and other than the clubhouse man, who was noisily arranging equipment in the adjoining room, they had the place to themselves.

Both men were still dumbfounded about how they got to the World Series against the New York Yankees. The Brooklyn Dodgers had led the National League race for most of the season, enjoying a comfortable lead along the way. However, starting in July, the Giants caught fire and steadily rose in the standings as they went 59-27 through the rest of the summer. It took a team effort to make up so much ground, but two players in particular ignited the spark: Monte Irvin and Willie Mays. Monte had destroyed opposing pitchers, driving in a hundred and twenty-one runs, which led the league, and socking twenty-four homers all while batting .312. At the same time, in his rookie campaign, after a slow start to the season, Willie added much needed speed, power, and the best defensive play many on the team had never seen before in their entire careers. As a result of these outstanding contributions and the "Never give up!" spirit provided by manager Leo Durocher, the Giants finally caught up with the Dodgers on the final day of the regular season, forcing a three-game playoff. The Giants' comeback was the talk of baseball, but that proved to be just a prelude.

The teams split the first two playoff games, taking the race down to a one game, winner-take-all contest. In the final game, the

Dodgers led 4-1 as the bottom of the ninth began. However, Alvin Dark singled to open the inning for the Giants. Don Mueller followed with a single to right. After Monte Irvin popped out to first for the first out of the inning. Whitey Lockman followed with a double, scoring Dark. However, Mueller, running as hard as he could to take an extra base, slid safely into third but in the process hurt his leg so badly he had to be carried from the field. The game had tightened, the score now 4-2, and fans for both teams stood, shouting and screaming encouragement to their respective teams. When play finally resumed, the stage was set for one of the most incredible finishes in baseball history. Bobby Thomson stepped to the plate, and on an 0-1 count drove a home run that barely made it into the left field stands, giving the Giants the pennant. Pandemonium erupted—raucous cheers from the Giants' faithful to the head-down, gut-wrenching sorrow felt by those who lived and died with the Dodgers' fortunes. With Thomson's home run, dubbed the "Shot Heard 'Round the World" by the media, the Giants were set to square off with the powerful New York Yankees.

"Hank—I still don't believe we got here," Monte said, turning to face his friend. "Can you believe it? I *still* can't. Seems like a dream."

Before Hank could respond, the locker room door opened and in walked Willie Mays, smiling broadly. "Had to get here," he said, plopping down heavily in front of his locker. "I don't want to miss anything. This is unbelievable." Realizing he had interrupted a conversation, he said, "Sorry—I'm just excited as I've ever been before in my life. I can't believe any of this. What were you talking about?"

Hank teased, "Mays, if that smile gets any wider, you're going to crack your ears. Settle down, Man. Just another game today. That's all."

"Just another—" was all Willie could get out before Monte chimed in. "Don't you listen to a thing he says. He's just funnin' with you. And besides, I'd bet money he's more excited than all the rest of us put together. I still can't believe how we got here."

"Bobby's home run, that's how," Willie said. "Never seen anything like it!"

"That's not what I'm talking about, Willie," Monte said, looking over at Hank. "I mean *here*. Took us two years. Two *long* years. But, we did it. Leo said we would, but I don't think he thought it would be this long."

"What are you talking about?" Willie asked.

Hank finally joined in. "What he's talking about, Rook, is that you wouldn't even be here if it hadn't been for us." When Willie stared at him blankly, he said, "You don't have a clue what I mean, do you?"

"Not really," Willie replied. "but I think I'm about to get educated."

Hank continued, "Back in July of '49 we were just like you— green, so excited just to be here in the Majors. The Giants got our contracts from Jersey City and brought us up together on July the 8th. I'll never forget that date. It was Monte's first time in the Big Leagues, and my second chance to make good." Turning to Monte, he asked, "Remember what Leo said that day? Remember what he predicted?"

"How could I forget it." Monte stood and began putting on his uniform. Turning to Willie, he said, "He told everyone on the team to treat us like everyone else. We were the first Blacks for the club, and we were a *big* surprise to all our new teammates. But Leo said they needed to give us a chance—because we'd help them win games and put money in their pockets. I don't know how much Leo liked us at first, but I know he loves his money, and he must have believed we'd help with that. He sure went out of his way to make us feel part of the team."

"That wasn't his biggest prediction that day," Hank added. "He said we'd help them to the pennant and World Series. Turns out he was right about that, but it's taken a lot longer than I expect he thought at first." He pointed at Monte and laughed softly. "Kid, you should have seen him shaking in his shoes that first day we showed up. Leo made us each say something to the team. I thought Monte was going to faint dead away—dead as a mackerel."

"I was not!" Monte shot back. "I was just shy back then is all."

"Shy, my foot. Thought you were going to throw up right in the locker room."

"What happened?" Willie asked, still seated and hanging on every word.

"It was like this," Hank said, turning to Willie. "Leo gave his little talk and told everyone we were here to stay—and to give us a chance. I'll always be grateful to him for that. He didn't have to do it. But then he told Monte he had to introduce himself, and you know what he did? All he said was 'I'm Monte, and I'm here to play ball.' That was it. Everybody waited and waited for him to say something else, but that was it. I finally had to jump in and save him!"

Willie laughed as Monte interrupted, "And what a great help you were. You made us both look like fools."

"What'd he do?" Willie asked.

"Oh, not much. He just said, in not so many words, something like this: 'Gentlemen, your worries are over. I'm here now. Why, in no time at all I'll be tattooing that right field wall with line shots. I once hit a homer so far—"

"Very funny," Hank cut in, as Willie's laughter grew louder. "At least I said *something*. I wasn't no mute like you. Whatever you want to say about all this is fine, but to me, we deserve this. We've done pretty good since we got here. We've helped, each in our own way."

Just then Leo Durocher stepped through the door, stopped in his tracks, and said, "What's going on here? You should be resting. What in blazes you doing here so early?"

"They were just telling me how lucky you are they came to the team two years ago," Willie replied, laughing again. "Said you wouldn't be here without 'em.'"

Leo shook his head. "Willie, I told you not to listen to those two." He pointed at Hank. "Especially him. And don't ever turn your back on him." He paused, turned serious, and said, "Well, they're about right—if that's what they said. I knew Monte was going to help us right from the start. Wasn't so sure about Hank. Had heard he could be a bad one."

"Me?" Hank said in mock horror. "Not me! Why, I'm—"

"We all know what you are," Leo interrupted. "But, enough of this *old home week* baloney. We've got the Yanks starin' right at us, and we better play better than ever or they're going to kill us. That's what you should be talking about—preparing for."

He walked over to Hank, handed him the lineup card, and asked, "How you feelin' today? You want in on this?" Hank's name was penciled in at left field and batting 3rd. "Mueller's leg is so bad he can barely stand up. He's tough as nails, but I doubt he'll be able to play at all in the series. I need somebody who can give me the same hard production he's done all year. Can you do it? Can I count on that?"

"Skip, you just let old Hank at those Yanks. By the time I get done with 'em, you won't even remember how to spell Mueller's name. You've got nothin' to worry about. Nothin'.'"

"Humble as ever," Leo said, reaching over and swatting him on the shoulder. "But we're *all* going to need your confidence. Nobody figured we'd be here, but here we are—and I don't want to be embarrassed. We've got to show we deserve this, that it wasn't just a lucky home run put us in."

Monte finally spoke up. "We'll be ready. I'll talk to everybody when they get here. They already know what we're up against. I'll just remind them—and tell them if they don't step up, I'll put Hank on 'em. That'll light 'em up."

"Couldn't hurt," Leo said, moving back toward the door. "I don't care what you do, but help me get them ready. Those Yanks—"

He left without finishing his thought.

....

The Brooklyn lineup card read as follows: Eddie Stanky, leading off and 2nd base; Al Dark, shortstop; Hank Thompson, right field; Monte Irvin, left field; Whitey Lockman, 1st base; Bobby Thomson, 3rd base; Willie Mays, center field; Wes Westrum, catching. Dave Koslo, the Dodgers starting pitcher, was batting ninth.

The game started at 1:15, and before many of the Yankee fans could get settled in, the Giants made two quick outs in the top of the first against Yanks' starter, Allie Reynolds: Stanky grounding to short and Dark flying out to deep right. However, Reynolds was showing very little command of his pitches and walked the next batter, Hank Thompson. With Thompson taking a huge lead, Monte Irvin drilled a single to right field, sending Thompson to third. Whitey Lockman followed with a ground rule double that scored Thompson, with Irvin having to stop at third on the play. That brought up Bobby Thomson, hero of the playoff game that got them to the series.

Thinking too much about Thomson, Reynolds quickly fell behind two balls and no strikes. During those pitches, Monte noticed that after Reynolds took the sign from his catcher, he looked at the ground a couple of seconds before going into his long, looping windup. On the third pitch, the instant Reynolds looked down after getting the sign, Monte took off for home. Reynolds didn't even know he was stealing until Monte was nearly half way down the line. He rushed his delivery, but Monte, sped home, sliding toward the top of the plate and away from Yogi Berra's tag. Home plate umpire Bill Summers shouted, "Safe! Safe! Safe!" as a jubilant Irvin jumped up, brushed himself off, and ran toward the dugout. Yogi Berra protested mightily that he had tagged Monte out, but to no avail. The Giants were up 2-0, and the fans who had made the trip across town to help make up the 65,000 in attendance cheered so loudly that time had to be called before the next pitch could be thrown. Reynolds, clearly rattled, walked Thomson, which ignited the Giants fans yet again. Willie Mays followed and crushed a fastball to deep right, where it was caught by a leaping Mickey Mantle. The inning was finally over, but what followed created excitement no one expected.

The Giants, having been fired up by both Monte's pregame talk and taking their quick lead in dramatic fashion, practically ran from the dugout out to the field for the bottom of the first and began their warm-up throws. Monte, in left, threw over to Willie, in center, who tossed the ball to Hank, in right field—who threw all the way back to Monte to start the sequence again. When the Giants' starter, Dave Koslo, finished his warm-up pitches, young Mickey Mantle dug in for the first post-season at-bat of his career. He flew out to right on the third pitch of the game. Phil Rizzuto followed with a single to left, but he was stranded at first when the next two batters, Bauer and DiMaggio, went out on weak fly balls. The inning was over quickly and the Giants retained their 2-0 advantage.

When the Giants were back in the dugout, they noticed newspaper photographers crowding around both side entrances to their dugout, jockeying for position, their cameras held high. Monte, Willie, and Hank were the last to reach the dugout, and as soon as they were in range, camera clicks came fast and furious. No one on the Giants had realized it, especially not Durocher, who was craning his neck the farthest out the dugout to see what was going on, but by making out the lineup card the way he did, he had just fielded the first all-Black outfield in Major League History. However, the scribes had taken note, and their focus was now not on the game, but on the history unfolding right before them. It wasn't until one of the photographers nearly fell out onto the field while screaming for the three outfielders to scoot together for a picture that they understood what had just taken place. The three men paused a moment as picture after picture was taken. While doing so, Monte was the first to speak. "How about that," he said, breaking into a smile while turning to Hank and Willie.

"Get in here, you three!" Leo barked, a smile betraying his real feelings. "We've got a game to win."

"Yes, Mr. Durocher," Willie said, ducking into the dugout. "That's what we're gonna do!"

….. ….. …..

The Giants went on to win that first game, 5-1. In addition to stealing home during a World Series game, the first time anyone had done so in thirty years, Monte also slugged four hits. However, despite their quick start, the Yankees prevailed in six games. Still, Monte led all batters with a .458 average, and Hank set a new World Series record by drawing seven walks. They lost the series, but they helped change the face of the game when they took the field with Willie Mays in that first game, adding another first and knocking down yet another wall.

Monte Irvin played eight seasons in the Major Leagues, compiling a lifetime batting average of .293, with 99 home runs and 443 runs batted in. Combined with his years in the Negro Leagues, Puerto Rican League, and Mexican League, his career was impressive by any standard. Thus, in 1972 he was inducted into the Mexican Professional Baseball Hall of Fame. The following year, 1973, he joined the ranks of the National Baseball Hall of Fame, voted in by the Negro League Committee. Years later, in 1997, he also became a member of the Cuban Baseball Hall of Fame.

Following his baseball career, Monte continued to be active in baseball, first by serving as a scout for the New York Mets organization. Then, in 1968, Monte became the first Black executive in Major League history, serving as a Public Relations Specialist for the Commissioner's office. He also served on the Hall of Fame Committee on Veteran Players. He continued in those roles until his retirement in 1984. However, even in retirement, Monte couldn't break himself away completely from baseball. He made appearances and worked on special projects for the Commissioner's office right up until his passing on January 11, 2016, at age 96.

NOTE: *For the sake of historical accuracy, it should be mentioned that while most baseball historical societies and organizations list Monte Irvin as the first person of color to play for the New York Giants organization, many feel that distinction should go to Hank Thompson. Monte and Hank had their debut with the Giants on the same night, July 8, 1949. That night, Thompson was the starting third baseman and appeared on the field before Irvin. Monte didn't enter the game until serving as a pinch-hitter in the 8th inning. Why, then, is Monte still listed more often than Hank as the pioneer here? Possibly because Hank Thompson had already played in the Major Leagues and had broken the color barrier for another team, the St. Louis Browns, in July of 1947. Others suggest Monte's contract was acquired first by the New York Giants, thus making him the first person of color in their organization. Whatever the rankings, both men were instrumental in changing Major League Baseball forever.*

1955 Topps #100, Monte Irvin
Courtesy of The Topps Company, Inc.

4

Sam Jethroe

Boston Braves

Sam Jethro with his 1950 Boston Braves teammates (Sam top row, far left).

Sam Jethroe's father, Albert Jethroe, started playing catch with his son and teaching him the fundamentals of baseball when Sam was just five years old. At the same time, he took Sam as often as he could from their home in East St. Louis, Illinois, across the Mississippi River to sit in the "Colored Only" section of Sportsman's Park, so they could watch both the St. Louis Cardinals and the St. Louis Browns play. After returning home, Sam and his boyhood pals would play pickup games against other boys in the surrounding neighborhoods, among them Hank Bauer, who went on to an outstanding Major League career. These experiences forged in Sam a love for the game that drove him all through his childhood and early teen years. He knew he'd most likely never be allowed to play on the same field with his childhood heroes, most notably Dizzy Dean, Rogers Hornsby, and George Sisler. However, he soon learned of the Negro Leagues and began following their teams, vowing that one day he would make a career playing for one of them.

After graduating high school, he began playing semi-pro ball for several area clubs and was scouted by several Negro League teams. He soon signed a contract with the Indianapolis Clowns and later joined the Cleveland Buckeyes, where his career really took off. Always a swift runner, he built his reputation as one of the fastest runners—if not *the* fastest man—in the league. The reputation fit as he led his own team in stolen bases every year and the entire league most seasons. After playing nearly seven years of outstanding baseball in the Negro Leagues, where he won the batting title two years and set numerous stolen base records, Sam caught the eye of the Brooklyn Dodgers who purchased his contract. However, by that time, the Dodgers had already signed several players of color, were loaded with talent—especially in their infield—and did not see a good fit for Sam with the Major League club. As a result, they traded him to the Boston Braves, who assigned him to their Triple-A club, where he tore the cover off the ball and, again, led the league in stolen bases. After many years of perseverance and holding fast to his childhood dream, he made his Major League debut with the Boston club on April 18, 1950. However, his path to the Big Leagues might have been quite different if another organization had made a decision to sign him five years earlier.

….. ….. …..

April 11, 1945
Boston, Massachusetts

Sam Jethroe entered the lobby of the Melbourne Hotel, a "Colored Only" establishment at the southern edge of the city proper and walked, a suitcase in each hand, toward the front desk. Just as he set down his suitcases, a voice from the other side of the room called out, "Hey, Jet! Not you, too!"

Marvin Williams stood up from his chair, walked over to his dear friend, and shook his hand firmly. "You've got to be here for the workout, right?" he asked, reaching out and playfully straightening Sam's tie.

Sam brushed his hand away. "If that's why you're here, they sure are scraping the bottom of the barrel!" Both men burst into laughter.

At that moment both men flinched as they heard the crack of suitcases slamming to the stone floor.

"Way below the bottom of the barrel," a voice called out. When they turned, they saw Jackie Robinson, arms folded, shaking his head, and smiling broadly while resting his right foot on top of his large suitcase.

"Now, there's a picture for you," Sam said to Marvin, laughing and pointing to Jackie. "Times gotta be tough for that old-timer. Look—he's working as a bellboy now. What's the matter? Baseball not work out so good for you?"

"Very funny, Jet," Jackie said, kicking his suitcase across the floor toward Sam. "Careful picking it up. You might drop it. How many balls you boot last year? Led the league in errors, didn't you?"

Marvin stepped over, placed his hand on Jackie's shoulder, and hugged him. "Good to see you, Jack." He stepped back and jerked his thumb toward Sam. "Well, I know why they asked *you and me* here. We're great, after all. But what about that skinny little runt? What's he doing here? Why *him*?"

Just as Sam started to reply, the clerk repeatedly rang the bell on the counter. "Gentlemen!" he shouted. "Are you checking in? If so, step forward. There's a line forming behind you. What'll it be?"

"Checking in," Jackie replied as he elbowed his way between his friends and pounded his right hand on the counter. "A room away from the street," he said to the clerk. "Can't stand noise. I need my sleep, especially tonight. I've had a long trip."

"You don't like noise?" Sam chided, righting Jackie's suitcase and shoving it across the floor toward him. "Why, you snore like a buffalo. Kept the whole second floor of the Algonquin Hotel up all night last year if I recall. I'll never forget—"

Marvin cut him off. "I remember that. That was at the All-Star game in Kansas City. I heard it, too. Was that *him*?"

They laughed again as Jackie playfully threw several punches at Marvin.

"Gentlemen!" the clerk said again, this time his voice sterner.

"OK—OK," Sam said, waving his hand at the clerk. Turning to his friends, he said, "I tell you what. Soon as me and Jackie get our rooms, let's all come back down and eat at that coffee and sandwich shop next door. I'm starved. Sound good?"

"You're *always* hungry," Marvin teased. "Got to keep up, what, all hundred and twenty pounds of you drippin' wet? Bet you really have to work at that."

Sam glared at him. "At least I'm not getting a gut like yours."

"Why, you little . . ." Marvin said, moving toward him. The clerk started ringing the bell again, but it didn't do any good. They kept up the barbs until Jackie stuck out an arm and quieted them both.

While signing the register, Jackie said, without looking up, "Don't know about you two, but I was told to be here in the lobby at six sharp. They're sending somebody to meet me. How about you?"

He looked at his watch. "That's about half an hour. I'll take up my gear and be right back down."

"I was told the same thing," Sam said, looking over at Marvin, who nodded. "So, let's hurry up and get settled and get back here. We can wait on the couches over there by the window. Then maybe we can figure out what this reunion is all about."

Jackie reached over, grabbed Sam by the shirt sleeve, and pulled him to the counter. "Sign in!" he commanded. The others who were waiting to check in applauded. All three men turned . . . and bowed.

....

The Boston Red Sox of the American League had invited three players from the Negro Leagues to work out and show off their skills to their coaches. The Red Sox general manager, Eddie Collins—one of the greatest players of his generation, a member of the National Baseball Hall of Fame, and now considered one of the best judges of player talent—had spent the better part of a month combing through scouting reports on the players on the rosters of all Negro League teams. The reports had been put together hurriedly and didn't contain the depth of detail typically written up for minor league and major league players. Still, after much scrutiny, he finally settled on three to bring to Fenway Park.

The player he was most interested in was Sam Jethroe, who was reportedly twenty-three-years-old and known as "Jet" and "The Comet" because most believed he was the fastest runner in all of the Negro Leagues. He had led the league in stolen bases each year he had been in professional ball. He was a switch-hitter with occasional power who also sprayed the ball to all fields and hit for high average. He was known as a tough out, especially in pressure-packed situations. What stuck out most in the scouting report, though, was a section the Red Sox general manager just couldn't get out of his mind: "A terror on the basepaths. Rattles other team. Ignites rallies with his swagger." Sam was slated to be the starting centerfielder for the Cleveland Buckeyes in the upcoming season.

Collins was also impressed by the report on Marvin Williams, twenty-five, who was the star second baseman for the Philadelphia Stars. Powerfully built at 6'1" and 190 pounds, the righty slugger had a sharp batting eye and a natural, fluid swing that allowed him to clout home runs to all fields. While other teams feared him most for this powerful bat, he was one of the best fielding second basemen. His soft hands and wide range turned many hard-hit grounders into easy outs. The report also described his "soft spoken and calm demeanor that may at times make him seem lazy—but competitive fire is there underneath."

The last player invited for the workout was Jackie Robinson, who almost wasn't included because Collins didn't know what to make of the mixed reviews in the scouting reports. Jackie was the oldest of the group at twenty-six, but one scout had questioned whether he was actually much older than the listed age. Another scout had described him as "loud and potentially a trouble-maker" although no specifics were given. However, all who had seen him play were of the same opinion when it came to his skills on the diamond: he was a "four-tool" player who could run, throw, hit, and hit with power. And, like Sam Jethroe, he was very distracting to pitchers when on the basepaths. Jackie was a multi-position player for the Kansas City Monarchs, one who looked good no matter where he was placed in the field.

When all three men had returned to the lobby and settled in, each facing the door so as not to miss the Red Sox representative who would soon be meeting with them, Jackie was the first to speak. "Do either of you have even the faintest idea why we're here? All I was told was the Red Sox wanted to take a look at me, whatever that means."

Marvin Williams replied, "Well, one look at you will be enough, I imagine. That ugly mug of yours would scare the skeleton off an iodine bottle."

Jackie scooted forward on the couch and kicked at Marvin, catching him just below the knee.

"Ow! That really hurt!" Marvin shouted as he rubbed his leg.

"That's enough of that," Sam said, calmly, admonishing them both as he noticed the desk clerk glaring at them again. "If you'll stop all that and shut up a minute, I'll tell you what I *think* is going on here. At least I'll share what I've been told."

Jackie and Marvin learned forward, and Sam continued, lowering his voice so no one else in the room could hear. "I got a call from Wendell Smith. Writes for the Pittsburgh paper, the *Courier*. Always does the best coverage of the Negro League teams. I've known him a long time, and he's good and fair in what he says."

He lowered his voice even more. "So, Wendell called me out of the blue the other day and asked if I could give him a quote about being invited here to Boston. I didn't know what he was talking about and told him so. He was really surprised nobody had talked to me, so he said he'd do his best to fill me in."

"So, what *is* going on?" Marvin asked, as he and Jackie moved their chairs closer.

"This is what I know—from Wendell. I'm going to start by saying I don't know whether this is a stunt or it's the real thing. I guess we'll find out tomorrow. Anyway, Wendell said some Councilman or Alderman named Muchnick here in Boston is a strong supporter of rights for everybody, especially Negroes, and he threatened the owners of the Red Sox so bad it scared 'em to death. Seems he told them he was going to join up with a bunch of churches that want to stop baseball on Sundays here. According to Wendell, the churches here have a lot of power and support of plenty of public officials. So, this Muchnick says to the Sox if they didn't give an "opportunity" to some Black players, they'd shut down Sundays at the park. Wendell didn't know exactly what 'opportunity' meant, but here we are. I guess we're getting ours, whatever that is."

"Wait a minute," Jackie cut in. "You trying to tell me that Boston is thinking about signing players like us? You're out of your mind. It doesn't get any more *separate* than in this town. This is worse than down south."

"I know," Sam said, nodding toward Jackie. "This may turn out just to be a bad joke on us. Likely it will. But . . .." Here his voice trailed off for a second before he continued, his face serious, his voice strong, "Just what if it *could* be true? Times are changing. Not fast enough, but the war is still turning everything upside down. Remember that one-armed outfielder the Browns had? How about that pitcher—I *think* he was with Cleveland—who was missing part of a leg? Why, most of the players in the Major Leagues can't hold a candle to the teammates we've got right now. It's going to happen. If not now, then soon. It's got to."

Marvin finally spoke while Jackie sat there shaking his head. "You know, this could be it. Colored units have served all through the war, and I've even worked in a munitions plant in the off seasons. Maybe this is their way of showing appreciation for everybody pitching in, that everyone has earned a chance."

"You don't really believe that," Jackie cut in. "You're still dreaming. Not happening. Not now. I think this is some big publicity stunt that they think will help them somehow. If it's true about churches putting on pressure to sign us, this is probably just a way to shut 'em up. When I got my phone call, I figured it was some public relations gimmick to try to get more Blacks in the stands. You mark my words—there's a money reason behind this somewhere and *not* a social one. I can't see anything else that fits."

"Now, let's stop a minute and think about this some more,"

Sam said, scooting his chair even closer. "Jackie, you're one of the best all-around players in the league. I respect you, but I *hate* playing against you. You're that good. And you, Marvin, you hit the longest home run I've ever seen. That was the one in Kansas City that cleared the wall, and nobody ever found the ball. Never seen power like that any time either before or since. Nobody wants to see you coming to the plate. Heck, I back up at short when I look in and see you." Here he paused and smiled. "And I guess I've got one or two skills that keep me drawing a paycheck, and I plan on being around a long time."

Marvin interrupted, "Hate to admit it to your face, but you're fast as they come, and you get other teams so mad when you're on base that fights break out all the time. You can play on my team any time."

"Thanks," Sam said, "but I don't want this to sound like I'm patting us on the back. Not my purpose. I'm saying this because it makes sense the three of us are here. Think about it. We—us three— could sure show these Boston baked beans a thing or two about playing this game. I'd have called *us* if I was in charge of this club. Oh, there are other guys we know who should also be sittin' here, but think about? Because some others might be just as good or better, but *we* are the ones who can change games in a hurry—because of the way we play the game. This isn't braggin'. It's the truth—and that's why this might be real and not a stunt."

"I still think you're out of your mind," Jackie said, leaning back heavily in his chair. "You tell me you honestly believe in your heart you can see us up here and on the same playing field with the Boston Red Sox. I don't see it. I don't see how it can happen. Not now, anyway."

"Listen to what I'm saying," Sam said. "Yeah, it might be a bad joke on us. It might be to keep baseball on Sundays—or something else. But what if there's even a slight chance? We *have* to do this, no matter what comes of it. Most of me agrees with you, but let me ask you this. Do you know anybody else from the Negro Leagues who has been in Fenway Park without having to buy a ticket? Know anyone who has put a foot on that field? If nothing else, whatever happens tomorrow, we'll have stories to tell. I'll be there tomorrow, and I'll be ready, whatever they want me to do."

"Me, too," Marvin said, without looking up. "Got to give it a chance. We got to. If it ain't coming real now, it will someday. Maybe this'll help."

Jackie leaned forward again. "You two have lost your minds. What world do you think you're living in?"

"Then why are you here?" Sam asked. "Why did you agree to come? If you thought this was all some bad joke, why'd you get on a train and come all that way?"

All were silent a moment until Jackie blew out a loud breath and said, just a hint of a smile on his lips, "Because you might be right. I still don't think so, but . . . .."

At just that moment, a tall, thin man wearing a sharp, tailored suit accentuated by a large, red bow tie walked into the hotel, looked around briefly, and walked briskly toward them.

"I'm Robert Quinn, traveling secretary for the Red Sox," he said, stopping a few feet from where they were seated. "You the players?"

"I'm Sam Jethroe. This is Marvin Williams—and that's Jackie Robinson. Please sit down, here. There are a few things we'd like to ask. First of all—"

"I'm not here for questions," Quinn interrupted, his voice clipped. "I'm just supposed to give you these and give you some directions." He reached in his pocket and pulled out three large envelopes. "Inside you will find more than enough for reimbursement for your travel to and from, per diem for meals and hotel, and general expenses. I'm sure it'll be more than satisfactory."

He handed each an envelope. "Tomorrow morning be at the south entrance of the ballpark at nine sharp. Don't be late. Someone will be there to unlock the gate and let you in. If you're late, you'll stay locked out. That person will take you to the locker room where you'll have ten minutes to change into your uniforms. You were told to bring your own, and I'll assume you did."

Jackie raised his hand, but Quinn ignored him. "I've been told to tell you you'll run, hit, and throw. Some coaches will be there to watch. That's all I know." Jackie raised his hand again, but Quinn glared at him and added, his voice more than a little condescending, "I'm assuming you've been on a streetcar before. In the morning, go down to the corner and get on. It's a straight run to the park. Tell the conductor to let you know when to get off. Think you can do that?"

When Quinn paused, Jackie jumped in. "Mr. Quinn, we're perfectly capable of getting ourselves there in the morning. You just make sure there's someone there to let us in—because we won't wait. *That* you can count on."

"Mr. Quinn," Sam said when he could get a word in. "Can you tell us anything, *anything* at all, about why we're here?"

Marvin nodded and added, "Please, Sir."

Quinn pulled up his left sleeve and looked at his watch. "Wouldn't know about that. Not my job. They'll tell you tomorrow." After readjusting his sleeve, he said, "That's it, boys. You're on your own now. I'm headed home."

Jackie stood and blocked his exit. "You'll want to take the streetcar. It's down on the corner."

Marvin also stood. "It's that big, boxy contraption on wheels. You do know how to ride one, don't you?"

Sam, while standing, glared at them both. "Thank you, Mr.

Quinn. Appreciate the money. Appreciate your time. Thanks for coming." He reached out to shake Quinn's hand, but Quinn was already spinning around and heading for the door.

Marvin pointed to Sam's outstretched hand, laughed softly, and said, "What, you getting' ready to pump some water?"

Turning to his friends, Sam said, "You two shouldn't have said that. You know that, right?"

"All I know is I'm . . . scared," Marvin said, sitting down again.

"You—*scared*?" Jackie said. "I don't believe it. Scared of what?"

Standing again, Marvin grimaced and, fighting back a smile whined, "Will you hold my hand when we ride that nasty streetcar tomorrow?"

Sam rolled his eyes and groaned. "Let's get something to eat. It looks like we got enough meal money to lay out a spread. You coming?"

Both nodded and pointed toward the door. "After you, Jet. Just lead the way."

….. ….. …..

The next morning, they met again at the coffee shop for a light breakfast before heading to the park. Sam suggested they leave the hotel just before eight to give them plenty of time to get across town and to the south entrance of Fenway Park. Each carried a small suitcase with his gloves, shoes, and uniform.

As they boarded the streetcar, the morning temperature was in the upper 40s, with light rain and a stiff breeze filling the air. "My hands are cold!" Marvin shouted as he rubbed them together. Sam and Jackie agreed while rubbing their hands on their pant legs.

"Great day for baseball," Jackie said, looking out toward the sky.

"*Any* day is a great day for baseball," Sam said. "What, you're going to melt?"

"No—I'm afraid I'm going to freeze. Think of how your hands are going to sting when you hit a ball," Jackie said while making the motion of a swing and follow-through.

They rode the rest of the way in silence until Fenway came into view. "Conductor!" Sam shouted. "Our stop!"

Just as Quinn had said, one of the groundskeepers, an older man wearing faded overalls and a wide-brimmed rain hat, was waiting for them at the gate. "I'm Gus. You boys follow me," he said. "This way. I'll take you to the locker room."

They walked under the stands and through a long tunnel before they came to a door on the right. Gus opened it and motioned them inside. "Watch your heads and mind the steps," he cautioned as they slowly entered the room.

Once they were inside, Gus waved and said, "I got to get to work. Good luck." When they reached the middle of the room, Marvin froze in his tracks. "Would you take a look at this. This is the *locker* room? Looks more like a hotel lobby. Look at the seats, the tables, those cabinets over there. And look at the showers through there. A whole room full of 'em! Ever seen anything like this before at a ballpark?"

"Shake the straw out of your hair," Jackie admonished. "This is why they call it the *Big Leagues*."

Sam piped up, "Knock it off. We can look around later. We're supposed to get out on the field, remember? I'm takin' the locker over here by the door. Let's get dressed before somebody sees us in here and throws us out. Let's at least look like ballplayers."

Marvin shook his head. "This is better than my boarding house room. What does a man have to do to work here? Sign me up."

Each quickly got into uniform: Sam in his Cleveland Buckeyes flannels, Marvin in his Philadelphia Stars uniform, and Jackie in a jersey emblazoned with "Kansas City Monarchs" across his chest. Sam finished first and picked up a couple of balls from a bucket by a set of steps. Turning to Marvin and Jackie, he said, "Until somebody gets here and tells us what to do, we might as well make ourselves to home. I'll be right back. I'll see how we get out of here." Not more than a minute later he returned, grinning, and announced, "Come on. You've got to see this."

The steps led into the dugout and, as they approached the rail, they stopped and stared, taking in as much of the park as they could from their vantage point.

"Take a look," Sam said, moving toward the steps that led up to the field. "I've seen some fine places to whack a ball, but this takes the cake. Just look at this. Come on—follow me."

As they stepped out of the dugout and walked onto the field, Marvin was the first to speak, and he did so matter-of-factly, as if he were describing a familiar location. "Let's see. Looks like just over 300 feet down that left field line. And a wall. A *big* wall. Look at that. Must be thirty or forty feet high. I could tattoo that—regular. Center is deep. Indention out there—not rounded or square. There's like an extra cutout. Right field line right at 300. Short. Made for your switch, lefty swing, Sam. Not a problem."

When they reached the first base line, Marvin swung around and continued, his voice still even, almost subdued. "Our stadium in Philly could sardine in about eight thousand. Least that's what they brag. This place would hold, what, four or five times that—at least. Never seen the likes of it."

"It's the infield impresses me," Jackie interrupted, jumping over the first base line and moving toward second base. "Throw me a ball," he called over to Sam, who looked around first before tossing him one. "Smooth as silk," Jackie said, bending down and brushing his hand across the grass. "Of course, the rain has helped. Still, like a pool table. We need this at our stadium."

They continued to study their surroundings until Sam spoke up. "We better get warmed up. Somebody's bound to be here in a few minutes. Let's throw a few—and stretch. Watch the grass. Jackie's right. It's slick."

Sam trotted over to short, Jackie to second, and Marvin moved over to first. "Let it rip!" Sam yelled. "Throw it around." Marvin then skipped a grounder over to Sam, who tossed to Jackie, who flipped the ball back to Marvin. They repeated this several times, quickly picking up the pace. They stretched between throws and tried to warm quickly, a tough task in the light rain and early morning chill. Each time the ball was returned to Marvin, he paused just long enough to point out another feature of the stadium, from the smooth infield dirt to the number of rows of seats in the first level in the stands to the wide expanse of foul territory on both sides of the field to the view of the towering buildings beyond the right field wall. "Never. Never seen anything like it," he repeated over and over.

After catching one toss from Sam, Jackie playfully threw wide of Marvin, the ball coming to rest at the foot of the dugout. Marvin jogged for the ball and called back, "Funny man. You're a bag of fun." As he reached down for the ball, three men came out from the locker room and walked up the dugout steps toward him. All were wearing Boston uniforms. Not sure what to do, Marvin just stood there—and waved.

The tallest of the three was Hugh Duffy, the spry seventy-nine-year-old infield coach for the Sox. He motioned for Sam and Jackie to come over, and as they approached, he said, "I'm Duffy. This is Del Baker, our third base coach, and Larry Woodall, coach at first."

Sam introduced himself, then Marvin and Jackie. After they shook hands, Duffy said, "We're to take a look at you. Sorry about the stinkin' weather, but we'll just have to make do. First thing we'll do is—"

Jackie cut him off and said, "Excuse me, Sir. If you don't mind, I'd like to ask you something. Nobody's said a word to us. Why *exactly* are we here? What's this all about?"

Duffy glanced quickly at the other coaches, cleared his throat, and replied, "Like I said, we are supposed to look at your skills. Hitting, running, fielding, throwing. That's what we've been told to do. Somebody else will come down and visit with you later after we're finished. Let's—"

This time it was Sam who interrupted. "Are you looking to sign some Negro players? Is that why you brought us here? I think it's only fair that we—"

Larry Woodall stopped him. "We're always looking for talent. We hear you three are some of the best in your league. We've been told to see if that's true. What else happens isn't up to us. Somebody will come down and talk to you later on. Our general manager is in his office. It might be him. But, before that, we've all got work to do, if you're ready."

Before anyone could ask another question, Duffy said briskly, "Let's do some hitting first. Larry will pitch to you, and Del will catch. Just regular batting practice. Take some hacks and show us what you've got. There's a bag of bats over by the railing. Pick one that suits you. You, Sam, you go first. Understand you're a switch hitter. Show both sides, OK?"

Motioning to Marvin and Jackie, he said, "You two. Head out to the outfield to shag and throw the balls back in. Fire 'em in. Show us those arms. Throw 'em home—if you can." His voice wasn't condescending, but it wasn't encouraging or warm either. He gave a direction, plain and simple.

When everyone was set, Sam stepped into the batter's box and took a few righty practice swings. "I'm ready," he finally called out. Larry Woodall took a half windup and tossed in a pitch right down the heart of the plate. Timing it perfectly, Sam pulled the ball high toward dead left field, the ball finally striking loudly near the top of the high wall. He smiled, turned, and looked at Duffy, who was standing just off to the right, but Duffy made no comment or eye contact. He kept his gaze straight ahead. Sam hammered line drives on the next two pitches, one right down the line and the other deep into left-center.

"That's good!" Duffy called out, "Now lefty."

"I'm just getting warmed up," Sam turned and said, spinning his bat and digging in again.

"Never mind. Seen enough. Switch around now. Show me what you've got."

Once ready, Sam called out to Larry, "Right down the pipe. Let's go." He fouled the first pitch straight back. It bounced off the wall and rolled back almost right at Duffy's feet. He didn't bend down to pick it up. Sam stepped out and waved Marvin over toward right-center. "Here it comes," he yelled.

Two sharp line drives followed, both right at Marvin, who quickly threw the balls back in.

"That'll do," Duffy said, waving Jackie in from the outfield. "Grab your glove and take his place out there."

"That's it?" Sam asked, twirling his bat. "That all you want to see? I've got good power from the left. I can show you—"

"That's fine. Maybe later. Next man up right now. Grab your glove and get out there."

Jackie held up near second base so he could ask Sam why he didn't hit more. Sam looked back at Duffy before replying, "Beats me. Maybe I impressed him. I think I did pretty good after the nerves settled."

Jackie shook his head and laughed as he continued jogging to home plate. He was also thrown six balls. He deposited the first two well over the left field wall. After the second one, Jackie glanced back and saw the coaches looking at each other, but none said a word as he continued. The next three swings produced sizzling line drives, two of them to left, and the other right up the middle. The last pitch was popped up high above third base. He stepped in for more, but Duffy said, his voice expressionless, "Nice hitting. That'll be enough. Next man in." He called out to Marvin that it was his turn. Jackie flipped his bat toward the dugout and trotted toward the outfield.

Marvin, in his nervousness, swung late on the first pitch and lined the ball into the stands behind first base. He looked over at Duffy, who finally smiled. "Take your time. Settle in." Settle in he did. The next pitch rocketed over the tall left field wall. Five line drives followed, sprayed to all fields.

Duffy called them all together as the other coaches gathered around. "Each of you take a base, and let's look at some grounders. Grass is wet, so we'll do just a few." Sam reminded him he *could* play infield positions, but most of his professional experience was as an outfielder, especially in center field. "This'll tell me enough about your glove," Duffy replied. "Why don't you take shortstop."

When they were positioned—Sam at shortstop, Jackie at second, and Marvin at first—Del Baker sent each three hard-hit ground balls right at them. Their range wasn't challenged at all. After each catch, they flipped the ball to Duffy, who tossed it back to Del, and the process repeated until Marvin caught the last of his grounders. No one had booted a ball, but the chances hadn't been tough, either.

"Come back in!" Duffy called to them. "Let's do some runnin' now." As all gathered around, he continued, "Look, normally we'd mark off a hundred yards, but the field's too wet. Let's just see how you do from home to first base. That should give us what we want to know. You first," he added, pointing to Sam. "Hear you move right along. That right?"

Sam replied, "Get your watch ready. I'll let you decide."

Duffy walked down to first base, took out his stopwatch, and shouted, "Get ready!" He then counted backward from three, and when he got to "Go!" Sam, from the left side of the plate, was off. His foot touched the bag at 3.8 seconds, which put him in the upper tier of players Duffy had clocked in his long career. All he said when Sam got back to home plate was, "That was good. Very good. Now, wait over by the dugout."

Jackie ran next, his time at 4.3, also a very fast clip. Marvin slipped right out of the box and nearly went down. Sam and Jackie both turned away to hide their laughter. Marvin's time was 4.7, very good considering the rough start. Duffy made a few scribbles on his clipboard, then walked over to them. "That's it for today. Thank you for coming." He turned to Dell. "Go with them to the locker room. Get 'em a bar of soap and three towels. You boys feel free to shower up and get dressed before you leave."

Sam just stood there, staring blankly at him. He looked over at Marvin and Jackie, who were doing the same. "Wait a minute," Sam said as Duffy and the others started walking away. "Is that all you want to see? We didn't really have a chance to show you our game—what we've got. Can we hit some more at least?"

"You did fine," Duffy replied. "I've been around the league a long time. Doesn't take much for me to size up players. No need for more hitting or running. I've seen enough."

"And what did you decide?" Jackie asked, the irritation clear in his tone. "What's your report going to say? What did you *see* from this?"

Duffy toed at the soft dirt and said, "I saw three fine ballplayers. Didn't see any warts. You three can play. I've no doubt of that."

"Then what happens next?" Sam asked, moving toward him. "You said somebody was coming down to talk to us. Should we just wait here?"

Duffy looked first at his coaches before replying. "Opening Day is little more than a week away. Everyone's busy. Our general manager is around here somewhere, but I'm sure he's up to his neck in work. I'll give him my report. Don't worry—we'll call you." He looked at his watch. "Again, thank you for coming. Appreciate it." He then turned and headed quickly toward the dugout. Larry Woodall followed close behind. Del finally said, "Well, you heard the man. Let's get to the locker room. Follow me."

Sam didn't move. Instead, he looked slowly around the ballpark, finally stopping when he got to the high wall in left. "You know," he said to the others, "I could really put some dents in that. I know it, sure as fact."

Jackie walked over and grabbed his arm. "Me, too," he said, quietly. "But it doesn't look like any time soon."

Marvin joined them. "My swing's made for that. Could hit it twice a day and three times on Sunday."

"You're *still* dreaming," Jackie said.

"Maybe—maybe not," Sam replied. "I still don't know what this was."

"You heard what he said," Jackie cut in, sarcasm filling his voice. "He said, 'We'll call you.' Only problem is, he didn't say *what* they'd call us."

"I think we already know the answer to that," Sam said, dryly. "But the question for me is are we good enough to play here?"

"We are," Marvin said. "You know it—I know it."

Taking one last look around, Sam turned to his friends. "Let's get out of here. Need to get home. Our season starts soon, too."

Marvin took a final look at the area around second base and said, to no one in particular, "Sure would be nice."

Sam grasped his shoulder and said, "Let's go. We've got ball to play." He turned to Del. "We're not showering. Don't come along. We'll change quick and find our own way out."

"Suit yourself," was all Del said before turning and walking away.

"Suits me just fine," Sam said. "If we need anything, don't worry, *we'll* call you."

....

A call from the Red Sox never came. Councilman Muchnick had backed off from support of those who wanted to stop Sunday ballgames, so the regular schedule went on as planned. The Boston club had been true to their word. They did invite several African American players in for a look. Whether anyone high in the organization ever studied the report of the events at Fenway Park on the morning of April 12, 1945, is still not known. However, two great ironies grew from that day. Boston was the first to bring in players from the Negro Leagues for a tryout; however, they were the *last* Major League team to add a person of color, in 1959, twelve years after Jackie Robinson stepped on the field for the Brooklyn Dodgers in 1947. Five years after the tryout at Fenway Park, Sam Jethroe did become the first African American to play for Boston, only it was for the *Boston Braves* of the National League—*not* the Red Sox. It is also interesting to note that on that cold, dreary April morning in 1945, it was Sam Jethroe the organization had wanted to see the most. He had already earned the reputation, as one scout put it, as a "Fireball" on the diamond. Through their inaction at that time, the Red Sox missed signing some of the greatest talent in the Negro Leagues.

After signing with the Boston Braves and making his Major League debut on April 18, 1950, Sam put up spectacular numbers his first season, a season which culminated in his becoming, at age 32—although most thought he was just twenty-eight—the oldest Rookie of the Year in MLB history. That season he hit .273, led the league in stolen bases with 35, had 58 runs batted in, slugged 18 home runs, and scored a hundred runs. The next year his stats were almost the same, and a bright future seemed certain. However, likely because of spending six years in the Negro Leagues and his time working up through the minors, his prime years were behind him. Injuries increasingly cropped up, greatly lessening his time on the field and lowering his production. By 1953, a stomach illness and other medical woes caused his batting average to dip so low he was demoted to the Braves' Triple-A club, where he eventually appeared to regain his batting stroke. However, the Braves' scouts were not convinced he would ever return to anything close to his Rookie of the Year form, and he was traded at the end of 1953 to the Pittsburgh Pirates. Both his medical condition and fading skills followed him to Pittsburgh, where he played in just two games at the start of the next season before calling it a career.

Following his playing days, Sam fell on difficult times when his home burned down and his business, "Jethroe's," a neighborhood bar and steakhouse, faced closure because of financial and legal complications. He hadn't played in the Major Leagues long enough to qualify for a pension, which would have helped him greatly. Seeing few options, Sam filed a suit against Major League Baseball in which he requested pension benefits for former members of the Negro Leagues who, because of limited opportunities of the day, had not been able to play in the Majors long enough to meet the qualifications for pensions. His case was thrown out but, several years later, in 1997, Major League Baseball did start providing funds for former Negro League and other older players who had not been able to receive pensions. Sam may not have won his first case, but his actions eventually led to the assistance provided to many others, making him a groundbreaker in yet another way. Sam Jethroe passed away on June 16, 2001, at age eighty-four.

1951 Bowman #242, Sam Jethro
Courtesy of The Topps Company, Inc.

6

Minnie Minoso

Chicago White Sox

Minnie Minoso with his 1951 Chicago White Sox teammates
(Minnie middle row, 3rd from left).

Minnie Minoso was born Saturnino Orestes Arietta Armas in Perico, Cuba, where his family worked in the sugarcane fields. The date of his birth has long been a source of both mystery and humor. In interviews, Minnie himself often provided different dates with the range typically falling somewhere between 1922 and 1926. What *is* known is that Minnie, who later took the surname of his natural father, Minoso, quit school at an early age so he could join his father in the fields. By doing so, he hoped to build up his slight frame to

73

strengthen himself so he could be more competitive in the sport he dearly loved: baseball.

The strenuous work in the hot and humid sugar fields was good for Minnie's physical development. When not working, he played in pick-up baseball games with friends, relatives—*anyone* he could find in the neighborhood—often playing deep into the night. His batting and fielding prowess soon caught the attention of the Cuban semi-pro leagues, and he was signed by Marianoa, a powerful team in Havana. His first year there, the Cuban Professional League voted him Rookie of the Year, an auspicious start to his career. Impressed not just by his baseball skills but also by the way he carried himself and his obvious love of the game, scouts for the New York Cubans of the Negro Leagues offered Minnie a contract, which he accepted in the spring of 1946. He played three seasons with the Cubans and was known as the "Cuban Comet" because of his speed on the base paths. He became one of the better players in the league and a crowd favorite wherever he played.

However, the New York club was in serious financial trouble, so in 1949 they sold Minnie's contract to the Cleveland Indians, who assigned him to their minor league affiliate in Dayton, Ohio, where he tore the cover off the ball, hitting over .500 in limited play. That impressed the organization so much he was brought up to the big club briefly that same year. At this time, Minnie was playing third base. Because the Indians were deep at that position, he was sent back to the minors to learn to play the outfield. Minnie was a quick study and played well, but Cleveland traded him to the Chicago White Sox after the 1950 season. His play was so impressive during spring training in 1951 that he was called up to the big club on May 1—the first person of color to play for the organization. He went on to become one of the most beloved players in White Sox history.

....

June 17, 1951
Shibe Park, Philadelphia, Pennsylvania

Minnie Minoso was absolutely destroying American League pitching. At the start of the second game of Chicago's double-header with the Philadelphia Athletics, he stood among the league leaders with a batting average of .365. He also led the league in triples, stolen bases, and being hit by pitches, having been plunked eight times already at this early point of the season. The latter accomplishment was the direct result of his bravado and taunting of pitchers while on the bases. Especially while on first he would start increasing his distance from the bag, inch by inch, rattling pitchers and daring them to throw over.

Earlier in the season, while Minnie was on first base after a single, the opposing pitcher, Hal White of the Detroit Tigers, threw over eleven times in a row trying to catch Minnie—before making one pitch to the plate. When White finally did make his first pitch, Minnie promptly stole second, causing Hal to charge Minnie, who was still brushing himself off after popping up from his slide. Second base umpire Larry Napp stepped between them as both benches emptied and rushed toward the field. No punches were thrown, but White let loose a string of words so blue that Napp started laughing, which made Hal even angrier. Minnie just stood there, shrugging his shoulders, as if asking, "What's the big deal? Isn't this just part of the game?" White's glare told him the two had vastly different views on the subject.

Minnie had already become a fan favorite, a relationship that started building from his very first at-bat for Chicago when he hit a towering home run on the first pitch thrown to him. He also ran the base paths with wild abandon, not always successfully, but with a flair and excitement few had ever seen before, even his own teammates. Before games, fans showed up to the park early to watch the club take batting practice. Others arrived early to watch Minnie "practicing" crashing into the right field wall to prepare himself to grab potential doubles and triples. He threw balls high into the air so he could practice diving catches. After each crash into the wall or diving slide in the outfield grass, he would playfully roll on the ground, flailing his arms out as if the wind had been knocked out of him. The crowd roared its approval.

His teammates gravitated to him, in awe of his pure joy in the game and how seriously he treated his opportunity with the club. Each day they couldn't wait to see what he'd be wearing when he stepped into the locker room. His shirts were typically multicolored—most would describe them as "loud"—some with flowers or trees, others more like walking rainbows. One had a cluster of parrots across the chest. Minnie favored wide-brimmed hats and sported a different one every day. His pants were always pressed so crisply the pleats appeared razor sharp, and his shoes were shined and buffed so heavily the light in the room reflected off them as he walked. Minnie was teased about his attire every day, but he would say, "Dress good—play good!" then smile and start dancing his own version of the cha-cha until he got to his locker. It wasn't long before several of his teammates started falling in behind him and formed a conga line: Nellie Fox, Chico Carrasquel, and Joe DeMaestri usually leading the way and urging others to follow. Normally, such behavior by a player new to a team would have been considered completely inappropriate, but Minnie's captivating smile and genuine love of the game were contagious—and exactly what the club needed.

Manager Paul Richards, normally a conservative sort and a stickler for rules, borrowed one of Minnie's biggest hats before an afternoon game. He waited until everyone had gone out to the dugout and then emerged, the hat tilted jauntily to the side. When the team saw him, to a man they laughed, cheered, and shook hands with both Minnie and their manager. After that, they went out to the field and crushed Cleveland, 12-1. A week later, while in Boston to play the Red Sox, Minnie took five of his teammates to a hat store he had heard of, the Levine Hat Company, and bought them hats—and not just the run-of-the-mill variety. All had colorful bands and long, bright feathers, very much in the style worn by Minnie. Later that day when the group showed up to the locker room, their teammates erupted in laughter. Playing loose, they won that game, too.

Even the umpires didn't know what to make of Minnie. When he would argue a call on the field, he'd let loose a diatribe that was part in English, part in Spanish, and yet another part a combination of both. He always kept his distance from them so he could wave his arms wildly as he spoke, and his tone was never threatening. On occasion, his teammate and close friend, Chico Carrasquel, would run out of the dugout to help translate what Minnie was saying, but Chico, not wanting Minnie to get in trouble, started "filtering" what was being said—to the point it sounded like Minnie was agreeing with the calls and saying what great umpires they were. Minnie didn't know what was going on, but everyone else did, including the umps, so the arguments usually ended up with smiles all around.

In just under two months, Minnie had helped set a new tone and atmosphere both within the team and among the fans in the stands. One of the Chicago newspapers even started a "Minnie Watch" in the sports pages to make it easier to follow his exploits. The only dark cloud hanging over his arrival to the team was the fact he couldn't stay in the same hotel as his teammates when they were on the road, and they missed him. Minnie didn't like it, but he knew there was nothing he could do, so he didn't balk when he was sent to live with host families in the Black community where the team was playing. His teammate, Chico Carrasquel, from Venezuela, who was light-skinned and described by the team as "Spanish," *was* allowed to stay with the team, but he took it upon himself to do everything he could to keep Minnie connected to his teammates at such times. Chico often picked up Minnie so they could eat together and go to movies, and it wasn't long before other members of the team joined in as a way of showing their support and respect. Minnie reciprocated by taking them with him to local restaurants that served dishes common to his native Cuba, so he could share with them some of the history and culture of his homeland.

In fact, Minnie's teammates became very protective of him. He led the league in being hit by pitches and, as direct consequence, Chicago pitchers suddenly found themselves at the top of the league in "retaliatory" pitches to opposing batters. It wasn't long before every time Minnie was hit, players on the other team started looking around the field as if trying to figure out which of them would be batting in the next inning, thus adding a bullseye to their backs. When his own pitcher plunked someone in return, Minnie made no outward expression. But when the team returned to the dugout, Minnie would walk over to the pitcher and hand him a cigar, grinning the whole time. It was a gesture that surmounted language and helped cement the bond between Minnie and the team.

There was another, more tangible, way Minnie changed the team and added a new level of competitive spirit and drive. His antics on the base paths were bad enough, but pitchers also knew the distractions were one of the main reasons the batter behind him in the lineup, Eddie Robinson, Chicago's first baseman, was clobbering the ball. Because pitchers were losing focus while pitching to him, Eddie was currently batting .311, almost forty points above his career average and was among the league leaders in home runs. The addition of Minnie to the team had been a blessing for Robinson, who now feasted on pitches that were rushed and lacked their usual movement. The tandem of Minnie and Robinson pushed opposing pitchers near the boiling point of frustration when Chicago's top of the batting order came up.

The mood was now light in the Chicago clubhouse before the start of the second game of the twin bill. In the first game of the day, Chicago had won 4-0, but not without more than a little discomfort thrown Minnie's way. He had been drilled in the back by a Carl Sheib fastball in the first inning. He responded later by driving a single to left in the 7th. Once on base, he increased his lead more and more, taunting Sheib and causing him to make six throws to the bag before he turned his concentration to the plate. Minnie increased his lead even farther after that first pitch, daring Sheib to try to pick him off. Seven more throws over followed, each time Minnie just making it back safely, frustrating Sheib to the point of distraction. Minnie was finally erased on a double play, but while crossing the field near the mound on his way back to the dugout Carl glared at him and suggested he not dig in too deeply the next time the two faced each other. Minnie just smiled broadly and kept trotting to the dugout. Now, while stretching to get ready for game two, his back was tight where he'd been hit. However, he didn't care. The victory, and his part in it—bruise and all—had run first place Chicago's record to 38-17 and put them a full three and a half games ahead of the second place Yankees. To Minnie, that was all that mattered.

The Philadelphia fans, frustrated by his success against their club, had just about had it with Minnie as he came up to bat with one on in the first inning of the second game and booed him loudly and unmercifully. Some shouted sharp expletives and crude comments about the color of his skin. Minnie showed no outward reaction as he dug into the batter's box and waited for Philadelphia's pitcher, Alex Kellner, to check on the runner at first and then go into his windup. Kellner was a tough right-handed pitcher who had earned the reputation as someone who didn't mind throwing at hitters, no matter the count or the situation, just to let them know who was in charge when he was on the mound. He was also pitching this season with a huge chip on his shoulder. Arm trouble the previous year had resulted in his leading the league in losses by a starting pitcher, and he was more intense than ever while trying to put that lost season behind him. Minnie knew this, but it didn't bother him in the least as he took his practice swings. To Minnie, *how* he got on base wasn't nearly as important as just getting *on* base. If he had to take a fastball off his arm or back, so be it—as long as it started or kept a rally going.

As Minnie readied himself, the runner on first, Nellie Fox, also swift on the bases, took a long lead, drawing a throw. Minnie stepped out of the box, took two more practice swings, and dug back in. On Kellner's next pitch, Minnie lined a sharp single to right field. Fox had such a good jump he easily made it to third. As soon as the ball was thrown back in, Minnie called time and walked over to his first base coach, Lum Harris, to make sure he had seen the sign for the next play correctly. Kellner seethed and gripped the ball tighter as Minnie took his time walking back to the bag.

As Eddie Robinson, batting cleanup, dug in and waited for the first pitch to him, Minnie faked taking off for second base even before Kellner set himself on the mound. It startled him, and he quickly stepped off the rubber and fired to first, just a split second late to nab Minnie. Minnie stood up, brushed himself off, and the pitcher and runner stared intently at each other, Minnie smiling and Kellner scowling. The challenge was on. The gauntlet had been thrown down.

Minnie took a long lead, inching slowly farther out, swinging his arms back and forth to keep himself balanced and ready to zip either direction. When it looked like he was going to run, Kellner turned and fired to his first baseman, Ferris Fain, who slapped the tag as quickly as he could toward Minnie, who had to dive head-first back to the bag. The first base umpire shouted, "Safe!"—drawing protests not just from Fain and Kellner, but also from what sounded like every fan in the stadium. The roar was so loud that Minnie called time and walked over to his coach, again to make sure he had the correct sign. Minnie nodded, went back to the base, and started his lead again. Just as he stepped a few feet from the bag, Kellner whirled and fired again, hoping to catch Minnie napping. It did catch Minnie a little off guard, but he made it back standing up. Fain slapped a tag on him three times before tossing the ball back to his pitcher. By the way Fain blew out a breath as he retook his position, Minnie knew he had rattled them exactly to the point he wanted.

All the while, Eddie Robinson kept backing out of the batter's box and taking practice swings to keep himself to the ready. He was used to Minnie's torturing pitchers and knew if the interplay lasted long enough, the pitcher's concentration could lag to the point he would be served up a nice, fat fastball. He could look just for that one pitch. A curve or change-up wouldn't be thrown because the extra second the ball would take to get to the plate could make the difference in whether Minnie was thrown out if he took off for second. Eddie was a left-handed batter, which meant Minnie's view of the catcher was partially blocked when he was into his lead, so he had to remain extra vigilant.

Kellner again went into the stretch, holding his glove still just above his belt, and watched Minnie edge farther and farther out. This time he threw toward home, rushing his delivery, which surprised Minnie, who decided in a split-second not to run. The pitch was a ball, high and inside. As soon as Athletics catcher Joe Astroth caught the ball, he stood and fired a strike down to first, hoping to catch Minnie taking his time getting back to the bag. This, too, caught Minnie slightly off guard, and he had to dive toward the outfield side of the first base bag to give him the extra time he needed to avoid Fain's sweeping tag. The play was close—so close even Minnie thought he was out. But Ed Hurley, the first base ump, dramatically swept his arms over and over, at the same time yelling, "Safe! Safe!" The boos rained down again, but this time the shouts came at the umpire, who motioned toward the base as if indicating Minnie's fingers had hit the corner of the bag just before the tag got there.

When Hurley looked up, Philadelphia's manager, Jimmy Dykes, was standing right behind him, screaming at the top of his lungs, but the sound was drowned by the roar of the crowd. Hurley took a few steps back and waved him away just as Kellner and Fain joined in, surrounding him. Larry Napp, umpiring at second, ran over, separated everyone, and cautioned them they were all close to being thrown out of the game if they didn't get back where they belonged. Minnie just stood on top of first base, folded his arms, and smiled as the scene unfolded before him. Dykes glared at him as he finally started back toward his dugout. Kellner slapped the ball violently into his glove and spat toward Minnie, just missing his shoe. Minnie looked down at the ground for a second, then back at Kellner. He smiled again, this time as toothy as he could, which caused Kellner to stop and start back toward Minnie until Fain stepped in and urged him back to the mound.

Minnie knew he had them. As Kellner set himself and went into the stretch, Minnie didn't take quite as long a lead as before— because he knew he didn't have to, knew he wasn't going to need extra time. Just as Kellner, still seething, started his leg kick, he saw out of the corner of his eye Minnie was already well into his dash toward second. The play wasn't even close. When Pete Suder, Philadelphia's second baseman, took the throw, he didn't even bother making a tag. He just stood there, holding the ball and staring down at Minnie, who was already shaking the dirt from his uniform. Kellner walked halfway toward second, stopped, and yelled, "Gimme the ball! What, are you a statue?" He didn't even look at Minnie.

The A's pitching coach walked slowly out onto the field to settle down his hurler, who was walking in circles around the mound while rubbing up the ball. After a few quick words of encouragement, the coach trotted off, and Kellner, now appearing focused again, shook off several signs from his catcher, reared back, and fired a fastball that Robinson didn't quite center. The popup that followed was so high it brought more than a few *ooohhhs* from the crowd, but the third baseman settled under it for the second out. Don Lenhardt was then intentionally walked to load the bases, but on the very next pitch, Jim Busby grounded to first. Kellner had been rattled, but he still got out of the inning without a run scoring. While heading toward his dugout, he called out, "Minoso!" Minnie looked over, but Kellner didn't add anything else. Instead, he shook his head and muttered something Minnie couldn't quite make out.

The pace of the game picked up, and the score was still knotted at 0-0 when Chicago came to bat in the bottom of the third inning. On the second pitch of the inning, Nellie Fox grounded sharply to the second baseman, who easily threw him out. Then, as Minnie walked toward the plate, a low rumble spread through the stands, finally becoming a cascade of shouts at Minnie that rang down to the field. Adding further drama to the moment, Kellner called his catcher, Joe Astroth, to the mound, put his arm around his shoulder, whispered something to him, then walked behind the mound to rub up the ball. In the third base side box seats, a few fans stood. Other clusters soon followed all around the stadium. There were very few in the park who didn't know what was going to happen next.

The crowd grew even louder as Minnie stepped in the box and dug in, taking the last of his practice swings. When he was ready, to the surprise and dismay of many, Kellner stepped off the rubber, walked behind the mound, and this time picked some dirt from his cleats, as if he had all the time in the world. Minnie knew what he was doing. So did everyone else. Those in the Chicago dugout all got up and moved toward the rail, bunching together so that all had a good view of the field.

When Kellner was finally ready, he went into an exaggerated, full wind-up, and with all the strength he could muster let loose a fastball that rode up and in, catching Minnie on his left cheek just below his left eye. The instant Minnie knew the ball was tailing in, he lunged backward, which fortunately resulted in the pitch not hitting him squarely. Still, the force was such that he went down, fast and hard, to the dirt at his feet. The pain was excruciating, and as soon as he ungripped his bat he clutched at his face and writhed back and forth across the plate. To a man, the members of the Chicago White Sox rushed from the dugout, first toward Minnie, but then suddenly changing direction, charging at Kellner. The Philadelphia dugout also emptied, and the melee was on.

Don Lenhardt, Chicago's burly left fielder, was first to reach Kellner and took a roundhouse swing at him, just missing when Kellner ducked at the last second. The two crashed together, wrestling each other to the ground as members of both teams joined in with shoves, shouts, and a few punches of their own. The crowd erupted again as the umpires quickly interspersed themselves in the mob and started pulling players away from each other. Finally, after third base ump Charley Berry managed to separate Kellner and Lenharadt and threatened to eject them both—and anyone else who continued to fight—all started settling down. There were no ejections, although most of the Chicago players were screaming for

Kellner to be thrown out. The umpires just waved them away while saying that any other trouble would result in wholesale ejections. The Sox players didn't like it, but they also knew there was nothing else to be said.

Minnie, still clutching his cheek, was now sitting up on top of home plate while the trainers from both clubs knelt down and checked him over. As both teams finally started heading off the field, Paul Richards called Chico Carrasquel over to walk with him to home plate so he could interpret.

"What's it look like?" Richards asked his trainer as he bent down to see how Minnie was doing. Minnie looked up at his manager but didn't say anything.

Gene Taylor, Chicago's trainer, replied, "He's lucky. *Very* lucky. Glancing blow. Doesn't look like anything's broken, he's going to be plenty sore tomorrow. Already starting to swell. Take a look for yourself."

Richards gently pulled back Minnie's hand and studied his cheek. "Son, you OK?" he asked. "Geez—that's going to be some shiner. You've had enough. I'll have Taylor take you back to the hotel and tend to this. You can rest and heal up, so we can have you ready for our next series against the Yanks."

Richards looked up at Chico and asked him to find out how much Minnie had understood. Chico spoke to him in Spanish until Minnie, surprising all, jumped to his feet. In perfect English, he looked at his manager and said, "Coach, I'm not coming out! I'm not! I'm staying here." Minnie broke free from the grip of the trainer and headed toward first base.

Richards blocked him, wrapping his arms around him. "Whoa! Wait! But you're already black and blue!"

Minnie looked at him curiously. Chico, sensing that his friend didn't fully understand, said a few more words to him. Minnie replied, and when he did so, Chico started laughing, loudly.

"What is it?" Richards demanded. "What'd he say?"

Chico, struggled to stop his laughter. "Minnie said, 'Well, I'm black. I don't know about blue.'"

Richards shook his head. "What else did he say?"

"He said he's going to first base because if he leaves the game, it will spread around the whole league, and every time in every city, they're going to try to—what's the word? —*intimidate* him. He won't let that happen and says no matter what you do, he's going to take his base."

"But look at that face!" Richards shot back.

Minnie put his hand on his manager's shoulder, as if trying to comfort *him*, and said, "Minnie is OK. You'll see." Without another word, he trotted toward first. The Philadelphia fans—violating baseball tradition—did not applaud when they saw Minnie was going to remain in the game. Instead, it almost sounded to everyone that a collective gasp was let out as Minnie touched the first base bag, as if they couldn't believe what they were seeing.

Ed Hurley, the home plate umpire, said to Richards and Chico at the same time, "Your man has guts. I'll give him that."

"Yes, he does—and then some," Richards said. "Maybe more than good sense. I know he's right. Let's just keep an eye on him."

Hurley nodded. Chico walked with his manager back to the dugout as Minnie stretched and ran in place at first base while waiting for play to resume.

Minnie took his lead, again inching out as far as he dared. Kellner didn't throw over, but he did step off the rubber, making Minnie retreat for a moment back to the bag. The crowd again started yelling at Minnie, whose face was swelling so rapidly he was having a difficult time seeing out of his left eye. Because of his injury, he hadn't been given the steal sign, so this time he settled for an average lead, allowing Kellner to finally throw to the plate. When he did, Robinson laced a fastball to center field. Minnie was off with the crack of the bat and easily made it standing up to third, where he rounded the bag and pretended he was going to try for home as the relay from the outfield skipped toward the mound. When the shortstop finally grabbed the ball, time was called.

Kellner had been backing up home plate, and as he walked back toward the mound he swung to his left, bringing him only a few yards from Minnie. He paused for a moment, glared at Minnie, and continued to the mound. Kellner's concentration and focus were gone. This became even more apparent when the next batter, Don Lenhardt, doubled to deep left field, scoring Minnie and sending Robinson all the way to third. As Minnie touched the plate, the crowd let loose. The cries weren't directed to their faltering pitcher. Rather, they wanted one last dig at Minnie, who simply ignored them. The trainer was waiting for Minnie at the dugout steps and, while urging him to take a seat, applied an ice bag to his cheek. However, he wasn't seated long. On the next pitch, Jim Busby socked a home run deep into the left field stands, scoring Robinson and Lehardt ahead of him. Chicago now led 4-0.

Jimmy Dykes scrambled to get one of his best relievers, Morrie Martin, warmed up in the bullpen before the game got completely away from them. However, before Martin could get his arm loose, the next batter, Chico Carrasquel, singled to left. Phil Masi fouled out, but Chicago's pitcher, Luis Aloma, added the final insult—a line drive single to center. Dykes had seen enough and, as soon as the ball was thrown back in, he started walking slowly toward the mound. Kellner, still seething, handed him the ball without a word, looked toward the Chicago dugout and scowled as he headed for his dugout. In the ultimate insult, the Chicago players turned their backs dugout to him.

Martin retired the next hitter, finally drawing the inning to a close. When Chicago's starter, Luis Aloma came back to the dugout to get his glove, Minnie took him aside. Luis was also from Cuba, so there were no communication issues. Minnie told him in no uncertain words he wasn't to retaliate on his behalf. When Luis looked confused, Minnie said, "This game is not over. We're only three and a half games ahead of the Yankees, and our next series is against them. We *need* this game. Let's finish them off right now, and the next time we play them we can do something. Please."

Chico Carrasquel had overheard the conversation and relayed a summary of it to his manager, who nodded approvingly. "He's right again," he said, pointing toward Minnie. "Good sense. Good team player."

From there on, the Athletics, sure at least one of them was going to be drilled at some point, spent the rest of the game in tentative batting stances at the plate. They managed just four more hits and never threatened to score. On the other hand, Minnie retaliated in his own way by putting on quite a show, going four for four, with two RBI's, three runs scored, and a walk on top of everything else. In his last at-bat, in the top of the 9th, his left eye was almost completely swollen shut. He still managed to lace a single to center. As he rounded first base, pockets of Philadelphia fans across the stadium finally rose to their feet and applauded—not the man, but his heart. Minnie quickly tipped his cap, then took his longest lead of the day, drawing another throw as he dove safely back to the bag. When he looked up, his teammates were all applauding.

The final score was 9-0, with Luis Aloma going the distance and allowing just five hits. His was an outstanding performance, but after the game everyone gathered around Minnie, both to congratulate him and check on his health. When Richards came over and asked how he felt, Minnie, holding ice to his cheek, looked up and replied, "We won. All I care about. That's beautiful. It's beautiful!"

Each of his teammates, in turn, shook his hand before heading to the lockers. They had won the double header, but on this day, they had accomplished much more than that. Thanks to Minnie, they were now, more than ever, a team, in *every* sense of that word.

....

Minnie Minoso went on to play in seventeen seasons in Major League Baseball, eleven of those as a starting player. He played for the Cleveland Indians, Chicago White Sox, St. Louis Cardinals, and Washington Senators—some of them multiple times. Minnie appeared in 1,835 games, and his career statistics include a lifetime batting average of .298, 1,963 hits, and 186 home runs. However, those numbers hardly tell the story of Minnie Minoso. He was one of the most exciting players of the 1950s and early 1960s, many seasons surpassing or falling just short of the accomplishments of players such as Mickey Mantle, Ted Williams, and Stan Musial. *The Sporting News* named him Rookie of the Year in his first full season, 1951, through a vote made by American League players. He also made the All-Star team seven times, led the American League in triples three times, stolen bases three times, batted over .300 nine times, and was hit by pitches 192 times (10th at the time in Major League history). In addition to outstanding natural talent on the field, he was also flamboyant and a constant irritant to other teams when on base. He was a popular teammate wherever he played and was adored by fans who appreciated the energy and excitement he generated.

In spite of all that, Minnie Minoso's professional baseball career is an extremely complicated one to summarize and do justice to, for several reasons. First, he was the only player to take the field professionally in seven different decades, from the 1940s up to 2003. When he was in his 50s (his actual age on each occasion is still up for debate), the Chicago White Sox brought him back for cameo appearances on the field in 1976 and 1980. In his 1980 appearance, he knocked a base hit, becoming one of the oldest players to do so in MLB history. In 2003, when 77 or so, he suited up as the Designated Hitter for the independent St. Paul Saints of the Northwest League—and drew a base on balls, for which he received a five-minute standing ovation. In addition, he played everywhere from Cuba to the United States to Mexico, and played exceptionally well every place he landed. These accomplishments earned him enshrinement in the Cuban Baseball Hall of Fame in 1983 and the Mexican Professional Baseball Hall of Fame in 1996. On top of all that, when he first retired from Major League Baseball after the 1964 season, he immediately went to the Mexican Baseball League, where he played and coached nine more seasons. He never left baseball, and baseball never left him. Starting in 1976, he worked for the Chicago White Sox organization the rest of his life, first as a coach and then as an ambassador, not just for their own team, but for baseball at large. Finally, in 2008 he was awarded the "Jackie Robinson Legacy Award" for lifetime achievement.

Today, many passionately believe that Minnie should be in the Major League Baseball Hall of Fame in Cooperstown. Why he isn't there is a mystery to those supporters. They believe comparison of Minnie's record with others of his era leave no doubt he is worthy of membership, especially among those whose careers straddled the Negro Leagues and the Major Leagues. Perhaps it is the fragmented nature of his playing career—that he played in so many leagues and that he did not play longer in Major League Baseball—that continues to be held against him. In the end, he will be remembered as a genuinely kind and caring person who played for the fans—and who provided inspiration and support for the many Latin players who came after him, many of whom refer to him as the "Latin Jackie

Robinson." Minnie Minoso passed away on March 1, 2015 behind the wheel of his car, while on his way home from yet another baseball-related function. Minnie probably wouldn't have had it any other way.

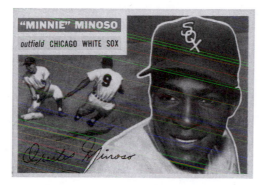

1956 Topps #125, Minnie Minoso
Courtesy of The Topps Company, Inc.

7

Bob Trice

Philadelphia Athletics

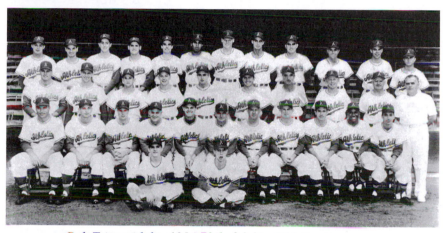

*Bob Trice with his 1954 Philadelphia Athletics teammates
(Bob top row, 6th from left).*

Bob Trice grew up in Weirton, West Virginia, where he had fallen in love with all sports by the time he started school. When he finally reached high school, his skills had developed to the point that he served as captain for his high school baseball, football, and basketball teams. The talented three-sport athlete became a local legend, and several college and professional teams courted him. However, at age seventeen Bob felt compelled to help the war effort and joined the Navy, serving until his discharge in 1946. As soon as he returned home, he took a job working alongside his father in a steel mill but immediately realized it was a mistake. After just one day, Bob decided to quit and at least try to follow his dream of making a living in baseball.

Bob joined a local semi-pro team, which used him all over the diamond: at first base, in the outfield, and even on the pitching mound. He played so many positions so well that he caught the attention of scouts for the Homestead Grays of the Negro National League. Because of his natural athletic ability, the Grays offered him a contract without even having a specific position in mind for him.

From there, Bob's professional baseball career took off, but initially there were more than a few bumps in the road. The Grays had few openings in their regular lineup. However, they did need pitching, and because Bob had shown some talent there while playing at the semi-pro level, the club decided to see what he could do on the mound. They knew he would not be a traditional power pitcher, but he did have a sharp-breaking curveball and a slider that often buckled the knees of hitters from *both* sides of the plate. What he lacked in speed he more than made up for by keeping hitters off-balance and unsettled at the plate. Bob was a quick study, and soon he was relieving anD0020then starting for the team. He had found the position where he would become a star.

After another season with the Grays, Bob moved on to play for several other teams before finally being signed by Ottawa of the International League, an affiliate of the Philadelphia Athletics. With Ottawa in 1953, Bob took the league by storm. He led the league in wins with a 21-10 record, was on the All-Star team, was named Most Valuable Pitcher, and was even crowned Rookie of the Year. The pitching-starved Philadelphia Athletics took note and invited him to spring training the following year. After an outstanding performance in the spring games, he made the big club. On September 13, 1953, Bob became the first person of color to play for the Athletics.

....

July 10, 1954
Connie Mack Stadium, Philadelphia, Pennsylvania

The Philadelphia Athletics had just lost to the Boston Red Sox 5-3 in a wild back and forth game. With the score knotted at two runs each at the end of nine innings, the Red Sox took the lead in the top of the 10th only to have the Athletics respond with a run of their own in the bottom of the inning. In the 11th, Boston got the go-ahead run on a walk with the bases loaded, which caused Philadelphia's manager, Eddie Joost, to fling a fungo bat the full length of the dugout, just missing several heads along its flight. A sacrifice fly followed for Boston's final run. In the bottom home half of the inning, the Athletics got the tying run to the plate, but a quick double play ended their threat—and the game. The loss dropped their record to 30-47, miring them deeper into 7th place. In a quiet clubhouse after the game, most players showered and headed quickly out of the park before their manager could call a meeting to dress them down for their sloppy play.

Just under an hour after the end of the game, only the manager and a handful of players remained. One of the players, Bob Trice, had stalled his departure, hoping he could squeeze in a private moment with Joost. He sat in front of his locker and made a half-hearted attempt at reading the local newspaper while waiting for the others to leave. Bob had read the same news story about a fire in a local factory three times before he rolled up the paper, slapped himself hard on the right leg, and stood up, his emotions racing. It was time he talked to his manager. After looking around to make sure no one else was in the immediate area, he walked to Joost's office and knocked softly on the door.

"Yeah, what is it?" Joost called out in a gravelly voice.

"It's Trice, Bob. Can I come in for a minute? It's important."

A few seconds later, Joost swung open the door. "I'm looking at lineups for tomorrow. Doubleheader. Always a headache. *You're pitchin' the first game.* So, this better be good. What do you want?"

Bob leaned against the door frame. "Got something on my mind. Skip, I know you're busy, but if you could just give me a few minutes, I'd be grateful."

Joost thought about chasing him off, but his curiosity set in. "What are you doing here? It's late. Aren't you going back to your hotel? Or, are you just going to sleep *here* tonight? Why don't you—"

Bob knew that sarcastic tone of voice. Joost called on it every time the team suffered a bad loss. Bob cut him off. "I'm getting ready to head down to the streetcar stop. I'd just like a minute. Please."

Seeing the worry on Bob's face and hearing the concern in his voice, Joost waved him in as he turned back toward his desk. "Well, come in. But make this fast. Take that chair over by the file cabinet."

Bob closed the door, walked across the room, and sat down, speaking the minute he was settled. "Skip, I'm just going to say this. I just don't feel right, and I don't know what to do about it."

"You sick? You look OK. I can get Murphy up here. I swear the man *never* goes home. He's not just a trainer. He was a medic during the war. Seen it all from what I hear."

"No, I'm fine. Well, I'm not fine, but I'm not sick, either. It's just that . . .."

"Trice, what in the world are you talkin' about. Spit it out."

Bob locked eyes with his manager, his heart pounding. To this point, he felt his relationship with Joost had been as friendly as could be expected between a player and a manager. They didn't speak often, but when they did, Bob believed a trust was developing between the two. The last thing Bob wanted to do was set that back, but he also knew if anyone in the organization would understand what was in his heart, his manager would be that person.

"Skip, this isn't what I thought it would be. Oh, I knew it'd be different up here in a lot of ways, but I guess I didn't understand what was going to happen. I just don't feel right at all." He paused and looked down at the floor before continuing, this time his voice very matter-of-fact, "I'm not sure I want to be here."

"Look, we've talked about this before," Joost said, scooting his chair out from behind his desk and closer to Bob. "Some of these cities have got that rule. I'm sorry you can't stay with us sometimes when we're on the road, but we can't do anything about it right now. Just the way it is. You know that."

Bob leaned back in his chair and shook his head. "That's not what I'm talking about. That's not why I'm here, but . . . it's a part of it. Seems like our travelling secretary—what's his name? Jamieson? There are still too many towns that don't have hotels where I can stay, and he's always fixing it up with a family so I can stay with them. But all he ever says is the same thing, 'You'll like them. They're *Black*.'"

"Honestly, Skip, I can't stand most of the people where I stay when we're on the road. Just because our skin's the same doesn't mean we're going to like each other. I'm nothing to them but the five bucks a day they get for giving me supper and a place where I'm out of sight. I don't like it, but I've been trying to live with it. But that's not why I'm here. There's so much more. There's . . .."

When he hesitated, Joost asked, his voice softening, "What do you want me to do? Bob, if I can do it, I'll try. I hope you know that."

"I honestly don't know. There's so much, and it's *all the time*."

Joost had been holding a lineup card and a pencil, but he set them next to him on the table and crossed his arms. "Let's have it. I want to know."

Bob loudly blew out a breath, and replied, "Thanks. I guess I just want to say a few things, and I hope you'll understand."

"Go on. Tell me."

"Skip, I'm not a snitch, a tattle-tale, and I'm not ungrateful. I want that out first so this doesn't sound like I'm complaining about anyone in particular. I know I wasn't the choice of a lot of people around here. As it worked out, I was the first on this team. It wasn't my choice. I was happy where I was in Ottawa. I was told to report here, and I did. What I didn't know was how much I'd be by myself, and I wasn't used to that at first, and I'm still not now. I'm grateful the club signed Vic Power before the season, but he's from Puerto Rico, and we have very little in common. He's about the only one I talk to, and we don't understand over half of what the other is saying because of the language.

"The other guys all have roommates on the road. I get *host* families. The others get to eat together, go to the movies, play cards, shoot the bull. I can't do any of that because I'm not here most of the time. I'm not saying they don't want me around. I honestly don't know one way or the other for most of them. Oh, I know some are mad I'm here, but I don't get many chances to find out about the others. I think I get along fine with most, but it's hard to tell."

Joost leaned back. "I wouldn't worry about that too much. Most of them don't like me and don't want a dang thing to do with me after we leave the park. I don't like that either, but it's part of the job and the way it has always been. That's just baseball."

"I understand that, Sir, but *you* have a choice. You *could* be with them more if you wanted to try. I can't. Before I got here, I loved the game. Baseball was my whole life. I know the International League, and my Monarchs team before that, aren't the same, but we always had fun and played loose. We were serious about winning and hated it when we lost, but if we did lose, we didn't cut open every moment of every game to figure out what happened. I mean no disrespect to you, but seems like we do just as much talking as we do playing. We study and study and study. I know why we do it, and it's probably a better way. I'll admit that. But it sure isn't as much fun."

Joost stood up, walked behind Bob's chair, and picked up a file folder. "It doesn't matter whether it's the minors, the Mexican League, or wherever—baseball's the same. It *should* be the same. We all might go about it different, but winning is still why we're here. It might seem to you we spend too much time on strategy, but I want you to think about the competition we face every day—no matter what team we're playing. They can all beat you. I just picked up the scouting report for the Sox that I was given the other day. I've studied it six ways from Sunday because it might help. We try everything we can to get an edge, and that takes meetings and scouting reports and pullin' together. It might not be for you, but that part is fun for *me*. That's what I'm paid to do. I want my players to draw close and believe in what we're doing to try to win. Don't you want that?"

"Yes, I do. Please don't misunderstand me. Everything you just said is right. I know that. It's just that up here baseball isn't as much fun for me. Maybe it's because I don't have anyone to talk to most of the time, but when I go to the park, it's like going to a job I've never had before, and I don't feel the joy or excitement I always felt. I just feel . . . *sad* most of the time. Here, I feel like it's just work."

Joost laughed. "It *is* a job. It *is* work. *Hard* work. And, do you know how many out there in the minors and behind every bush would give their eyeteeth to be here right now, sittin' right here in this locker room? Most of them will never make it because it *is* hard. They might even have enough talent to play, but they'll never get a chance. Do you know how lucky you are? To be on this team? In this league? You sit there and say you aren't having fun. Baseball is more than just having fun, and you know that. So, what is it you're really saying? There has to be more or I'm really missing something."

Bob tensed up for a moment and wondered if he'd gone too far, had crossed a line. "Maybe I should go," he said, pulling his legs together so he could stand. "I'm sorry. I—"

"No, let's keep going. I need you on this ball club. Let's talk this out more. I know you've had a rough stretch and have lost a few in a row, but you're still one of the best pitchers I've got, even on your worst day. Heck, you're leading the team in wins right now. I haven't patted you on the back much, but I don't do that with anybody. Maybe I should have said something more. I don't know."

"Thanks for saying that, Skip. I don't need pats on the back. That's not what I'm getting at. You're one of the best managers I've played for. That's the gospel. I'm talking about something else. Every day I go out on the field, I know what's going to happen. I try not to pay attention to it, but it's hard not to."

Here Bob chose his words carefully. "I know you've heard about the letters and calls I get. At first, they put a scare in me, but now I try to put them out of my mind. Still, when I pitch, sometimes I look around the stands and wonder if one of them will be waiting for me after the game. That's a heck of a thing to think about when I'm on the mound. Hard to shake. I'm not a coward. If I could see them coming . . . but I can't, and I think about that a lot."

When Joost didn't say anything, Bob continued. "And, then there's the name calling and the shouts from the stands. I've gotten used to that everywhere I've played. It's nothing new. Yes, I know they scream everything bad they can think of about Italians when DeMaestri makes an out or an error. The same for Jacobs and Limmer about their religion when they upset the fans. But with them, it's just a dig—not personal. And this isn't just when we're away. The fans here at home do this all the time, too. So, I know I'm not the only one, but it's the way they scream at *me* that gets me and is something I've never had before. It's the hate that's there. The hate. If I do good, they say I'm lucky. If I flub a play or make a bad pitch, it's because of my color—like it's a disease that causes me to lose my skills in a snap."

Joost started to respond, but Bob didn't give him a chance. "Even my own teammates. It's the little things. Most wait until I'm out of the shower after a game before they go in. They don't ask me to play cards or checkers in the clubhouse. Most don't talk to me. I don't think they're being purposely mean to me. I think they just don't know what to do with me."

Joost finally raised a hand and stopped him. "Look, I know it hasn't been—*still isn't*—easy for you. But it's not easy for anybody, no matter who they are. The fact is, when your game is there, you're really good. When the change, curve, slider are working, your fast-ball catches batters off guard, and they're kept off balance. Then you shine. You're 7-7 right now! Think about that. If it weren't for you, we'd be in the cellar. There's been a bad hop here, a bad call there, and you've thrown your share of gopher balls already this year, something we're going to have to work on. But, all in all, I think you're making progress and you'll get better. I'm counting on that. We all are."

Both men were startled when the office door flung open. The Athletics' regular catcher, Joe Astroth, walked in, stopped when he saw them, and said, "Oh, I'm sorry. Didn't think anybody was here. I saw the lights on and thought I'd look just to make sure. You two OK?"

"Astroth, you should be home now," Joost replied, sharply. "Double header tomorrow. What in blazes are you doing here?"

"Forgot my wallet. Third time this year. Always put it above my locker so I don't lose it, and then I forget it. Go figure. My wife'd kill me if I showed up without it." He looked back and forth at Joost and Bob. "You sure everything's OK?"

Joost studied him a minute before saying, "Joe, take a seat. You're already late gettin' out of here, so a couple more minutes won't matter." When Joe was seated, he said. "Let me ask you something. Be honest now. What do you think of Bob—his pitching? I want you to tell me—and Bob. Let's hear it."

Joe looked back and forth between the two, not sure what he was supposed to say. When he didn't say anything, Joost spoke again. "This isn't a trick question. Just give me a scouting report on him. If you were on a team facing us, what would you say?"

Obviously still uncomfortable and avoiding looking at Bob, Joe finally spoke. "Well, first thing is he has a pretty fair curve. Two, really. One roundhouse and one over the top, twelve to six. If batters don't know it's coming, buckles a lot of knees."

Finally looking at Bob, Joe hesitated until Joost urged him to continue. "And his slider is a *sweeper*. Both righties and lefties hate it. Hard to get the barrel on it. If he's going good with it, they'd be lucky for a loud foul. He's also got a good change of pace because his arm motion is same as the fastball. Throws the timing off really good. They swing through it like windmills."

"Any faults? How would you tell batters to hit him?" Joost asked.

"Fastball is nothing to write home about, but it'll do because he uses it to set up the slower stuff. But, if the fastball isn't being thrown for a strike so he can get ahead, you can sit on the curve and time the slider pretty good. I'd tell my hitters to wait him out. That is, take a few pitches and see what he has going. If he's off that day, sit back and clobber him."

Bob finally spoke up. "Joe, why haven't you ever said anything like this to me before? What you say is true—I've no problem with that. It's just that we could have talked about what we wanted to do if I was off—if I needed to adjust during a game. If you know all this, then the others do, too. Why don't we ever talk about this? Sure would help, don't you think?"

Joe sat there, staring straight ahead at his manager, as if asking how he was supposed to respond. Seeing how uncomfortable the situation had become, Joost spoke up, directing his words to Bob. "I think what Joe is trying to say is you can be *predictable* when you start slipping in a game. Guess I've noticed it, too, but the same can be said for almost all pitchers, after all."

Bob started to speak, but Joost held up his hand and turned to his catcher. "So, Joe, what do you think about Bob's future with us? Think he'll get better? I know he's sittin' right here in front of us but be honest."

Joe shifted in his chair. He looked at Bob and said, "He can play. He's got moxie." He paused and turned back to Joost. "He needs to stay more focused, in the game more. His mind wanders sometimes, doesn't bear down when he should. Sorry. That's just what I think."

"I take no offense," Bob said, moving so he was right in front of Joe. "I wish you'd said some of this before." Joe didn't respond. He just shrugged his shoulders and looked back at Joost.

"No matter," Joost said. "We get the point here. Joe is in position to judge you the best. What he says make sense, and if you think about it, I think you'll agree." He turned back to Joe. "You better get home. Mary will skin you if you don't hurry. See you tomorrow. Oh, by the way, you're catching the first game." He smiled broadly and pointed to Bob, "He'll be pitchin'. You two might want to have a cup of coffee before the game. Maybe say a few words to each other?"

Joe nodded, first to Joost and then to Bob, and without saying anything left the room.

As soon as he was gone, Joost turned to Bob. "Here's what

I want you to do. Go home and get a good sleep. Sleep on it. Tomorrow, give me your best. If you do that and you still want to go back to Ottawa, I'll see what I can do. My money's on you realizing you need to stay here. You can't throw this away. *This* is your future. I think you'll figure that out. We'll talk after the game tomorrow."

Bob stood and reached out to shake his hand. Joost shook his hand, firmly.

....

The next day, Sunday, July 11, 1954, was stiflingly hot the second the sun started rising. There was no breeze, and the humidity rose quickly. By game time, the thermometer settled in at ninety-three degrees.

As Bob finished the last of his warm-up pitches before the start of the game, he noticed his jersey was already soaking wet and after the inning he'd have to get to the locker room for a replacement.

He and Joe had not met before the game to talk strategy and go through the Red Sox batters. Bob had wanted to, but every time he approached Joe, Joe was busy with another task and said, "We'll see if we have time later. Give me a minute." The minutes stretched to game time, and both took the field without so much as a nod to each other.

The Red Sox shortstop and lead-off hitter, Milt Boling, swung at Bob's first pitch, a slow curve, and lofted it to short right-center, where A's centerfielder Bill Wilson made a one-handed running catch. He threw the ball back in as the crowd cheered and finished settling into their seats.

The next batter, Jimmy Piersall, also swung at the first pitch, a fastball that caught just the outside part of the plate, and smashed a sharp grounder to the second baseman. Spook Jacobs booted the ball, allowing Piersall to reach safely. On the road, the play would have been ruled an error, but the hometown Official Scorer declared it a hit. Ted Williams dug in next, and on a 1-1 count singled to right. Piersall stopped at second. Bob wasn't pitching badly, but his curve didn't have its normal snap, and the slider wasn't sweeping. As the next batter dug in, Joe thought about going to the mound to tell his pitcher to slow down, take a breath, and do what he does best: change speeds more effectively. However, he didn't move from behind the plate. Instead, he called out, "Two on! Bear down! Let's go!"

Sammy White, the Sox catcher, swung late at a 2-0 pitch and fouled it to the first baseman. Two outs. Billy Goodman, their first baseman, stepped to the plate, dug in, took his customary three practice swings, and was ready. He took two quick strikes, both sliders that caught the inside corner, before timing a hanging curveball and driving the ball just over Bob's head and into center field. Piersall scored easily, and Williams took third. After gathering himself and wiping the sweat from his hands, Bob threw a slider to Jackie Jensen, their centerfielder, who drove it high and deep to left. At first, most thought it would clear the wall for a three-run homer but, at the last second, timing his jump perfectly, Philadelphia's left fielder, Gus Zernial, caught the ball in the very tip of the webbing of his glove. The crowd cheered again as the Athletics came in for their half of the opening frame, down just 1-0. It could have been much worse.

The Athletics' leadoff hitter, Spook Jacobs, walked on four pitches, but he was stranded at first as the next three batters went out on easy fly balls. Bob was headed back to the mound before he had a chance to change his shirt.

In the top of the 2nd, Bob gave up a double and walked a man, but three hard-hit balls resulted in outs, keeping the score 1-0 in favor of the Red Sox. Bob and his catcher didn't speak between innings. When the Athletics were at bat, Bob sat alone by the water cooler, largely ignored by the rest of his teammates, who cheered each other on and joked with one another. His manager was the only one to acknowledge him. Joost did so by patting him on the back and saying, firmly, "Bear down today. Show me what you've got."

The score remained the same as the Sox came to bat in the top half of the third inning. The inning started oddly, with Athletics' first baseman Lou Limmer catching the last of the infield warm-up throws and, as he turned to toss the ball into the dugout, stepped awkwardly on the side of the first base bag, turning his ankle and falling in pain to the ground. The Athletics' trainer ran out and checked the injury as Limmer writhed in pain in the soft dirt around the bag. Joost also ran out, and Bob and the others in the infield walked over to see what was going on. By the time Bob got there, Joost was motioning Don Bollweg to get loose and take over at first. The trainer and Joost then helped Limmer to the dugout. The umpires allowed Bollweg to throw the ball around a few times to warm up, but because this was the first game of a doubleheader and the day was going to be long, the home plate ump soon motioned for Bob to get ready to start the inning. He asked for a couple of warm-up pitches because of the delay, but his request was denied.

Still thinking about his first baseman, Bob looked in and saw Ted Williams digging in the batter's box. Bob gave Williams—judged by most as the best hitter in the league, possibly in all of baseball—nothing to hit, walking him on four pitches. Bob started off the next batter, Sammy White, with a hard breaking slider, and Sammy clubbed the ball to deep center, where it was caught just a few feet from the wall. The crowd had grown silent, anticipating a home run, then cheered loudly as the ball was caught. The next batter singled on a hanging curve, sending Williams to third. Jackie Jensen followed, taking two curves that ended up high and inside before doubling into the right center field gap, driving in two runs. A groundout to short followed, but the batter after, Grady Hatton, lined a bullet to center, scoring Jensen. Their pitcher, Frank Sullivan, then hit a fly to deep center, and the inning was over, but not before Boston had scored three runs, increasing their lead to 4-0.

As Bob walked slowly from the mound to the dugout, Joost waited for him at the top of the steps. "Got to keep the ball down, Bob. Pitches are up today. We'll try to get some runs back now. Take a seat. Drink some water. Towel yourself. Heat's bearing down."

His words were meant as encouragement, but Bob knew he didn't have it today. His pitches weren't sharp, and his motion, for whatever reasons, didn't feel fluid, normal. He didn't have the *touch* and couldn't get enough change in speed to keep the hitters off-balance. As Bob sat alone next to the water cooler, he pounded his pitching hand in his glove, grimaced, and glanced over at his catcher, who was gulping down a cup of water. "What do you think, Joe?" he called over, hoping to strike up a conversation. Joe flung the rest of his water to the dugout floor before responding. "Not good. Catching too much of the plate. Not foolin' 'em today."

"Suggestions?" Bob replied. "Something you think we should try?"

"I'll think on it. Top of their order coming up. Second time through. They'll be hackin'."

Nothing else was said between them. The Athletics went out in order in the bottom of the third—and quickly: a ground out to third, a pop up to left, and a strikeout. Joe finally looked over at Bob and pointed out to the mound, urging him to walk ahead of him and out of the dugout.

It didn't take long for Boston to strike in the fourth. Bolling drilled a changeup to left to open the inning. Bunting for a hit, Piersall was thrown out, Bolling moving to second. Ted Williams, who had been hotter than usual over the past week, was intentionally walked. Sammy White dribbled a grounder back to Bob who rushed the play, bobbled the ball, and threw wildly past first, allowing Bolling to score all the way from second on the error. Goodman was next. He scorched a rocket that glanced off the outstretched glove of the diving second baseman, loading the bases.

Joe took off his catcher's mask and slowly walked out to Bob to deliver a new baseball. Once at the mound, he looked at the runners at each base before saying, "Joost signaled for a stall. Romberger's warming up and needs a little more time. Looks like we just didn't have it today."

"Appears that way," Bob said, also looking at the runners. He was tired—not just physically, but in ways he couldn't quite put into words. Rather than being upset with his performance, he was angry with himself—for not following his gut and his heart. On the mound, in this game, wasn't where he wanted to be. At that moment, he thought of Ottawa in the International League. Of being named Rookie of the Year at that level the previous season. Of joking with his teammates there. Of waking up every day anxious to get to the park to have the camaraderie and fun that always seemed to meet him as soon as he stepped into the locker room. Now, however, that was a distant memory, one he kept going back to when he should have been striving to achieve in the present and striking into the future.

"No place to put him," Joe finally said, pointing to Jackie Jensen, who was striding toward the plate. "Try the slider, low and away, and see if a double play shows up. If it doesn't . . .." He didn't finish the thought.

The first pitch to Jensen was to be a hard slider low and away. Instead, the ball rose up and in, almost hitting him. Joe took an extra second before firing the ball back to Bob, as if to say he needed to bear down on the next pitch. Bob went into the stretch, looked at the runner at third, and let loose another slider, this one catching too much of the heart of the plate. Jensen drilled it into left-center, scoring both Williams and White.

Bob had backed up the plate, but by the time he was halfway back to the mound, Joost was already there, waving toward the bullpen. Bob paused a moment when he saw him, then continued walking slowly until he reached the edge of the mound. Joost was rubbing up a new ball but suddenly stopped and said, "That's it for today. Grab some bench. Romberger's coming in." His words were low, but firm, his tone one of disappointment.

"Sorry, Skip," was all Bob said before turning and walking toward the dugout. He passed Joe, who was on his way to the mound, but neither looked at the other.

The dugout was silent as Bob walked down the steps and sat alone again by the cooler. No one said a word to him. Instead, all eyes were focused toward the mound as Joost and Joe gave instructions to their relief pitcher. Once play resumed, on Romberg's first pitch, Ted Lepcio doubled off the center field wall, plating Goodman and Jensen, driving the score to 9-0. A walk and two groundouts later, the inning was finally over. The line score for Bob was nine runs, eight of which were earned, on ten hits and three walks—in three and a third innings. It was, by far, his worst outing of the year. The Sox continued to pour it on in the later innings, scoring nine more times. The Athletics managed five hits but no runs. Final score: 18-0. Bob took the loss, dropping his record to 7-8.

Just over five minutes after the game was over, Joost walked into his office and slammed the door shut behind him so violently the whole room shook. The players were quiet, knowing better than to joke around and visit after such a lopsided defeat. A small sandwich buffet had been prepared for them so they could grab a quick snack before the second game, and they had lined up, slowing moving along the tables, as they heard their manager let loose a tirade they knew was directed at them.

Bob had started toward the end of the line when he suddenly stopped, put down his plate, and headed for his manager's door. Joe DeMaestri, the A's shortstop and one of the few teammates ever to draw him into conversation, stuck out an arm to block his progress. Bob pushed his arm back and said, "It's OK. I need to go in."

Bob knocked softly, opened the door, and walked right in. "Skip," he said, looking right at Joost. "It's time. I want to be sent back to Ottawa."

Joost sat down heavily in his chair, crossed his arms, leaned back, and replied, the disappointment still ringing in his voice, "I'll arrange it. Don't want anyone here who doesn't want it. I thought you'd give everything today. Thought you'd be ready. Just what was that out there? That's all I want to know."

Bob avoided the question. "I need to go back there and get back to the game again. I think I can do that. I'll work on my delivery. I'll get my motion back where it should be, and I'll work on all my pitches. I know what an opportunity I've been given. And, I appreciate it. I appreciate your support. I just wish I hadn't let you down."

"You didn't let *me* down," Joost said, shuffling some papers on his desk. "No, you let yourself down. I don't think you gave it a chance after times got tough. You're going to have to live with that."

Joost stood up. "You'll get sent down, but there's no guarantee you'll ever get back up here. None at all. You'll have to work twice as hard—and show that you've changed everything, not just your pitching, but your attitude. That's a tough road. Most don't make it back."

"That's a chance I'll have to take. I'm no good to you here. I'm no good to myself. I need to get everything back where it was, and I can't do that here."

After a long and uncomfortable silence, Joost finally spoke. "You're on the bench for the second game. I'll talk to the general manager tonight."

Bob walked forward to shake his hand and said, "Thanks, Skip—"

Joost cut him off and refused his hand. "You don't thank me for this. You don't." He sat back down and filled out the line-up card for the second game.

….. ….. …..

Bob's wish was granted, and he was sent back to Ottawa of the International League. There, he pitched very well and appeared to regain the form that had brought him so many accolades in previous years. The game was fun again, and each day he couldn't wait to get back to the park. In the offseason, he joined Roy Campanella's "Barnstorming" team, and among his teammates were Larry Doby and Monte Irvin. He played well, but during one outing he felt something pop in his pitching arm. At first, the injury bothered him as only a tightness that would go away a day or so after pitching. He thought he was fully recovered when he was invited to Spring Training with the Athletics in 1955. There, he impressed his manager and coaches with not just his pitching, but his new attitude and confidence, earning him another chance with the team.

However, he hurt his arm again in an early outing, and his performance dropped off almost immediately. He was switched to a bullpen role, but even that didn't allow him enough time for his shoulder to heal properly. After just four games and his earned run average ballooning to 9.00, he was sent to the Columbus Jets of the International League, where all hoped he'd regain his form. He didn't. His performance there was so poor he was demoted to Class-A ball, where he was soon given his outright release. He never pitched in the Majors again. His career pitching mark ended at nine wins and nine losses—and many questions about what might have been. Even though he was in almost constant pain every time he pitched, he still managed to play three more years, his time split among the minors, the Panamanian League, and the Mexican League. Finally, in 1959, he called it a career.

After retiring, he stayed active in sports through semi-professional basketball and coaching high school baseball. When his playing career ended, he was asked many times if he ever regretted asking the Athletics to send him back to the minors. His reply was always the same: "No—never!" In the minor leagues and leagues around the globe, he rekindled his love of the game and found the inner peace he desperately sought. In 1988, at age 62, Bob Trice, the first player of color to don the Philadelphia Athletics uniform, passed away after a short bout with pancreatic cancer.

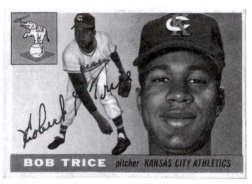

1955 Topps #132, Bob Trice
Courtesy of The Topps Company, Inc.

8

Ernie Banks

Chicago Cubs

Ernie Banks with his 1954 Chicago Cubs teammates (Ernie top row, far right).

Ernest Lee Banks didn't care much for baseball as a young boy. His dad had to bribe him with money and sweet treats just to play a game of catch. While in high school, Ernie favored basketball, football, and track and lettered in all three. Because his high school didn't have a baseball team, during the summer he played softball for a church team. He soon discovered he had much better skills than his friends, including pretty fair hand-eye coordination that made hitting easy for him. He then joined the Dallas Black Giants, a local semi-pro baseball team and became a standout.

After high school, Ernie continued playing semi-pro baseball, and during one of those games, James "Cool Papa" Bell, one of the greatest players in Negro League history, spotted him. Impressed with Ernie's hitting and fielding, Mr. Bell recommended him to the Kansas City Monarchs of the Negro National League. Ernie had wanted to study theology and become a minister, but the enticement of playing with a professional team made him put those plans on hold. In 1950, at age nineteen, he put on a Monarch's uniform. By his own admission, his skills were raw at the time, but the older members of the team took the likable teen under their collective wing and taught him to play the game with pride, toughness, and confidence.

After three short years, with a stint in the Army thrown in the middle, Ernie had improved to the point the Chicago Cubs purchased his contract. By this time his skills were so impressive the Cubs called him right up to the big club, making Ernie one of only a handful of players from the Negro Leagues never to play in the minor leagues. On September 17, 1953, Ernie Banks became the first person of color to play for that storied franchise. His first game for his new team was one he'd never forget. Before that game, Jackie Robinson, one of Ernie's heroes and idols, stopped by to congratulate him. Jackie also took Ernie aside and suggested he "listen and learn" as much as could—and let his on-field performance do his talking for him. Ernie followed that advice, and his play the rest of that season was so good he earned the starting shortstop job. The following year he became the Cubs' quiet leader, respected and adored by fans and teammates alike, a role he'd continue for years to come.

....

May 12, 1970
Wrigley Field, Chicago, Illinois

Ernie Banks sat alone in the far corner of the dugout watching large puddles form on the tarp stretched loosely over the infield. Rain had been soft and steady the better part of the morning but the forecast called for clearing around noon—about an hour before the scheduled start of the game. He sighed as a streak of lightning cracked across the olive-green sky. Right after the low rumble that followed, he looked farther up in the sky and said, almost in a whisper, "Please. Please." Folding his arms, he closed his eyes and leaned back against the wall of the dugout. All he could do was wait.

Waiting had not come easy for him of late, and he was certainly not alone in that. For the past three days, everywhere he went impatient friends, fans, and members of the media shelled him with questions: "When you gonna hit it?" "Are you nervous?" "Is the pressure getting to you?"

He had hit his last home run, #499, on May 9 in the seventh inning off Don Gullett of the Reds. A hanging curveball. The second he touched home plate that afternoon the congratulations started building. The opposing catcher, Johnny Bench, had started to shake his hand, realized what he was doing, quickly stepped back, covered his mouth with his glove and said, "Congratulations, Ernie. One more and you're off to Cooperstown." At the same time, the home plate umpire, Satch Davidson, stepped around to brush off home plate, blocking Ernie's path as he did, and added, "Happy for you. Nice goin', Ern."

Reporters swarmed his locker after the game with congratulations and questions, of which the most frequently asked was, "What will #500 mean to you?" Not yet ready to talk about that, he stalled them by repeating over and over, "Icing. That's what it'll be." By the looks the scribes gave him, he could see most were confused by the response. Ernie just smiled and started answering other questions.

That was two games ago. Two *long* games—because #500 wouldn't come. Was he pressing too hard? Were pitchers not giving him much to hit because they didn't want to be in the books as the one who served it up? Or, as he was feeling more and more the case, was his swing slowing more rapidly than ever? He was thirty-nine now, and the swing wasn't crisp and tight as it once was. Whatever the reasons, the drought continued, spotlighted every day in the papers by a sentence at the end of the game coverage write-up: "No 500 again today"—a tag that made Ernie feel more and more he was letting everyone down.

He had ended the previous season sitting on #497. Some wondered if he'd just call it a career. Others felt he should continue the chase to become only the ninth player in Major League Baseball history to join the "500 Club," along with the likes of Babe Ruth, Mickey Mantle, Ted Williams, Willie Mays, and Hank Aaron. Some suggested his skills were eroding to the point that however well-intentioned a return would be, he might embarrass himself and possibly the game itself. The latter didn't know what was in Ernie's heart. He wanted this achievement not just for himself, but for the history of the game—and all that he would represent in that history.

Once the current year started, he took thirteen games to reach #498; #499 had taken twelve more after that. Twenty-five games to get two homers wasn't the plan. What if it took even longer for the next one? Ernie shivered at the thought.

He opened his eyes to check the sky again and saw Ron Santo walking slowly toward him.

Mustering as serious an expression as he could, Santo asked, "So, what's new, Banks? Anything goin' on in your world?"

Ernie shrugged. "Oh, nothin' really. Just the same old thing. Just the usual."

"Well, I still say it was nice of everyone to give you a *special day* today. That was pretty considerate, you know."

"What are you talking about?" Ernie asked, squinting at him. "I didn't hear anything about it. Didn't see nothing in the papers."

"You've probably been too busy to notice. Today, in your honor, is Senior Citizens Day. Fitting, too. What are you now, forty-seven, forty-eight? I know you're not a day over fifty, right?"

Ernie picked up a fungo bat that had been leaning against the corner of the dugout, pointed it at Ron, and said, "This is for your skull if you don't pipe down. Understand me?"

"Just trying to help is all." Ron smiled and pointed out to the left field bleachers. "But, in all seriousness, today's the day, right?"

"You, too!" Ernie snapped back. "Why don't you—"

"Whoa! Just foolin.'"

Ernie looked down at the puddle forming at his feet and said, quietly, "Sorry. It's just, well . . . .." His voice trailed off.

"I know. We all do. That's why everybody's down in the locker room. Wanted to give you some time alone. I came out to check on you, to see if you wanted a sandwich or something to drink." He paused a few moments. "Or, how about if I bring out four or five reporters to share this special time with you? They can sit right there next to you. You'd like that, right?"

Both laughed heartily as Ernie pointed to the bench. "Sit. But don't bother me anymore."

"Me? Would I do that?"

As Ernie was about to respond, thunder echoed through the stadium, the floor of the dugout vibrated under their feet. Santo didn't say anything. He knew how badly Ernie wanted to get out there—to get this all over with.

Just then Frank Secory, scheduled to be the second base umpire for the game, ducked in the other end of the dugout, startling them both. After brushing rain from the brim of his cap, he said, "What you think, Ern? Want me to call it a day?"

Ernie sat straight up and started to reply, but Santo pushed him back and said, "Frank—you do that and I'll personally club you. We can't take much more of this guy. He's driving us nuts! And besides, that ain't rain. It's angel tears. They're so happy about Ernie they're crying their eyes out."

When he could finally get in a word, Ernie turned to Ron and said, "Oh, nuts, am I? And you're my friend?"

Frank grinned and shook his head. "Well, I guess I can wait a little longer to decide. Might blow over. Can't wait too long, though." He waited for another round of thunder to fade. "Ern, do you remember I was there when you hit your first? That was, what, 1953? I remember I was crew chief that day, behind home plate. You were a skinny little runt—couldn't have weighed more than a sack of potatoes. When you hit that ball, I couldn't believe it made it out. Just barely made it over the way is how I recall it. But that was Sportsman's Park. *I* could have hit one out of there."

Ron chimed in, "It was a cheap one, was it? He's been hittin' those for a long time, hasn't he?"

Ernie laughed. "Cheap! That one left the stadium if *I* remember right and bounced across the street. Nothin' cheap about it. And, yeah, I remember you were there. Didn't you also ring me up twice that game on balls about a foot outside? I've always said you need specs, even back then."

Frank waved his hand as if to brush Ernie's words aside and said, "Say, just thought of something else. You could hit it today, and with this weather, we might not make five innings. Would wash it out, you know. Would have to do it twice. That could take a *long* time." He shook his head. "Could happen."

"You tryin' to kill me?" Ernie said, falling heavily back against the dugout. "I wouldn't have thought about that in a million years. Thanks. Thanks a lot."

"Don't mention it. Always glad to help out, especially at a time like this." Turning to Ron, he said, "Keep an eye on him. He doesn't look so good to me."

They all laughed as Frank hurried up the steps and walked over to check the tarp.

When he had gone, Ernie rolled his eyes. "That was a big help."

"He was just trying to loosen you up. He's usually all business, so that was pretty great of him. We're all rooting for you."

They sat there a few minutes in silence, watching Frank tugging here and there at the tarp to keep it stretched over the infield dirt. Ron finally turned back to Ernie and asked, "Tell me about your first. I can't believe Secory was there. Do you remember anything about it?"

Ernie kicked at a small puddle near his left foot and looked out at the clouds rolling by. "I can see that day like it was yesterday. I don't know where the time has gone. Secory was right—1953. Right at the end of the season, September 20. We were playing the Cards, and Gerry Staley was pitching. I hated facing him. He was a tough righty who threw a nasty knuckleball at the oddest times, so you never knew when he'd float one up there. He could also be wild with his fastball, so it wasn't smart to dig in much. You never knew what he was going to throw. Anyway, the count was in my favor, and he shoved a knuckleball that didn't knuckle much up there, about eye level. I got the barrel on it, but I didn't think I'd hit it that hard. I was almost at second base when I realized I had lofted it out to Grand Avenue. Nobody really said anything about it because we were getting clobbered that day. I was pretty happy, but everybody else just wanted to forget the game—and fast. You know how it is after a good drubbin'." He shook his head. "Man, that was a long time ago. A *long* time ago."

Ron put his hand on Ernie's shoulder. "But what a career. You're one of the best, my friend—of all time. It's an honor to play with you. I know how lucky I've been to share the same uniform."

"Thanks, Ron. Appreciate it." He laughed softly. "I almost didn't come to the Bigs, you know. Didn't want to play for the Cubs at all."

"What do you mean? What are you talking about?"

Ernie laughed again. "I was having the time of my life playing for the Kansas City Monarchs in the old Negro National League. Greatest bunch of guys I've ever known. We had Elston Howard and Curt Roberts on that team. We hung around together after about every game. I was just a kid. I was nineteen when I signed in 1950, and I was like the little brother most of my older teammates never had. They looked out for me, and I loved them all. I got paid almost nothing, but I didn't care. They knew how to play ball and to have fun doing it. Going to the ballpark every day felt like Christmas. I just figured I'd play my whole career there. Never really thought much about coming up here."

He got up and stretched his arm out of the dugout to check the rain. "I remember after three years with the Monarchs, my manager, Buck O'Neil, called me into his office and told me Chicago had bought my contract. I cried when he told me. I cried right there on the spot—and begged him not to make me go. Can you imagine? It wasn't that I was scared. I just didn't want to leave everybody. I loved it there." Ernie shook his head and smiled at the memory as he sat back down.

"You're kidding!" Ron said. "You really didn't want to get to the majors? When I got my call, I cried, too, but it wasn't because I was sad. I cried because I wasn't going to miss those rotten ballparks, the dives we stayed in on the road, having only enough money to eat tomato soup made from ketchup. I couldn't wait to leave all that."

"I was just a kid. I had all these big brothers who had helped me learn what the game was all about. They were my family."

"What happened when you got here? How long did it take you to get over all that?"

"I've *never* gotten over it. I still miss those days. I love it here, but there was something special about that time in my life that will always be with me."

Ron leaned forward. "But think of all you've accomplished here. That's pretty darn special, too. I didn't realize some of it until I read that piece in the paper yesterday. Thirteen times on the All-Star team, twice Most Valuable Player, Gold Glove, and you led the league for a long time in intentional walks, which shows how much pitchers respect and fear you. On top of all that, this is your eighteenth season! Good grief! I'll never get close to any of that, and I think I'm pretty fair myself. You've got to be proud. I know we're all sure as heck proud of you."

"I'm just happy to still be playing," Ernie said, almost sheepishly, deflecting the praise. "I'm thirty-nine, and I know there probably isn't that much longer for me. I'd like to get to twenty years. That's a nice, round number. It'd also let me stall some. I don't know what I'd do if I couldn't come to the ballpark anymore."

Ron gripped Ernie's shoulder, giving it a quick shake. "You shouldn't be thinking about that. Not now. You're going to be around a long time. I just know it. What you need to think on now is Pat Jarvis. He's on the hill today for the Braves. He's *really* good. That fastball of his gets up there in a hurry. And he throws it high, about here."

Ron waved his right arm back and forth almost neck high to illustrate. "I don't think I've ever hit even a loud foul off him. But today I'm going to lay off the high stuff. You watch—today's going to be my turn. And I have the feeling yours, too."

Ernie mocked a swing with his arms close to his chest. "He's going to jam me—in tight. He'd do it anyway, but everybody's doin' it this season. They all think my bat's slowed. Can you imagine?"

Ron laughed. "No, I can't imagine. You look like you're still swingin' pretty good to me."

"I'm going to step back just a shade in the box, and if I get that high, hard one, I'm going to kill it. You watch."

"I believe you just might." Ron stood and started walking back toward the clubhouse, calling over his shoulder, "You better. I don't think I can't take this pressure anymore."

Ernie laughed and flipped the fungo bat toward him. "Santo, I swear—one more word out of you . . .."

The sound of Ron's laughter faded as he hurried down the steps back into the locker room. As soon as he had gone, the smile started disappearing from Ernie's lips. He looked out onto the field, then up to the sky. He exhaled loudly before saying to himself, "Today's the day. This'll do."

He stood up and made his way toward the locker room.

....

Jack Brickhouse, long-time television play-by-play announcer for the Chicago Cubs and close, personal friend of Ernie Banks, reached out and grabbed the microphone, as if to steady himself. He was rooting for Ernie as much, if not more, than anyone in the ballpark— and hoped his quest for the 500 plateau would end with this at bat. It was the second inning and Ernie's first time at the plate. There were two outs, nobody on base, and the Cubs were behind 2-0, the result of a Ken Holtzman wild pitch with the bases loaded in the first inning and an error on the same play.

The crowd was small because of the morning's weather and the threat of more showers by evening. By the last turnstile count, there were just 5,264 fans in attendance, but nearly all were now on their feet, cheering and urging Ernie on as he slowly stepped into the batter's box. He kicked at the dirt with his right foot, making a small groove where he could anchor the cleats of his shoe. He tapped his bat twice on the top edge of the plate, backed out quickly to stare at Pat Jarvis, the Braves starting pitcher, and took two long, slow practice swings before clutching his bat tighter and taking his stance.

Jarvis went into his windup and let loose a blazing fastball right down the heart of the plate. Ernie, swinging just a millisecond late, fouled the ball back and to the right. He knew he had just missed centering a pitch he could have hammered, so he slowly stepped out of the box, exhaled loudly, and looked out again at Jarvis. Tony Venzon, the home plate umpire, threw a new ball out to the pitcher, and Ernie dug his cleats even deeper into the soft dirt.

Jarvis looked in for the sign. Bob Tillman, Atlanta's catcher, put down his right index finger and quickly flicked up his right thumb: high fastball. The pitch that followed was tantalizingly high but just a shade outside. Ernie started his swing, but with his reflexes as sharp as ever, he held up just in time. The count was now one ball and one strike.

Ernie backed out of the box again, adjusted his helmet, tapped his bat once on home plate, and took two more low practice swings to balance himself.

Jarvis toed the rubber and looked in for the sign. Tillman waggled his right index finger until it slapped against his left leg, then flicked it up several times. The message was clear: fastball, high and tight.

Jarvis nodded and went into a full windup. The pitch was up but didn't slide in as much as he had wanted and stayed too far toward the middle of the plate.

Ernie, his stance now slightly back to give him more room to extend his arms, swung and caught up with the ball right on the sweet spot of his bat.

The minute contact was made, Jack Brickhouse leaned forward, squeezed the microphone even tighter, and shouted, "That's a fly ball, deep to left! Back, back! That's it! That's it! Hey, hey! He did it! Ernie Banks got number 500! A line shot into the seats in left! The ball tossed into the bullpen!"

The crowd stomped their feet, clapped, and shouted, "Ernie! Ernie!" as he rounded the bases. His teammates ran out onto the field and gathered at home plate, ready to celebrate and savor the moment with him.

As Ernie touched third base, Jack Brickhouse picked up the mike again and shouted above the joy of the delirious crowd, "Everybody on your feet! This is it! Wheeee!"

....

Ernie hit twelve more home runs that season, finishing with a career total of 512, ninth on the all-time home run list of the time. His last came on August 24, 1971 at Wrigley Field in the bottom of the fourth off Lynn McGlothlin of the Cincinnati Reds. The Chicago faithful gave him a standing ovation that lasted so long he had to exit the dugout and motion for them to quiet down and let the game resume. It was a fitting tribute and a fine exclamation mark for a remarkable and distinguished career. He retired as a player at the end of the season, but he wasn't finished with baseball, and baseball wasn't finished with him. Almost immediately he stepped into the role of ambassador and unabashed cheerleader for the Chicago Cubs organization and Major League Baseball as a whole, drawing large crowds everywhere he went. He typically ended his sessions with fans by shouting his trademark phrase, "Let's play two!"

After his playing days, he was involved in business ventures around Chicago and Los Angeles including purchasing automobile dealerships, serving on the Board of Directors of the Chicago Transit Authority, and investing in the insurance business. As was the case when he was on the field, he worked tirelessly to achieve success in all his ventures. In 1977, he was elected to the Baseball Hall of Fame in his first year of eligibility. He was also the first player to have his uniform number retired by the Chicago Cubs. Later, in 2013, he was awarded the Presidential Medal of Freedom for his work in the world of sports, quite an honor for someone who didn't even understand or like baseball when he was a youngster. Ernie Banks passed away on January 23, 2015 at the age of eighty-four. Because of his accomplishments and his on-field grace and dignity, he was, and always will be, known as "Mr. Cub."

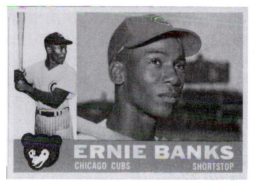

1960 Topps #10, Ernie Banks
Courtesy of The Topps Company, Inc.

Curt Roberts

Pittsburgh Pirates

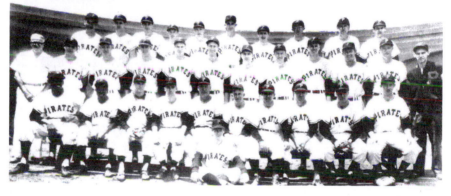

Curt Roberts with his 1956 Pittsburgh Pirates teammates
(Curt bottom row, 2nd from left).

Most of the pioneers who followed Jackie Robinson and helped tear down the color barrier in Major League Baseball knew they'd never achieve anything close to Jackie's accomplishments. Though highly skilled, some of these men remained average at best in their performance and potential. Curt Roberts was one such player.

Born in Pineland, Texas, Curt moved with his family to Oakland, California, where he became a standout on the high school basketball team. However, baseball was his first love, and right after graduation, he signed his first professional contract with the Kansas City Monarchs of the Negro Leagues. There he spent four years playing well and being mentored by veteran teammates such as Buck O'Neil and Satchel Paige. After the 1950 season, a Boston Braves scout saw him playing in the Mexican League and signed him to a minor-league contract. A year later, the Pittsburgh Pirates organization acquired his contract and assigned him to their high minors, where he built a reputation as a top-notch fielder who could also hit above average. Near the bottom of the standings, the Pirates of that era were constantly looking to upgrade their roster. In just such an effort, Curt was called up to the big club in mid-April of 1954. The night before the game he received a phone call from Jackie Robinson, who urged him never to give up on his dream, no matter what obstacles would be thrown in his path. The following day, April 13, in his Major League debut at Forbes Field, Curt tripled in his first at-bat and later doubled in the game. His future looked bright.

NOTE: *In the following scenes, when Curt Roberts is talking with Roberto Clemente, the conversations would have been in Spanish. At the time, Roberto spoke few words of English, and Curt was fluent in Spanish, the result of his study and practice of the language while in school and during his time playing ball in the Mexican Winter Leagues.*

April 2, 1955
Fort Myers, Florida

Branch Rickey, the Pittsburgh Pirates General Manager, slowly walked to his office door, opened it, and said to the young man sitting by himself in the outer office, "Curt, I'd like you to come in now."

Seven years before, Mr. Rickey had signed Jackie Roosevelt Robinson to play for the Brooklyn Dodgers, a signing that helped foster change not just in the game of baseball but in society at large. Mr. Rickey had taken quite a chance signing the first person of color to play in modern Major League Baseball. When Jackie finally took the field for that storied franchise, he wasn't the only one who received all manner and form of threats. To some, Mr. Rickey had opened a door they weren't ready to have opened. Instead of seeing a man who had changed the face of the National Pastime, they saw, as he was called in one anonymous letter, "The Great Satan." However, Brooklyn thrived after the color barrier there was crushed, and soon other teams followed their lead. After Mr. Rickey's tenure with Brooklyn, he became the General Manager of the Pirates, at the time a team mired at the bottom of the National League. Mr. Rickey continued to believe that when he evaluated players, the color of a person's skin or where he came from should not be a factor. To him, talent and potential were most important. As a result, soon after joining the Pittsburgh organization, Mr. Rickey signed the young man he had just invited into his office.

"Curt, please sit there—over by the window. I'll join you soon as I can pull around a chair. Beautiful day today. We should enjoy that wonderful breeze blowing in."

"Yes, Sir, Mr. Rickey." Curt stood and waited for Mr. Rickey to sit down before he did.

As soon as Mr. Rickey was seated, he asked, "So, how's your wife. Christine, isn't it?"

Curt took a moment and studied Mr. Rickey before responding. "The Mahatma," as he was respectfully referred to by his peers, had just turned seventy-four. The years and his intense work ethic had taken their toll, but he was as full of the fire and love of baseball as ever. Still, his once flowing, auburn hair had started to recede, his wild, bushy eyebrows had whitened at the edges, and the furrows below his eyes had deepened considerably, especially over the past few years. But, even to those who hadn't seen him in a long time, he was still immediately recognizable by his trademark large, tightly tied bow-tie that held the collar of his shirt pressed firmly against his neck.

Waiting until he was sure Mr. Rickey was settled comfortably in his chair, Curt finally replied, "Yes, Sir. She's fine. Can't wait to see her next week."

The second he had spoken the words, his breath caught and he felt light-headed. He had just stated what he *hoped* would happen the following week. He hoped with all his heart he'd performed well enough in Spring Training to make the team and travel with them as they opened the season. He had hit .343 in the spring games, and he felt his fielding around second base had improved another notch. Still, after a fast start in his rookie season the previous year, nothing seemed to go right as he lost his job as the starting second sacker, and his average dipped dramatically, ending up at .232 at season's end.

He believed the drop in performance happened because once the hits started coming further and further apart, he started pressing, trying too hard to climb out of his prolonged slump. However, the harder he tried, the deeper he dug a hole for himself. Now, sitting across from Mr. Rickey, he hoped his spring performance would be enough for him to get another chance. As Spring Training drew to a close, the uncertainty had been eating at him to the point he wasn't sleeping or eating regularly. He was exhausted in every sense of that word.

Sensing his unease, Mr. Rickey said, gently, "Relax. Take in some of that fresh air. We're just going to talk a while."

Curt exhaled softly and tried to appear more relaxed than he felt.

"Young man, we had great hope for you last year, and you didn't disappoint early on. Line drive hitter, occasional pop, and your work at second was just as we had expected. Very good. Very good."

Seeing he had Curt's full attention and hoping to put him more at ease, Mr. Rickey patted his own ample stomach. "Now my doc wishes I could shed a few pounds, but that's sure not the case with you. We list you at about five foot eight and a hundred and six-ty-five, but that's you dripping wet. Not much meat on you."

Curt, unsure of where Mr. Rickey's words were going, forced a weak smile.

"So, when the hot months came around, you faded. By mid-July you looked like skin and bones, and your swing and overall stamina faded. You couldn't help that. I know you tried. Hard. No problem with your attitude or your heart."

Mr. Rickey reached for a cigar, which he didn't light but used as a pointer as he spoke. "You've had a fine spring. I'd like to bet you start like last season and this time sustain that effort, but you came to camp even lighter. I had hoped you'd beef up and strengthen your-self over the winter. I'm afraid now your body won't hold up."

Curt interrupted him, "I really tried, Mr. Rickey. I just seem to have a hard time gaining weight. I can—"

Mr. Rickey waved his cigar, signaling Curt needed to stop and listen to him. "Last year, through the good and the bad, you did everything I asked of you. You didn't lose your temper when you faced the taunts and the threats I told you would be coming. And your effort was always clear. I have deep respect for you and what you've gone through. It's because of that we're now at a crossroads with your future. I'd like you to think long and hard about what I'm going to say to you now. If, after you hear me out, you'd like to talk it over with your wife tonight, I'll understand. I need your answer no later than tomorrow afternoon."

Curt straightened in his chair. "I am listening, Sir."

"One of the paths at the crossroads is to put our focus on you and your long-term future as a Major League ballplayer. If we go that direction, we'll send you down so you can build yourself up and gain the strength you'll need to push hard all season long—and *not* just the first months. You have the skills I look for and we need, but right now I'm not confident you can hold up. So, if we go that way, you won't be traveling to Pittsburgh with us. Now, this doesn't mean you'll never be back. I'd hope you would. But you definitely wouldn't start the year with us."

Curt lowered his head and started nervously tapping his right shoe on the floor. Seeing his agitation, Mr. Rickey asked, "Young man—your thoughts? What are you thinking?"

"I'm hoping the other path looks better to me. It's true I did wear down last year, but I know I can do better. I had never played that many games so many days in a row, so I didn't know how tough it was going to be. Now I do. I should have taken better care of myself. I know that now—and I'll do my best not to let that happen again."

"I'm glad you see that, Curt. As I said, if you strengthen yourself and monitor that, your future could be bright. But, you're not in that position right now. So, now I want to mention the other path. I'm not sure it's best for you, but it *could* be."

Curt leaned forward. "What else is there?"

"Well, you could stay with the team but not be our regular second baseman. This would buy you some time to get in better condition, but that's not why we'd be keeping you here. At least not the main reason."

"Then what would be?" Curt asked, stiffening again.

"I'm aware you've become good friends with Roberto Clemente. That is correct?" Curt nodded as Mr. Rickey continued. "His talent is raw, but he has potential to be a starter for us over the long haul if we can harness his gifts. To do that, we have to be able to communicate more effectively with him."

Mr. Rickey struck a match to light his cigar, but immediately blew it out. "You may already know where I'm going with this. This is where you come in. Your Spanish appears quite good. I've overhead you talking with Clemente around the batting cage, and others have told me you two talk nonstop in the dugout. *That's* what I need you to do. Nobody else around here speaks that language *and* knows what he's going to be facing this year. And you know what I mean by that. You had it thrust on you last year. I want you to help the coaches get through to him and help Haney get to know him better. Haney thinks Clemente's a loner and moody and not interested in learning. I don't think that's the case at all. You know him well. Do you?"

"He's not like that at all, Sir. He comes across that way because he can't talk to anyone, and he's always afraid of doing something wrong."

"Do you think you can help him? That is, do you feel you can help him and us with the communication?"

"I do. I like Roberto. He's still a kid, but he's a good kid. And I don't have to tell you about his swing. I wish I had it. He's pretty good as a fielder, too. I think he just needs time to learn our game, which he tells me is very different from the way he played it growing up. I wish you could have the same talk with him that you had with me and Christine last year when you brought me up. That helped me—more than you could possibly know. But I know you can't—because of the language."

He eased back in his chair and continued. "If you want me to, I'll do everything in my power to help Roberto make his way. We talk baseball all the time anyway. I'll make a better effort to help the coaches and others understand him—and him to understand them. I'd like to do that. It would help him. And I know it would help me because I'd have time to build my strength. I owe a lot to you, Mr. Rickey. I'd like to do this."

Though obviously pleased with Curt's sincere response, Mr. Rickey wanted his young player to fully understand the commitment. "What you decide should be what you feel would be best for you. I most certainly don't want you to feel you are being used as some kind of babysitter. And I don't want others thinking that. So, if this is the way we go, what you are doing will be our secret. Just between us. I'll publicly say we're giving you the opportunity to return to the form you had early last season and leave it at that. Now, you think you're up to this?"

Curt stood and looked out the window. "I want you to know how grateful I am for this opportunity, Mr. Rickey. I give you my word I'll give it all I have. I'll work into shape, and I'll stick close to Roberto. He's already going through a lot of what happened to me last year. Still happening to me. I'll do my best."

"Then it's settled." Mr. Rickey stood and said, "Tell your wife you're coming home to Pittsburgh."

"Thank you for believing in me," Curt said, stepping toward him.

"I'm not sure I'm doing you any favors. Time will tell. I wish you the best."

The two men shook hands.

….. ….. …..

April 16, 1955
Pittsburgh, Pennsylvania

Twenty-year-old Roberto Clemente used his fork to push his food slowly back and forth across his plate. "Your wife is a terrible cook!" he exclaimed to his dear friend and teammate, Curt Roberts. "What is this supposed to be? Never seen green meat before."

"Not so loud," Curt replied while smiling at his wife, Christine, who turned toward them after removing another dish from the oven.

"What did he say?" she asked, looking first at her husband and then at Roberto. "Does he like the new meatloaf recipe with the green beans inside? Found this dish in a magazine last week. Thought it might be nice."

"He said you look beautiful today. And he loves your cooking," Curt replied.

Roberto nodded toward Christine, rubbed his stomach, and forced a broad smile as he gulped hard and swallowed the food in his mouth.

"Good!" she said to Curt. Then, leaning close to Roberto, she said slowly and loudly as she placed a bowl before him, "You'll *really* like *this*. It's my new corn and carrot casserole. Put lots of spice in it for you because I know the food's pretty hot where you come from. Maybe it'll remind you of home." She then walked to the refrigerator to get a pitcher of iced tea.

Curt quickly translated her words while Roberto stared at the bowl. "She tries. She's a fine woman, and I love her—even when she serves up, well, I'm not exactly sure what this is. I didn't marry her for her cooking."

When Roberto was sure Christine wasn't looking, he turned to his friend, grimaced, raised his eyebrows, and said, shaking his head, "She's going to kill us."

Just then the Roberts' dog, a husky German Shepard, walked in from the living room. Roberto saw him and urged him over by snapping his fingers. Roberto made sure Christine wasn't looking as he scooped a handful of meatloaf from his plate and quickly offered it to the dog. Buck sniffed at it, looked up at Roberto, and ran out of the room. Curt howled and raised a hand to cover his mouth as Christine turned to face them again.

"What? What is it?" she asked, joining in her husband's laughter. "Roberto say something funny?"

Roberto smiled weakly as he kept his hand hidden under the table. "Nothing, Dear," Curt said, wiping his eyes. "Just thinking about something at the ballpark yesterday. Sorry."

When Christine turned away again, Curt whispered, "Just drop it. I'll clean it up later."

As Roberto did so, he said, "It's sticking to my hand. Now my hand's green, too!"

This time Curt laughed so hard he had to cover his mouth with his napkin. Before his wife could say anything, he said, his words muffled, "I'm sorry—I'm just excited tonight is all." He placed his hand on Roberto's shoulder. "He's playing tomorrow. His first game. Remember how special that was for me last year? Now it's his turn."

Roberto didn't know what his friend was saying, but he could tell by the smiles on his friends' faces and the way they were nodding their heads they cared for him and wanted him to feel welcome. He nodded toward Christine and said one of the few English phrases he knew, "Thank you—very much."

As soon as Christine sat down, Curt said to her, "Honey, please forgive me, but I'd like to talk to Roberto a few minutes. He's pretty nervous about tomorrow. You understand, don't you?"

She nodded as she offered Roberto more meatloaf, which he politely refused.

Curt turned serious as he said, "My friend, tomorrow's your big day. I know you're nervous, but you'll do fine. Just be yourself, and don't try to do too much. I'm also in the lineup tomorrow, so don't worry. I'll keep an eye on you from second base. If you have any questions while the game is going on, just yell 'em into me, OK?"

Roberto put down his fork and asked, "You're not joking with me, are you? Manager Haney really said I'd be playing? I don't want to be tricked, let down tomorrow. I want to be ready for my first game."

Placing his hand on Roberto's shoulder, Curt continued, his voice direct, "Fred Haney may be a lot of things, but he tells the truth, even though we don't always want to hear it so bluntly. Yes, you're in the starting lineup, and so am I. We've got a double header against Brooklyn, so Haney needs everyone to be ready. We get the first game, and I'm glad of that. Hate waiting around."

"But what if I do bad? I don't think Manager Haney likes me. He almost never looks at me, and when he does, he just points for me to sit on the bench. I don't think he wants me here."

"I felt the same way when I first came up last year. He was the same with me. Never had much to do with me. Never said anything when I did something good. I think that's just the way he is. Probably doesn't even talk to his wife when he's home."

The last comment got a slight laugh from Roberto, but he quickly turned serious again. "I don't want to make mistakes. I've waited too long for this day."

Curt could see his friend's obvious distress, so he changed the subject. He playfully smacked Roberto on the arm, and said, "Of course, you won't have a great start like *I* did in my first game. It was April 13 last year. Seems like yesterday. We are at Forbes Field and facing the Phillies and Robin Roberts, their ace. Ask anyone, he's the best pitcher in all of baseball."

Christine heard the name Robin Roberts and interrupted, "Oh, no—let me guess. Are you telling the story again of your first hit? The way you tell it, Roberts is the toughest pitcher of all-time, and you murdered him that day. Wasn't that the only hit you've ever had off him?"

"Never mind," Curt said, squinting at her. "I'm trying to loosen him up is all."

"You keep telling those whoppers and your nose is going to grow across this room."

"I'll tell the story *my* way, if you don't mind." He turned back to Roberto. "She was just asking me to tell the story of my first hit, and I told her that's what I was doing. Anyway, my first time up to bat I look out and there's Robin Roberts, glaring in at me. He's got a fastball that would take the letters off your uniform if it hit you. But I didn't care. I wasn't afraid. I dug in, making a deep hole in the back of the batter's box."

Here he stood, took his hitting stance, and went through the motions of warming up his swing. Christine shook her head and tried to get Roberto's attention, but his focus was completely on Curt.

"He went into that full windup of his, kicked his leg, and let fire a fastball that I heard as it whizzed by but didn't really see. He's that fast!" Roberto leaned closer as Curt continued. "I decided to step farther back in the box to give me an extra second to see the ball and, when he threw again, I saw it all the way to the bat—and clobbered it to deep right center field. I took off running and ended standing up on third base. Easy triple. I hit it so hard I didn't even have to slide. Now, that's what I call a good at-bat. You'll have to go some to beat that tomorrow."

Roberto looked at Christine as if wanting her reaction to the story. She had a pretty good idea what her husband had said, so she rolled her eyes and shook her head. "Don't you believe a thing he says about it. Yes, it was a triple, but he was so out of breath by third base he had to stop. Should have been an inside-the-park homer if you ask me."

"How can you say such a thing?" Curt asked, in mock horror. "I'm trying to build up this boy's confidence."

Roberto finally spoke, his voice cracking slightly, "Then I better hit a home run tomorrow. I want to do better."

"Roberto, I hope you do. Honestly, I do." Turning again to Christine, he said, "Roberto just said he'd like more of your meatloaf."

As she handed the platter to Roberto, he just glared at Curt, who again burst into laughter.

....

After Roberto left and they were clearing the table, Christine turned to Curt and said, "Look, he's a nice boy. I like him. But this is getting silly. He might as well just move in. He's *always* here.

Curt handed her a plate. "I know. But he doesn't speak English, so he doesn't want to go to movies or restaurants by himself. He just doesn't feel welcome anywhere, and he's scared. We've been there, *remember*? Remember all those southern cities when I was with the Monarchs? Same thing."

"Oh, I know—and I feel sorry for him, too. I do. But I'd like some time with my husband. *Alone*. You're going on the road soon."

"But he's just a kid."

Christine handed Curt a dish towel and said, "And what are you now? An *old man* at twenty-six? You know everything now?"

"You know what I mean," Curt replied, his voice softening. "He's getting the same treatment I got—and you did too—when you were with me last year." He leaned back against the sink. "Remember before the first game last year when Mr. Rickey asked both of us to his office. He said I had to keep my temper at all times and turn the other cheek. And you, too. I've talked to Jackie about it, and he said Mr. Rickey gave him and Rachel the same talk when he came up. Roberto doesn't have anyone to have that talk with him. They can't. The language won't let them. I've been asked to keep an eye on him, to help out as much as I can. I *need* to do this. I want him to know that he isn't alone."

Christine blew out a short breath and said, "You're right. I know it. It's just he's here *all the time*. We might as well adopt him!"

Curt laughed, pulled her close and hugged her tight. Before he could say anything, she said, "Well, since he's going to be back here tomorrow and tomorrow's going to be such a special day, I might as well bake him a cake so we can celebrate. What kind you think I should make?"

"Whatever you cook will surprise him. I'm pretty sure of that." Curt then fell into laughter again as Christine put her hands on her hips and glared at him.

....

April 17, 1955
Forbes Field, Pittsburgh, Pennsylvania

Curt and Roberto were playing catch just outside the dugout as the rest of their teammates continued their pre-game warm-ups out on the playing field. The Pirates were scheduled to host a double header against the Brooklyn Dodgers, who had won their first four games of the season. Pittsburgh, on the other hand, had yet to find the victory column and were already in last place in the standings, a location that had become all too familiar to them over the past few years. However, the contrast between the two teams didn't end there. Brooklyn had scored forty-one runs in their first four games. The Pirates had scored just nine and were still waiting for their bats to come alive. Manager Fred Haney knew his team needed a spark, and quickly, or they'd dig themselves a hole impossible to climb out of. That was running through his mind again as he prepared to take his lineup card out to the home plate umpire.

After catching a final toss from Roberto, Curt motioned him over.

"I know you're nervous. That's perfectly natural. Shoot—last year before my first at-bat, I threw up. I did. Honestly. Right in the dugout."

"That's supposed to make me feel better?" Roberto said, reaching for the ball and then tossing it back and forth from his right hand to his left. Roberto avoided his eyes, so Curt reached out, grabbed the ball in mid-flight, and said, "Slow down. Take a breath and listen to me a minute. You're batting third, right after Gene Freese. Frank Thomas is after you at cleanup. He's got the most powerful bat we have, so they won't want to face him with runners on base. So, you're going to get pitches to hit."

Roberto nodded he understood as Curt continued. "Johnny Podres is pitching for them, and he's tough as nails. Reaches far back into his windup, and that sometimes makes the ball hard to pick up coming out of his hand. Keep your hands back—and wait." Here he paused, smiled, and said, "But I clobbered him last year. Poor man flinched every time I came to the plate."

Roberto laughed, nervously. "I don't doubt it. If I was pitching, one look at you would sure scare me."

The nervous tension lessening, both laughed, muffling the sound with their gloves so as not to draw attention to themselves. Curt then spoke softly. "Take a moment now. Just for yourself. Stand over there by the railing and think about what you want to accomplish today. It's what I do before every game. Helps me focus, to shake off the rest of the nerves. Give it a try. It'll work for you, too."

Roberto didn't respond. Instead, he nodded and slowly walked away. Curt watched him lean against the rail and called over, "Hey—you've made it." Smiling broadly, he added, "This is *your* day."

Brooklyn didn't score in the top of the first as the Pirates' starter, Jake Thies, got three quick outs with just eleven pitches. Two of the outs were fly balls, but none were hit to Roberto, who was playing right field. After returning to the dugout, he pulled his bat from the rack and took a few short practice swings in the far corner of the dugout. Curt walked over and stood before him.

"Remember, my first time up I blasted a triple off the wall. Almost put a hole clean through it if I remember right. Don't want to add any pressure, but you think you can do any better? Home run first time?"

Roberto didn't smile. Already focused for his at-bat, he just shook his head and headed up the dugout steps to be ready when it was his time to move to the on-deck circle. The Pirates lead-off man, Earl Smith, flew out to right to open the home half of the first, so Roberto exited the dugout, stopped, turned to face Curt, and finally spoke, his voice full of the warmth of their friendship, "Thanks, my friend."

After Gene Freese lined out to deep center field, Roberto walked quickly to the batter's box, dug in, and took several vicious practice swings as he stared out at the pitcher. Curt crossed his fingers, at the same time noticing the fans to the left of the dugout scanning their programs to see who was at the plate.

The first pitch was a fastball, low and outside. Roberto had started to swing but held up just in time. Podres' second pitch was also a fastball, but this time right down the heart of the plate. Timing the pitch perfectly, he lined a rocket that ricocheted off a ducking Podres' glove and bounced toward Pee Wee Reese, the Dodgers shortstop. The ball was hit so hard it spun out of the webbing of Reese's glove and landed about ten feet to his left. By the time the ball stopped rolling, Roberto had crossed first base with the first hit of his career. No one in the dugout moved or made a sound until Curt raised his fist in the air and shouted, "Did you see that! 'Bout took Podres' hand off!" Standing on the first base bag, Roberto looked into the dugout, but he didn't appear to see Curt, who was furiously waving.

The next batter, Frank Thomas, tripled high off the left field wall, and Roberto scored easily. As he excitedly entered the dugout, no one congratulated him or offered any sign of acknowledgment—except Curt, who walked over, pounded him on the back, and said, "Only a single?"

Roberto reached for his glove before replying, "Felt like a home run to me. Felt good. *Now* I'm ready."

"I believe you are," Curt said. "Just might make a ballplayer after all. That is, if you listen to *me*."

Both men laughed heartily, then turned their attention to the field.

....

For the rest of 1955, Curt played only sparingly. Most of his time during the season was spent trying to work himself into better shape and teaching Roberto as much English as he could. However, he never again displayed the talent he had shown at the start of his rookie season. The following year he returned to the minors for good, playing well for eight more years before finally calling it a career in 1963. He and Roberto kept in touch regularly. Once, when the Pirates were visiting the San Francisco Giants, Curt was granted permission to go into the clubhouse before the game to surprise his old friend. It was later reported Roberto spent most of their visit calling teammates over, introducing them to Curt, and sharing with them what an influence he had on his career. It was the last time the two would meet.

On November 15, 1969, Curt and Christine were running an errand in the family car when a rear tire blew out. While Curt was jacking up the car, a drunk driver veered into him, killing him instantly. Curt was just forty years old. His final baseball stats read as follows: .233 lifetime batting average, 1 home run, 40 RBI, .969 fielding average, and 171 games played. At first glance, his record would seem modest at best. However, his accomplishments ranged far beyond just what he did on the playing field. Like his idol, Jackie Robinson, he served as a mentor and role model for many others on their road to the Major Leagues. That legacy remains to this day.

....

NOTE: *It should be mentioned that the National Baseball Hall of Fame, the Pittsburgh Pirates organization, and most baseball research groups designate Curt Roberts as the first African American to play for the Pittsburgh Pirates, which is an accurate representation. However, Roberts was not the first person of color to play for the team. That distinction belongs to Carlos Bernier, from Puerto Rico, who played in 105 games as an outfielder with the Pirates a year earlier in 1953. Many historians have, therefore, argued that Bernier should be recognized as the groundbreaking player for this organization. Several theories exist as to why Bernier's name isn't put forth more often. By most accounts, his time with the Pirates was nothing but tumultuous. He not only fought, and often, with members of opposing teams, but he also had nearly constant run-ins with his own teammates, which made him unpopular in all quarters. He had been suspended for punching an umpire in the face and frequently shouting obscenities at fans, which didn't make him the best representative of an organization. Other groups have pointed to his fair skin color as an important factor in their determination. Today, Carlos is often referred to as a "footnote" in baseball history.*

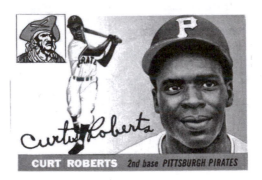

1955 Topps #107, Curt Roberts
Courtesy of The Topps Company, Inc.

9

Tom Alston

St. Louis Cardinals

Tom Alston with his 1957 St. Louis Cardinals teammates
(Tom middle row, 4th from right).

Tom Alston grew up in Greensboro, North Carolina, where he attended segregated schools that did not have baseball teams. Still, he loved the game and participated in neighborhood pick-up games every chance he got, often playing so late into the evening family members had to come looking for him. He was also an avid reader of newspapers, especially the sports pages, where he daily followed the exploits of his favorite Negro League players, often dreaming that one day he'd join them on the field.

Tom joined the U.S. Navy after graduating high school, and that's where he was first able to play on a regular team. He loved the experience of being with others who had a passion for the game and who could also give him advice about how to improve his fielding and hitting skills. After his discharge from the service, Tom started his college studies at North Carolina A&T, but his heart just wasn't in classroom work. He wanted to play ball. Soon, he began playing for regional barnstorming teams, including the Greensboro Red Wings and the Jacksonville (Florida) Eagles of the Negro Leagues. The pay wasn't much, but he didn't mind. He was doing what he loved. At the same time, the money he earned allowed him to continue his studies and earn his degree.

Just after graduation, an opportunity presented itself for Tom and several of his former teammates to sign with the Indian Head Rockets, a Canadian team in Saskatchewan. The Rockets were the best team in their league, and Tom became one of their stars, hitting for high average and dramatically improving his fielding skills. After the season concluded, Tom and several of his teammates were offered the opportunity to return to the United States to play for the Porterville (California) Comets, an all-Black team in the International League. There he hit over .350 his first season and displayed good power, hitting twelve home runs. After that season, the San Diego Padres of the Pacific Coast League purchased his contract. That next season with the Padres he continued his fine hitting, socking 23 home runs and driving in 101 runs, which brought attention from several Major League teams, especially the St. Louis Cardinals of the National League, who were looking to add power to their lineup. Not long after the Cardinals purchased his contract, Tom Alston became the first person of color to play for the franchise when he took the field on April 13, 1954.

....

January 20, 1954
St. Louis, Missouri

August A. Busch, Jr., owner of the St. Louis Cardinals, was, first and foremost, a businessman. He knew the more publicity he could garner the more his beer empire would continue to grow locally and nationally. He also knew negative news of any type caused a slide on the profit side of the ledger, and when that happened, he always fought hard with all his resources to change directions. His Board of Directors had recently shared some disturbing news, so he was bound and determined to snuff out the issue before it could take root any further. What they had said cut him to the quick. The Negro citizens of St. Louis, and in surrounding cities and towns in the Midwest, were not drinking his product as they had in the past—in protest. At the same time, fewer and fewer Negroes were attending Cardinal games at Sportsman's Park, which was also lowering revenue.

"Gussie," as he was known to friends and close associates, was sharp and shrewd when it came to a dollar, and anything that stood in the way of his acquiring those dollars was an obstacle that had to go, no matter what it took. He had discussed the current situation with his closest advisors, and they all said the same thing. St. Louis already had Black players when the St. Louis Browns put Hank Thompson and Willard Brown on the field in July of 1947. However, for the past seven years, the Cardinals had chosen not to do the same, a decision that was showing up where it hurt Mr. Busch the most: the profit/loss column.

He knew drastic action had to be taken and instructed his General Manager, Dick Meyer, to rectify the situation as quickly as possible by acquiring a Black player to help generate interest in the team. Dick immediately gathered his scouts and Cardinals manager, Eddie Stanky, to find out which player might best provide the solution. After a morning of heated debate, one name was settled on: Tom Alston, who was currently playing very well at first base for the San Diego Padres of the Pacific Coast League. Two hours later, Dick was on the phone with his counterpart with the Padres.

"John Dowd, my old friend, this is Dick Meyer. How you doing out there in all that sunshine? Life good for you these days?"

John had known Dick for many years and knew he wasn't calling just to inquire about his health. They were still close and dear friends, but business was business—and that never got in the way of their shared past. "I'm glad you called. It's been a long time. So, what do you want?"

"Why, John, what makes you think I want something? Can't old buddies just talk once in a while?"

"Not at the long-distance phone rates. You're so cheap you'd steal flies from a blind spider. I'm busy here. Let's get at it. What can I do for you?"

"Well, if you insist, I'll cut to the chase. I'm interested in one of your boys."

"No matter who it is, I'll take Musial in return. We'll call it even—straight up."

"Very funny. Seriously, you've got a big first baseman out there, I think his name's Allred or Allyton—or something like that—who we might be able to use."

John knew his friend was playing with him. "The name's *Alston*. Who you tryin' to kid? You studied him until you're half blind from reading. Why do you want him?"

"Well, you probably know we have put one of your old players, Steve Bilko, at first. He may have knocked the snot out of the ball in your league, and he does hit a fair number of homers, but he strikes out too much to play regular. Funny that you didn't mention that hole in his swing when you sent him our way."

John chuckled. "Must be that hot, humid air in St. Louis that's got to him. He was fine here. You must be killing him in that sweatbox you play in. But, I still don't get it. Why Alston?"

"We've been toying with the idea of a platoon where we switch in and out Bilko and somebody like Alston. That would give us plenty of power, and the competition wouldn't hurt either of them. Would take their play to a higher level, I suspect."

"I heard you were going to start playing Musial at first once in a while to save his legs. What happened to that idea?"

"Oh, we'll change Stan around from time to time. You know, give him a rest during double headers and hot weather, but we need to take care of the everyday lineup first."

John paused for a moment. He had the upper hand and knew it, "Since we're old pals, I'm going to give you a break. I think you can have Alston, but it's going to cost you. I mean *really* cost you. He's only twenty-two. Best years ahead of him, and he's going to be *good*. He hit right at .300 and pounded the ball last season, which I'm sure you know."

"You don't have to go into your regular sales pitch. I know I'm trapped. But, tell me this time. Does this kid have a hole in his swing as big as Bilko's?"

"What, would I sell you damaged goods?" John replied in mock horror. "What do you think I am?"

"Never mind," Dick shot back. "We both know the answer to that."

The men got down to business, moving their proposals back and forth like so many chess pieces, but John had the stronger game and position by default. After nearly an hour, they settled on a package of players and cash. The Cardinals would receive the services of Alston, but it cost them Dick Sisler, their starter at first for several seasons; Eddie Erautt, an important cog in their previous year's bullpen; two minor league prospects; and $100,000 cash. Sisler and Erautt didn't figure into the Cards long-term plans, but Dick knew the loss of the prospects and the cash addition would not please Mr. Busch. Still, he was ordered to "do whatever it takes" to close the deal, and that was the best he felt he could do under the circumstances.

The other baseball executives around the two leagues later called it a swindling. In the end, Mr. Busch said it was merely necessary business and justified it by saying to reporters, who quizzed him over and over about the trade, "Hell, I sell beer to everybody." His statement didn't make sense to the reporters, but it did to Gussie. It was his way of saying color didn't matter to him—in his players or his beer drinking customers—as long as the beer got sold. The Negro community immediately applauded him for the trade.

That afternoon, Mr. Busch ordered his executive assistants to set up a press conference during the next week at the Beverly Hills Hotel in Hollywood, California. He would fly out there himself because he knew it was time for a show. At the end of the meeting with his assistants, he barked one last command in his signature, gravelly voice, "And make sure there's plenty of Budweiser and caviar for all those reporters. Might as well get publicity for the brewery, too."

....

January 25, 1954
Hollywood, California

"So, my big-shot son says he's ready to play in the Major Leagues. Just what makes you think so?"

"Dad, you've seen it in the papers. I'm playing really good now. Hitting much better this season. And I've made only a couple of errors. The Cardinals say they liked the reports they got on me.

They wouldn't have traded for me if they didn't think I could play for them."

"Well, I'm telling you you're not ready. Those pitchers are going to throw you nothing but curveballs, and they are going to carve you up. You'll never get good wood on one. You're going to strike out like a windmill with that bat of yours, which is way too heavy for a decent swing, you know. Just you wait. They'll see you for what you are, and it won't take long. Sometimes you might be able to hit a fastball good, but you'll never hit for average up there. Not after those curves start coming, and they will, probably right from the start. You'll be back here shining shoes in no time at all. Your old team won't even want you, and then what will you do?"

"But the owner of the Cardinals—that Mr. Busch—called me personally and said he knew I was going to help the club. Knew I was going to hit and field and everything. Said he was sure. Wants me on the team—bad."

"He's just saying that. Do you really think he meant any of it? Look at you. You're still skinny as a fence post. I told you over and over to eat more and beef up so you'd keep your swing, but did you listen? And, what do you mean your fielding has improved? You still make too many errors on easy ground balls right at you. How many have you booted and then thrown away? Why, last season I saw you make two errors on one play at least twice. You call that good? The infield dirt at those Big League stadiums is different—all loose and raked out. You'll never keep your footing and will fall like dead trees all the time. Wouldn't surprise me if you led the league in errors before they send you out."

"I got a new glove, Dad. I'm breaking it in. It's got a deeper pocket, so I think it will help me catch better. I think my fielding will be OK. I think I'll be fine."

"You just keep telling yourself that, Son. You've got to keep your confidence. You know that. But, you've also got to be realistic so you don't get your heart broken. This is probably not going to work out. Oh, you've got some skills. I've always said that. But you never listen to me about what you can do to improve. You keep making the same mistakes over and over, so you might not ever get better. If you don't change your ways, you won't even be able to get on a semi-pro team. Nobody will want you. That's just the way it is."

"But Mr. Busch said he's going to ease me in slow this coming season. Let me watch and learn for a while until I get to know pitchers and ballparks. I can learn to play up there. I know I can."

"That won't make much difference. Like I said, you got to keep your confidence. But the odds are in favor of you taking a fall. If you don't hit, they will have you packing up and out of there faster than you can blink. I just don't see you hitting that curveball they'll throw up there. You'll see those curves in your sleep. You watch. Dad knows what he's talking about."

Tom Alston's mother, Anna, walked from the kitchen into the bedroom where Tom was sitting on a chair by a small desk. "Who you talking to, Tommy?" she asked, wiping her hands on her apron and looking around the room.

"I was just talking to Dad again. He just left. You just missed him. He always says his piece and then leaves in a hurry. You know him—never lets any grass grow under his feet. He was just talking to me about going to the Cardinals. Giving me his advice."

Mrs. Alston walked over to Tom and urged him to stand up from the chair. When he stood, she pulled him close, wrapped her arms around him, put her head on his shoulder, and held him tight. "Tommy, we've talked about this before. Your father's been gone these last four years. He passed and is now with the Lord. He was a troubled man, but he's in a better place now. We have to let him go. *You* have to let him go. We have to move on, Tommy. Please. Please do this for me—and for yourself. It's not good to be holding on to the past like you do. Promise me you'll try. Please do it for your mom. OK?"

Tom backed away slightly from his mother. "Of course, Mama. You always know what to say. Thank you for—"

"Besides," Mrs. Alston cut in, "We've got to get you ready. I know Mr. Busch sent me a train ticket so I could help you get ready for the big *press conference* tomorrow. Not sure exactly what that is, but I know we've got to get your clothes ready and you looking your best. He said he was sending over a speech for you to memorize. Did you get it? Have you practiced it?"

"It's on the table over there. I looked at it. It's a lot to remember. A lot to say. I'll need your help. Can we go through it tonight?"

"Why, of course we can. I'll be the audience. I'll be there tomorrow, so you can just pretend you're saying it all to me. It'll be fine. You'll see."

"Thanks, Mama. What would I do without you?"

"I've got the supper ready. You get those hands washed. A good meal will do you good. After we eat and the dishes are done, we'll get started. Now get at those hands!"

"I'm going" was all Tom said as he turned and stared out the window. He thought he saw his father running toward the streetcar down at the corner. "You'll make it, Dad," he said to himself. "You always do."

"What?" Mrs. Alston turned back toward her son. "You say something?"

"I'm coming. I'll get washed up."

"Get going! We've lots to do."

Tom took one last look out the window then headed to the bathroom.

….. ….. …..

January 26, 1954
Hollywood, California

August A. Busch, Jr. walked to the podium in the ballroom of the
Beverly Hills Hotel, looked around at the dozen local reporters,
including two from St. Louis, who had been gathered by his executive assistants and publicity department, and began addressing them.
"Gentlemen, first of all, make yourselves at home. We've servers
walking the room with caviar and the greatest beer ever brewed,
Budweiser." He waited for the servers to make their way through
the group and hand each a small plate of the caviar and an ice-cold
bottle of beer, which resembled hot dog and beer vendors hawking
their wares at a baseball game.

"Might be hard to scribble your notes with both hands full," Mr.
Busch laughed. "That's why I want you to relax. Our publicity people have put together materials for each of you with the particulars
of why we're here this morning. So, let's enjoy ourselves and talk
a little while. I just wanted to welcome you. Now I'll turn it over to
Dick Meyer, General Manager of our St. Louis Cardinals. "Dick—
the floor's yours. Grab a Budweiser on the way up here."

Dick hurried up to the podium, held up his bottle, and said,
"I thank you—and toast all of you who came today. Thank you."
Then, he turned serious. "This is red-letter day in Cardinals' history,
for a couple of reasons. First, we've just added a power-hitting first
baseman, one with great range around the bag and plenty of sock in
his bat. Last year, out here in the Pacific Coast League, he clubbed
twenty-three homers and drove in a hundred and one runs, all while
sparkling at first base. He's also a first-rate teammate who should fit
right in with the Redbirds."

After scanning the room and suggesting they try another
Budweiser, he continued, his words coming quickly, as if he wanted
to throw them out there and move on before questions could be

asked. "Tom is also a special addition to our club for another reason. He is now the first Negro to wear the 'birds on the bat' logo for our great organization. But that's enough of me talking about him. I'd now like to introduce all of you to the newest addition to our team, Tom Alston."

Dick started the applause, and Mr. Busch followed. A few of the sportswriters frantically tried sitting down their caviar and beer to join in, but before most could, Tom walked quickly to the podium, looked at his mother, who was standing at the back of the room, pulled the microphone up higher, and began reading his speech. "Good morning. I'm Tom Alston, and I'm grateful to be here. I want to thank you for coming."

He stumbled over a few words initially, but once he got rolling, his voice, while still somewhat shaky from the nervousness, evened out. "First of all, I want to thank the San Diego organization for everything they've done for me. I appreciate them so much. But I also want to give thanks to the St. Louis Cardinals, who are offering me the opportunity of a lifetime. Mr. Busch, Mr. Meyer, I want you to know I'll give it everything I have and do my very best to repay your confidence in me. I'm proud to be coming to such a great team, with such great players as Stan Musial and Red Schoendienst. They've also got a great manager in Eddie Stanky, and I won't let him down."

Mr. Busch and Dick Meyer suddenly stopped smiling and switched their attention from the writers enjoying their snacks to Tom as they realized he had stopped suddenly and was shuffling the papers in front of him, staring at them as if he had lost his place. An awkward silence ensued as Tom, now appearing panic stricken, looked first toward his mother and then at Dick for guidance. Mr. Busch sensed there was no way he was going to get back on track, so he moved toward the podium just as Tom spoke up. "I'm sorry. I just can't . . . I don't know—"

That's fine, Tom," Mr. Busch said while reaching for the microphone. Trying to make light of the situation, he said, "We didn't get you for your speech making. I'm sure your bat will do the talking quite nicely. Thank you for your very kind words. I personally want to welcome you to the Cardinals family." Addressing the reporters, he added, "How about some pictures, boys?"

Mr. Busch stepped forward and took Tom's hand, shaking it firmly for almost a full minute while photos were taken. Tom did his best to continue smiling, but his embarrassment over not finishing his speech was evident as he tried to avoid making eye contact with any of the reporters.

The sportswriter on the far left, one Mr. Busch didn't know, suddenly called out, "How about a question or two for Tom? Mr. Busch, would that be OK with you?"

Mr. Busch, still shaking Tom's hand, replied, "I think we've kept this young man at the podium long enough. And, besides, I want this gathering to be a celebration. So, here's what I suggest we do. Tom and I will mingle in with all of you, and you can ask a few questions while we do. Dick Meyer will join us, too. Drink up everyone—and don't let that caviar spoil. That's the best there is, you know. Enjoy yourselves."

As Dick came over, Mr. Busch put his arm around his new first baseman and led him down toward the reporters. "Thank you, Mr. Busch," Tom said, sticking close by his side. "I'm not much good at this. Never know what to say."

"Don't worry, young man. You just keep smiling. *I'll* do the talking."

Tom looked at his mother, who was still standing at the back of the room. She waved and urged him to get out among the reporters. He wanted to go hug her, to have her tell him again everything would be all right. As the reporters gathered around, he lost sight of her, which caused him suddenly to stop in his tracks.

"It's OK," Mr. Busch said, urging him to keep walking ahead. "Everything will be fine."

Tom wanted to believe it. But, at that moment, he couldn't. Instead, he thought of what his father had said to him, "You're not ready." He heard it over and over as Mr. Busch slapped him on the back and steered him through the line of reporters.

....

April 13, 1954
Sportsman's Park, St. Louis, Missouri

Just as Tom Alston stepped into the Cardinals locker room, Stan Musial, who had been waiting for him to appear, walked over to greet him. "Hi there, Tom," he said, warmly, extending his hand. "I know this is your first Major League game, so I wanted to be the first to wish you good luck—and lots of success."

Turning around to face the rest of his teammates, who were preparing for the day's game, he shouted, "Everyone! Look who's here! It's his maiden voyage. Let's all wish him the best."

The others stopped what they were doing, but nobody else walked over. Instead, some waved, others called over, "Hi, Tom," and the rest resumed their pregame preparation and rituals. It wasn't that they weren't happy to see him. They just didn't know what to make of him and didn't understand why he was there. They thought they already had a starting first baseman slated to start the season in Steve Bilko, but when all checked the lineup card as they arrived at the stadium, they saw Tom's name penciled in as the day's starter. The roster also contained several utility players who could take over at first when needed, so he didn't seem to fit in with that group, either. They also felt they had adequate bats off the bench for pinch-hitting duties. To most, why he was there was a mystery.

Manager Eddie Stanky came out of his office and saw Tom sitting at his locker. "Tom, you're at first and batting sixth today." That was all he said, and as soon as he'd finished, he headed out to the field. No one else spoke to Tom until they were all out on the field for the National Anthem. Rip Repulski, standing next to him along the first base line, shook his head and whispered to him, "Step back. Your shoe's on the line. Bad luck."

His words were prophetic. The first batter for the Cubs, centerfielder Bob Talbot, lofted a high pop foul that Tom settled under—and dropped—the first error of his professional career on his first fielding chance. Then, in his first three at-bats, Tom popped out to first in the second inning, struck out in the fifth, and popped out to first again in the seventh. In his fourth and last at-bat of the game, pressing too hard, he topped an easy grounder to second. He had not hit a ball out of the infield in his four trips to the plate. On top of that, the Cardinals lost a close game to their rivals, the Chicago Cubs, 6-4. After the game, he sat in front of his locker, just staring straight ahead as his teammates showered and dressed to leave the park. Stan Musial saw him, came over, and said, gently, "First game's always tough. Put it out of your mind. Go home. Get some rest." Tom thanked him for his kindness, but as he continued to sit there, he heard his father's words again, over and over, especially while seeing himself dropping the foul ball in the first inning. When he finally did shower and dress, he looked around the locker room and saw he was all alone.

Tom didn't play in the second game as Manager Stankey stuck to the platoon and started Steve Bilko at first base. Tom was back in the lineup for game three and went one for five, with his hit a long home run off Cubs reliever Jim Brosnan in a 23-13 demolishing that caused Manager Stanky to rant and rave so loudly in the dugout after the game a security guard came to the locker room to see that everything was OK. Tom had made four easy outs before the home run, and it was those easy fly balls he thought about as he walked out of the stadium.

The next day, Bilko again started at first base, but Tom was called on to pinch-hit in a close game with two runners on in the seventh. Against reliever Jim Davis, Tom crushed a fastball and sent it deep into the left field bleachers, putting the Cards ahead and on their way to their first victory of the season. In the clubhouse after the game, his teammates heaped on the congratulations and praise for his clutch hitting. Even his manager stopped by his locker and swatted him on the shoulder.

From there, Tom tore the cover off the ball, steadily raising his average until it hovered just above .400. The season was still young, but he had shown enough power at the plate and poise at first base for the Cardinals to trade Steve Bilko to the Chicago Cubs. Immediately after the trade, Mr. Stankey called Tom into his office, had him sit in front of his desk, and said, "First base is yours. Now, let's see what you can do without that shadow over your head. Get out there—and play ball!" Tom stood and smiled. He was finally happy for the first time in his Cardinal uniform.

····· ····· ·····

Sadly, that feeling didn't last. The trade of Bilko should have given Tom an extra dose of security, but it soon appeared to do exactly the opposite. As he faced new, additional pressure, his batting average plunged steadily, and his power numbers and fielding slipped as well. On top of that, opposing pitchers very quickly figured out there was a large hole in Tom's swing. He just couldn't lay off fastballs high and tight, and his strikeout rate soared so much that the Cardinals had him play in just 63 more games the remainder of the 1954 season. He ended up with just two more home runs and a season average of .246 while playing only occasionally in a utility role. The Cardinals also discovered a few months after the trade that he was really twenty-seven and not the twenty-two listed on the trade paperwork. When Mr. Busch found out, he was furious. He didn't mind so much the extra he had to give up to make the trade, but he now felt he'd been taken advantage of, something he wasn't used to.

Tom played parts of three more seasons with St. Louis, mostly at the insistence of Mr. Busch, who didn't want to release him until he was sure Tom had been given every chance to redeem himself. However, Tom never again achieved at a high level. His final career totals were 91 games played and a .244 batting average—not the statistics the Cardinals envisioned when they first acquired him.

However, the decline of Tom Alston's career is much more complicated than just a swift decline in his on-field performance. Throughout his career, he often heard voices both during and after games. He was finally diagnosed with significant psychological issues, which caused him to be institutionalized many times through the years. At one point after his playing days he tried, unsuccessfully, to take his own life. After another stint in a mental facility, he returned to his hometown and burned down his local church because of inner demons he could not control.

After his baseball career, Tom was never able to work for long before succumbing again and again to mental illness that prevented him from returning to anything resembling a normal life. For years he managed to get by on Social Security disability benefits and funds from Major League Baseball's "Baseball Assistance Team," an organization that provides help for former players in need. Finally, after a short battle with cancer, Tom Alston passed away, at age 67, on December 30, 1993. Today, a memorial plaque listing his role in helping knock down the color barrier in Major League Baseball can be found in the cement walkway just outside the west entrance to Busch Stadium, home of the St. Louis Cardinals. The plaque is only a few feet from the statue of Stan Musial, Tom's closest friend and confidant during his Major League career.

1955 Bowman #257, Tom Alston
Courtesy of The Topps Company, Inc.

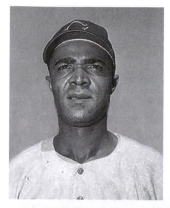

10

Chuck Harmon

Cincinnati Reds

Chuck Harmon with his 1954 Cincinnati Reds teammates
(Chuck middle row, 6th from right).

Chuck Harmon almost didn't become a professional baseball player—by choice. If not for World War II interrupting his college studies, he might very well have ended up with a career in his first love in the world of sports: basketball—*not* baseball.

Chuck grew up in a family of fourteen in Washington, Indiana. When he wasn't in school or helping take care of his siblings, basketball was his world. He loved the game so much he practiced day and night, eventually developing his skills to the point he helped lead his high school team to two championships. His play brought the attention of college scouts, and he played a year at that level before World War II intervened, during which time he served three years in the Navy. After the war, he accepted a minor-league contract with the St. Louis Browns organization. For the next five years, all in the low minors, he knocked the cover off the ball, hitting over .300 every year. However, frustrated because he was not being promoted to higher levels, he decided to try going back to basketball. In 1951 he attended a tryout for the Boston Celtics. His play was so good he made it through the first several rounds of cuts, but by that time he was already twenty-seven, and the coaches decided to go with younger players.

Fortunately, his baseball contract was purchased the following year by the Cincinnati Reds, who moved him up to their highest minor league affiliate, where he continued to excel. In 1953 he slugged 14 home runs, had 83 RBI, and again hit over .300. His effort was rewarded when the Reds invited him to spring training in 1954. After shining in the spring games, he made the team. Shortly thereafter, on April 17, 1954, Chuck made his Major League debut—and became the first African American to play for the Cincinnati Reds organization.

….. ….. …..

July 23, 1955
Polo Grounds, New York

As the Cincinnati Reds came to bat in the top of the 9th, most of the 4,373 fans who had come to the Polo Grounds to watch their beloved New York Giants rose to their feet, cheered, and applauded thunderously. Anticipation and nerves waved through the crowd as Giants pitcher Jim Hearn slowly strolled to the mound, carefully stepping over the first base line as he did so. For eight innings, he had held the Reds to a walk, a hit batsman, and only five balls that left the infield. The Reds' line on the scoreboard read 0 0 0—a no-hitter to this point. Hearn was thirty-four, a veteran of eleven Big League seasons, and one of the most popular Giants with fans and teammates alike. As he toed the rubber and started his warm-up tosses, the fans' cheers rose to a crescendo. He hardly noticed the sound, focusing only on his catcher's glove and the immediacy of the moment at hand. In his entire baseball life, from youth ball through all of his professional experiences, he had never come this close before, and he wanted this no-hitter as an exclamation point on the accomplishments of an excellent career.

Only moments before, as the Giants finished the bottom of the eighth, Hearn had been sitting in the dugout, alone, near the water cooler. No one spoke to him or made the faintest sign of recognition his way. And, in a time-honored baseball tradition, no one gave any indication a no-hitter was in the works. There was some light razzing of Sid Gordon, the Giants clutch-hitting third baseman, who had driven in both of their runs with shallow sacrifice flies but, other than that, all eyes were focused out on the field—and *not* toward Hearn, who sat quietly, running his right hand through his hair and staring at the floor. Yet, it was clear from their lack of attention, his teammates were rooting for him with all their might.

When Hearn made the last of his warm-up pitches, Gordon jogged over from third, took the ball from him, rubbed it up several times, and handed it back without making eye contact. Sid wanted his friend to have a quick moment to gather himself, to take in an extra breath and to focus. Jim, his voice, cracking slightly, said only, "Thanks" and turned toward home plate.

Joe Brovia was the first up for the Reds, pinch hitting for their starter, Joe Nuxhall. His manager, Birdie Tebbetts, urged him on, calling out, "Let's go! Need a baserunner! Bear down now!"

Hearn let loose with a roundhouse curve that caught Brovia by surprise. With a no-hitter on the line, he expected nothing but Hearn's best pitch, a heavy fastball. "Strike!" bellowed home plate umpire Bill Engeln. The ball was in Jim Katt's glove only a split second before he fired it back to his pitcher. Then, quick-pitching, Hearn again went into his windup and tossed up another curve, this one buckling Brovia's knees. "Strike Two!" Engeln shouted even louder, trying to be heard over the fans directly behind home plate erupting in cheers with each pitch. Katt again tossed the ball back as quickly as he could, not wanting to interrupt Hearn's rhythm and focus. Brovia had just finished digging his back shoe into the batter's box when Hearn let loose a blazing fastball. Brovia swung late and weakly tapped the ball to Wayne Terwilliger at second, who easily threw him out. The fans screamed and yelled their excitement, urging Hearn on through their heartfelt show of support.

The Giants' infield tossed the ball around the diamond as Cincinnati's next batter walked toward the batter's box. Birdie Tebbetts again went to his bench, this time calling on Chuck Harmon to bat for third-baseman Milt Smith, who had been in a deep slump. As Harmon dug in, Tebbetts called out, "Just get on! Just need a runner!"

Hearn looked in for the sign, nodded, and fired a fastball that just caught the inside corner. "Strike one!" Engeln called out as the cheering grew even louder. Katt tossed the ball back, and Hearn immediately looked in for the sign: two fingers down, the curve. Harmon caught the spin of the ball but still swung early, fouling it into the stands behind third base. As Engeln raised his arms and indicated the count was now no balls, two strikes, the fans in unison started stomping their feet and clapping even louder.

Hearn looked in again for the sign. Katt called for a fastball, and Jim nodded as he went into his windup. Harmon guessed the pitch and timed it perfectly, catching the ball on the sweet spot of his bat. A split second after contact was made, all eyes watched as the ball was driven into left-center field, a clean hit. The no-hitter was gone.

Hearn knew it at the crack of the bat. He turned slowly, watched the ball land in the outfield grass, bowed his head, let his glove fall to the ground, and just stood there as the ball was tossed back in to second base. The crowd, stunned, became absolutely silent. The only sound that could be heard came from the Reds' dugout, where several of the younger players cheered until the veterans waved them silent, indicating they needed to show respect for a valiant effort, even if it was on the opposing team.

A few seconds later the applause began, only in small pockets at first, but soon loud and boisterous from the whole stadium. Even several of the Reds' players tipped their caps to Hearn. Terwilliger tossed the ball back to Hearn, who looked at it as if it were partially the ball's fault his gem had ended. He waggled the ball in his right hand, indicating he wanted a new one, and tossed it to his catcher.

The next two batters made easy, routine outs, and the Giants won by the score of 2-0. The last play was a grounder to the first baseman, and Hearn had to cover the bag and receive an under-handed toss. As soon as the game ended, Hearn stood at first base and looked back to the outfield where the lone hit had landed. While he did, Chuck Harmon trotted by on his way back to the dugout. Out of respect, he didn't say anything to Jim about breaking up the no-hitter.

However, the fans were waiting for Harmon. As he neared the dugout, they started throwing bottles, food, wrappers, scorecard pencils—and every curse word and taunt they could muster at him. Chuck stopped short, ducked, and felt the steady rain of hatred pelt him. Their tone was so angry, so violent, that ushers immediately swarmed their direction to try to disperse them. Chuck's teammates moved to the edge of the dugout to get a better look, but none came to his aid. Instead, many laughed and shook their heads as Chuck started again for the dugout steps, a bottle glancing off the left side of his head as he did so. Once in the dugout, Chuck heard one voice much more powerful than the others bellowing, "You're a dead man!"

....

July 24, 1955
Polo Grounds, New York

Too frightened to move, Chuck Harmon gripped the training table tighter, his knuckles turning white. A man wearing a gray fedora that covered most of his face slowly opened the training room door just enough that he could slide inside.

Chuck's breath caught, and he started to bolt from the table just as the man shouted, "Don't move! Stay put!" Using the side of his right shoe, he slowly and deliberately closed the door behind him, the lock clicking loudly. Turning to Chuck again, he tilted his head back, revealing his face. He was young—early twenties at most—with rosy cheeks and just the faintest hint of a first growth of a mustache.

Still too stunned to speak, Chuck watched as he flipped open the flap of his briefcase, reached in, and started to remove something. Chuck, his head growing light and his thoughts jumbled, leaned slightly sideways, looked past the man toward the door, and desperately called out, "Officer! Officer!"

Caught off guard, the man flinched and dropped his briefcase, revealing what was in his hand. A pencil, short and stubby. The police officer who had been guarding the door was no longer at his post, so no one responded to Chuck's alarm. Instead, an awkward silence ensued as both men stared blankly at each other, each unsure what to do next.

The stranger spoke first while backing toward the door, his words coming in short bursts, his nervousness obvious. "I'm Colin Kent. Colin Kent. I'm——"

Chuck reacted to the first sound of his words by swinging his legs from the table down to the floor and bolting over to and behind the whirlpool tub. He grabbed a long-handled mop as he did and repeatedly jabbed it back and forth toward the man, urging him farther and farther away. His back pressed against the door; Colin fumbled for the door handle. He finally found it and frantically turned it side to side, but it was obvious the door was locked on the outside, giving no way back out.

"Get out of here!" Chuck shouted, brandishing the mop again. "The cop will be back any second!"

"I can't!" Colin shouted back, still wriggling the door knob. "It won't turn!"

"Keep away from me! I warn you! Don't you—" Chuck stopped in mid-thought as he looked down and saw that when Colin had dropped his briefcase, newspapers, notebooks, and different colored pencils had spilled across the concrete floor.

"Where's your gun? Your knife?" Chuck called out, his words now coming slower, his voice puzzled.

"Don'thaveone! I'mnotwhatyouthink. I'mnothereto...harmyou." Keeping his eyes on Chuck, he bent down and retrieved the items that had fallen from his briefcase. "I'm telling you the truth."

Chuck lowered the mop, resting its weight on the edge of the whirlpool. "Then where's the cop? Nobody's supposed to get in here. He promised he'd keep everyone out until the trainer got here for my rubdown. You're no trainer. Who are you?"

Laughing nervously and shaking his head, Colin replied, "I guess I'm an *idiot*. Thought I could sneak in for a scoop. Just wanted to talk is all."

"You're a *reporter*?" Chuck shot back, a combination of relief and exasperation filling his words. "Newspaper?"

Colin nodded, smiling weakly. "I swear—didn't mean to scare you. Didn't even know for sure you were in here. I knew they were hiding you out somewhere. I just wanted to get to you before the others did. We have an early edition, and I thought—"

Chuck cut him off, dropping the mop, its handle clanking sharply on the floor. "You're here for a story? That what you're telling me?"

Colin stood back up, leaning against the door again, his knees still weak. "Yes. That's the size of it. Guess I should have knocked."

Just then the door knob turned, and the door pushed Colin farther into the room. Both men jumped back, Chuck bending down to pick up the mop again and Colin pointing the sharpened end of his longest pencil.

"What the heck is going on in here?" Officer Johnson asked, looking back and forth from Colin to Chuck. "What is this?"

Realizing he was in no immediate danger, Chuck said, dryly, "Officer, as you can see, this man came in to stab me to death—with his pencil. He's the guilty party. No question about it."

Colin dropped the pencil and said to Officer Johnson, "I'm from the *Herald*. Just getting a story. You know me. You've seen me before. I'm Kent." He reached for his press pass and realized he had left it at home. "Remember?"

"Then what's all this? I could hear you two shouting all the way out by the peanut vendor. Nearly choked to death swallowing a shell when one of you screamed."

Chuck's voice grew louder as he asked, "Why'd you leave the door? You were supposed to stay here. Stay on guard."

Officer Johnson shrugged. "Keep your shirt on. I was just getting a snack." He turned to Colin. "How about if you watch him for me? I'll be just down the ramp so I can watch the game. It's about to start."

"Me?" Colin asked, again dropping his briefcase. "Let me get this straight. Somebody's out to kill him, and you want *me* to guard him? You out of your mind?"

"You're not supposed to be in here, right? You want a story, right? Then if you want something to write about other than me runnin' your sorry behind out of here, you'll stand the watch. Is there any part of that you don't understand, boy?"

"Wait a minute," Chuck interrupted. "This is ridiculous. *How* would he defend me?"

"He's got that sharp pencil, don't he?" Officer Johnson laughed heartily as he turned and headed out the door, calling back over his shoulder, "Don't get shot. Would ruin things for everybody."

Ignoring Chuck's calls of "Wait! Wait!" Officer Johnson slammed the door shut. His frustration boiling, Chuck said out loud and to himself, "Well, that's it. I'm locked in—again!"

Colin finally spoke. "What do you mean locked in? What are you talking about?"

"The door's lock is broken. It can be opened from the outside, but not from the inside. That means you're as trapped as I am." He looked directly at Colin. "It means if someone comes in to shoot me, you'll be in the line of fire, too. How about that?"

Colin jiggled the door knob again as Chuck mumbled, "This is great. Now I'm to depend on you to keep me safe. You and your . . . *pencil*."

"I'm not happy about it either. This is nuts. Somebody ought to turn him in!"

"Be my guest. Oh, that's right—you can't. We can't get out. We're trapped like rats in here."

"There's got to be some way out," Colin said, running his hands up and down the rim of the door frame.

"Already tried that," Chuck said, motioning at the same time for Colin to sit in a chair next to the rubdown table. "Might as well get yourself comfortable. First game of the twin-bill will start in a couple minutes. When it does, nobody'll come in here. We're stuck."

"But I've got to cover the game. I've got to get out of here."

Chuck laughed. "Looks like the only story you're going to get is in here. I'm almost afraid to ask you, but there's nothing else to do. Just what kind of story did you want from me?"

Realizing there was nothing he could do to get the door to open, Colin moved over and sat heavily in the chair next to Chuck. He took his hat off and tossed it on the table. "Well, I know about the threat, but that isn't exactly why I wanted to talk. Everybody else is going to write about that. I'm still pretty new at the paper and don't have my own byline yet. On top of that, I don't think my editor likes me much. Says I'm too young for this. Says he still doesn't know why the paper hired me. Says I'm not ready for big stories."

Chuck waved his hand around the room. "Well," he said, laughing. "You did get yourself trapped. That isn't going to help your cause much, is it?"

"No, it's not!" Colin said, defensively. "That's why I need something from you. Something good."

"What were you thinking about? What do you want to know?"

"Well, there's a pretty big group of Negro fans interested in you, not just in Cincinnati, but here in New York, too. We've got our own, and everybody seems to love Mays, but our Negro fans root for all the visiting players, too—like you. They want to know more about you. How you got started in baseball. What you like to do when you aren't playing. They want to know what kind of family you have. The human-interest side of all this."

"You're kidding," Chuck said, swinging around to face him. "No reporter has ever asked me *anything* before, let alone about my personal life. You'll *never* get it in print. Your editor will laugh in your face."

Colin blushed slightly. "Can't do any worse than I've done so far. I'd like to give it a try. That is, if you'll let me ask my questions. If I can get this done, the old man might start to take me more seriously."

"Or show you the door. Sure you want to go through with this? Might be the end of your job."

"Mr. Harmon, if you'll allow, I'll take a chance. It *could* end up good for me, and if it gets printed, I know many would like it. I don't have much to lose. What do you say? You game?"

Chuck shrugged his shoulders. "Oh, heck. Might as well." He pointed to the door. "It's not like we can do anything else. Fire away."

Colin opened a small notebook and prepared to jot down notes. "I'm not going to print anything about the threat except that one was made. As I said, the others will go into that. But just so I know, would you mind telling me what exactly happened and what's going on?"

"I'm really not supposed to talk about it, but if you give me your word you won't repeat this, I'll share some with you." When Colin nodded, Chuck continued. "If you were here yesterday, you saw what kind of reception I got after the game. I thought I'd been called everything, and I've had everything from rocks to spit flung at me, but I'd never experienced anything like that before. I understand part of it. From what I hear, Hearn is really admired around here, so I guess I burst a pretty good bubble. But that's my job. That's what I'm paid to do. So, the fans get mad at me. Fine. But apparently two of the faithful sent in very detailed letters saying they were going to do me in. Management didn't let me read the letters, but the FBI was called in early this morning. They said it was because of *how* the letters were worded. I've had all kinds of threats before, but these must have been different. Something in them scared both the Reds and the Giants, so here I am. And here *you* are. That's all I know—except they're supposedly following up some leads to find the writers. Meanwhile, they're hiding me, and I hate it."

"I'm sorry, Mr. Harmon. Nobody should have to go through something like this." He hesitated. "Do you think it was because of your . . . color?"

"I'm sure it doesn't help," Chuck replied, looking toward the door again. "Hate comes in all sizes and colors, doesn't it?"

"Mind if I use that in my story? That's good." Chuck waved his approval, so Colin continued. "Thanks for telling me. I won't print what you told me earlier. Promise. What I really want to know is how you got here. Well, not *here*. I mean, when did you first start playing baseball, Mr. Harmon?"

"First of all, you can call me Chuck. Skip the *Mister Harmon* business. I've never really told this to anybody up here. Again, nobody ever asked—but baseball wasn't what I really wanted to end up doing. I played high school basketball and wasn't bad. Our team won two championships, and I helped out enough that scouts from several colleges started coming to the games. The University of Toledo offered me a scholarship if I'd bounce a ball for them, so I took it. I was named All-American my freshman year."

"You went to college?"

The tone of the question didn't really surprise Chuck. "Yes, some of us . . . *baseball players* have gone to college. Or, did you mean something else?"

Colin fumbled with his notebook. "No. Just surprised. Well, not too many around here have been near a college campus. They wouldn't know how to find one with a compass. That's what I meant."

"I'm sure you did," Chuck said, drolly. "That was during World War II, and before I knew it, I was in the Navy. Served three years. Say, you might be interested in this for your story. While I was in the Navy, I played on an all-Black team when I was stationed near Chicago. My roommate then was Larry Doby. Plays for Cleveland. We had a lot of good ballplayers there."

"Wow! You're not kidding me, are you? I'm going to highlight that. Mr. Doby's a great player. Great hitter."

"Taught him everything I know," Chuck said, beaming. "He's turned out OK, I guess."

"And did you go to professional ball from there? Was that what got you started?"

"No. Went back to Toledo after the service, but I was too old then for scholarship money, so I had to find another way to stick around. That's when I got lucky and started playing for the baseball team I followed when I was growing up, the Indianapolis Clowns in the Negro League. The pay was good, but I had to hide out there, too."

"What do you mean—*hide out*?"

"I made good money playing baseball, but I couldn't use my real name or I'd have lost my amateur standing, which would have meant being banned from basketball. So, I quit baseball, went back strictly to basketball, but I couldn't make enough money to stay there."

"So, what did you do?" Colin flipped a page in his notebook.

"Luck again. I'll be the first to admit I've always been luckier than most. I didn't know it at the time, but a scout from the St. Louis Browns saw me play for Indianapolis. A month later he offered me a contract to play in their minor leagues and to try to work my way up. I was broke, so I knew I had to leave basketball behind. There are still times when I'm sad about that. Basketball was my first real love, but it just didn't pan out. Baseball did, and that first year in the minors I tore the cover off the ball and played all over the field."

Chuck laughed. "I was playing so good I thought I'd be with the Browns in no time. Well, four or five years later, I was still in the minors, being moved all the time to a different place, a different league. Played in the Three-I League one season, down in Tulsa the next—I've sure seen the country, that's for sure. I always hit above .300. Hit .375 one year. And, my glove was always my best skill, so that also helped."

"And you still didn't get called up? What happened? How'd you eventually make it?"

"The Puerto Rican Winter League happened, that's what. A couple of my teammates were going after a season was over, and I just sort of tagged along. I'm glad I did. It was fun there. Nobody worried about skin color, and everybody could eat, sleep, and travel where they wanted to. You just played ball. That was it. And the fans really love their teams down there and take care of the players if they get sick or need anything. If it had paid more money, I'd still be there."

Colin leaned forward, tapped his pencil on his notebook, and urged him on. "So, how'd you end up *here*? Give me the details."

"By that time, Cincinnati had bought my contract from the Browns. I still don't know why the Browns gave up on me. I hit everywhere they put me. But, that's baseball, I guess. Anyway, Cincinnati scouts liked what they saw when I was in Puerto Rico. My hitting was better than ever, and I played all outfield spots. Shoot—I even caught a couple of games, and jumped in as a relief pitcher once. I did a little of everything, but that wasn't all that unusual in that league. So, the Reds invited me to spring training in 1954, and I stuck with the team. I'm still not starting as much as I'd like, but I guess I'm still proving myself." Here he stopped to make sure he had Colin's attention. "Like you."

"I'd say you're right," Collin said, leaning back in his chair. "So, what *can* we do?"

Chuck stood up and walked toward the door. "In case you haven't heard, some of my teammates have started calling me 'Mr.

Glove.' I'm not hitting so good these days. Not like I'd like to—and they expect me to. I know my glove is what's going to keep me here for now. I can play anywhere they put me, and they know it. It isn't a great role, but it's one that will buy me time, time to see if the hitting can catch up. I've practiced my swing until my hands blister. I had my eyes checked. I've tried eating before games, not eating before games, every routine I can think of. So far, nothing's worked too long, but I'll keep at it. I've got to. How about you? What do reporters do to keep ready? What do you want next?"

"I've wanted to be a reporter since I worked on the junior high newspaper. It's all I ever wanted to do. Now, I'm here. What I didn't know was it's a lot tougher to stay here than it is to get here."

Chuck laughed. "I know. Same for me. And now . . . .."

"The death threats," Colin said almost in a whisper. "I am sorry. Wish there was something I could do."

"You're doing it," Curt said. "Maybe if some people see inside the uniform, if they take the time to get to know us . . . .. No, that would be too much to ask. I think it'll just take some time."

Colin snapped his notebook shut. "I think I have enough. I'll write it up later today. Sure can't get to a typewriter now." He looked around the room. "Thanks for talking to me. I appreciate it very much. One thing I can do is tell a good story. I'll give this one my best. I promise you that."

"Thank *you*," Chuck replied. "And I wish you luck. The best."

A long silence followed, each man just staring at the door. Colin finally looked at his watch. "Guess the game's in the second inning about now."

"No—I'd say the third. Haven't heard any big noise, so must be going fast. Likely a pitcher's duel."

After another long stretch of quiet, Colin asked, "What do we do now?"

"Give me a minute. I'm going to look for something. Our trainer always brings along a deck of cards wherever we go. Gives him something to do when he's not hovering over us. There it is!" he said, reaching high on a shelf to the right of the door. "How about gin rummy?"

"I'll win," Colin said, scooting over his chair.

"I can tell you're a real competitor," Chuck said, smiling and shuffling the cards.

"Takes one to know one," Colin shot back.

As Chuck started dealing the cards, an eruption of cheers rang out in the stands. Both men just looked at each other, and Chuck began to deal.

….. ….. …..

Colin's story was never published, and those who penned the threats were never caught. The FBI stayed with the team until they returned to Cincinnati for their next home stand. The first time Chuck took the field, boos rang out across the stadium, which in later years he said wasn't all that unexpected to him. Not long after the New York incident, his playing time dropped sharply. He played in just 96 games that season, eventually being sent back to the minors, where the organization hoped he'd rediscover his batting eye. The following season, after thirteen games with the Reds, he was traded to the St. Louis Cardinals where he was used primarily as a utility player. In 1957 Chuck was again traded, this time to the Philadelphia Phillies, where his career drew to a close at the end of that season. In four seasons, he had played in 289 games and built a lifetime batting average of .238.

After his playing career, Chuck worked as a baseball scout for many years—*and* a scout for the Indiana Pacers professional basketball team. He also worked many years in the legal system in and around Cincinnati, where he decided to make his permanent home. He spent a great deal of time helping out organizations for youngsters in the city. Chuck Harmon passed away on March 19, 2019, just a month before his 95th birthday. To the end, he was an ardent supporter of the Cincinnati Reds organization, helping them with promotions and events as often as he could. In recognition of this work, a special plaque honoring Chuck Harmon's accomplishments and pioneer work was placed above the main entrance to the stadium to be seen by generations to come.

....

NOTE: *Although Chuck Harmon was the first African American to play for the Cincinnati Reds, he was not the first person of color to play for the organization. That distinction goes to Nino Escalera, who was born and grew up in Puerto Rico. Nino appeared one batter before Harmon when they both made their Major League debuts in the same game on April 17, 1954. In the 7th inning of a game against the Braves, Escalera was called upon to pinch-hit for catcher Andy Seminick, and promptly singled to start his career on a high note. After he reached base, Harmon was sent up to hit for the Reds' pitcher, Corky Valentine. Chuck popped out to first base. When the inning was over, both men found themselves back on the bench for the remainder of the game. Chuck went on to play in parts of four seasons. Escalera's career ended after 73 games in 1954, during which time he had eleven hits, no home runs, and a .159 batting average. The highlight of his year—and his Major League career—came on May 22 when he became the last left-handed throwing player to play shortstop in a National League game. That may not seem much, but it placed him in the record books.*

After the 1954 season ended, Escalera returned to the minor leagues, where he played seven more years. He then became a scout for several organizations, continuing in that role for over twenty years. To this day, many historians consider Nino Escalera the pioneer in breaking down the color barrier for the Cincinnati Reds organization.

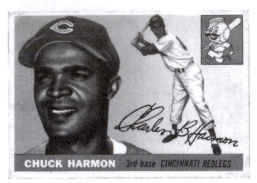

1955 Topps #82, Chuck Harmon
Courtesy of The Topps Company, Inc.

11

Carlos Paula

Washington Senators

Carlos Paula with his 1954 Washington Senators teammates
(Carlos top row, far right).

Carlos Paula was born November 28, 1927, and grew up in Havana, Cuba. He never cared much for school and dropped out in seventh grade. Big for his age, he started working, first in restaurants, then in manual labor jobs around the city. He even took up prizefighting to supplement his earnings. He also started playing baseball the year after he quit school when he saw several others in his neighborhood setting up a game. He loved the sport right from the start and vowed he would figure out a way to make his living with a bat and glove.

In 1952, Carlos' playing days in the United States began in Decatur, Illinois, with the Decatur Commodores, a Class D club in the Mississippi-Ohio Valley League. There he hit over .300, with good power and was voted to the All-Star team of that league. After just one season with the club, he signed on with the Paris Indians (Paris, Texas) of the Big State League, where he continued to hit well. At the end of the season, he returned to Cuba to play Winter Ball in the Cuban Professional Baseball League. Scouts for the Washington Senators attended several of his games and liked what they saw: an accomplished hitter and a fan favorite because of his aggressive base running and clutch hitting. They purchased his contract before the 1954 season and invited him to spring training.

As soon as the spring games began, Manager Bucky Harris grew more and more impressed by Carlos as he hit for average and power, ran the bases with great speed, and demonstrated a strong throwing arm. Carlos' new teammates dubbed him to reporters covering the team as "the most exciting player in camp." However, Harris felt Carlos would become an even better all-around player through a little more seasoning in the minors, so he was sent to their affiliate in the Sally League at Charlotte, North Carolina. At Charlotte, he led his team in most offensive categories, including extra base hits and home runs. One scout sent in a report that said Carlos had hit a home run of approximately six hundred feet. He was finally called up to the big club and made his Major League debut on September 6, 1954, becoming the first person of color to play for the Washington Senators. In that first game he had two hits, drove in a run, and seemed destined by teammates and sportswriters alike for a long career in the Major Leagues.

....

July 10, 1955
Griffith Stadium, Washington, D.C.

Carlos Paula and his dear friend and teammate Jose Valdivielso sat by themselves and ate their lunch in the box seats just above their team's dugout. The first game of their scheduled double-header with the New York Yankees wasn't to begin for about an hour and a half, so they each grabbed two ham and cheese sandwiches and a Coca Cola from the clubhouse and made their way up into the stands where they could visit in Spanish. Carlos and Jose knew their conversations in Spanish seemed to bother their teammates when they talked around them. Maybe the others thought they were talking about them, or maybe speaking their native language set them apart as *foreigners*—a word both had heard directed at them so many times they now knew the full weight it carried. Whatever the reason, Carlos and Jose went off by themselves whenever possible to relax so that everyone could be comfortable.

Carlos took a bite of his sandwich and said, matter-of-factly, "You know, I don't think Mr. Dressen likes us."

Jose laughed. "No—our manager doesn't like *me*. He *hates* you."

"But, why? What have I done?"

"Where do you want me to start? Let's see—last week you were on third and missed the sign for the squeeze play not once, but *twice* and were thrown out both times when you started running late. First time, Mr. Dressen just yelled at you. The second time he went crazy. By the time you got back to the dugout, he had already thrown bats, balls, gloves all over. A bat just missed my head! Might have killed me. He punched the water cooler, too, and hurt his hand bad. Been a long time since I've seen someone so mad."

"Anybody can miss a sign," Carlos said, defensively. "I just got confused. They're different here than in Cuba. Here there are too many to remember. At home, we have the same signs for everyone. Here, they give me one sign, you another one—nobody has the same sign for plays. Doesn't make sense. It makes it hard. He shouldn't have gotten so mad. He shouldn't *hate* me for that. Could happen to anybody, I think."

Jose took a long drink of his Coca Cola and wiped his mouth. "That's just the start. You're also late all . . . the . . . time. Late to the park, for practices, for meetings, getting on the trains. Want me to go on? You know that really makes him mad, right?"

Carlos shrugged. "I've *always* been late—all my life. Just the way I am. I don't think I can change now. And, it wasn't fair the other day when he yelled at me so bad. I had to call my grandmother in Havana. She's been sick. I was only half an hour late getting to practice. Why did he have to be so mad? I made it here in time for me to take some swings, and he still fined me twenty-five dollars. I just don't understand it."

Jose laughed again. "Because you told him back in spring training your grandmother died. Remember? I heard him talking to the other coaches about it. He knows. *That's* why he blew up."

Carlos picked up his second sandwich. "Well, that was my *other* grandmother."

Jose rolled his eyes. "Look, you're like a big brother to me— and you're my hero. You and Minnie Minoso. Both of you. I saw you both play in Havana when I was a teenager, and I wanted to be just like you two—but especially you. You were the most exciting player I'd ever seen. And, I've appreciated everything you've done for me since I got here. Even though I care for you that much, I have to be honest and say some things you may not like to hear."

"Go on. Tell me. I know you'll tell me the truth. Just say it. I won't be mad."

Jose swallowed the last of a very large bite he had taken, and finally spoke. "With all respect, seems like you need to pay attention more when you're in the outfield."

"What do you mean? I love playing there."

"I know you do. You have one of the best throwing arms I've ever seen. But that doesn't do any good or help the team if you're not sure of how many outs there are, or who is batting, or how many runners are on base. I turn sometimes and see you looking at people in the stands or playing with your glove. Mr. Dressen sees that, too.

"Remember last week when you threw the ball back in to second base after a single—while the runner who had been on second was racing toward home? I think you just forgot about the runner, but Mr. Dressen didn't. When the inning was over and we were coming back to the dugout he didn't say anything, but he looked at *both* of us like we were dirt."

Carlos tossed the rest of his second sandwich into the trash can next to the railing. "I just get bored sometimes," he began. "The game is *way* slower here. Too slow. These people think too much and don't have much fun. At home, we pitch the ball, we hit the ball, we catch the ball. Fast. And loose. Everything is so tight and wound up here—and looked at over and over. They make it hard to have fun, the way it's supposed to be. Am I wrong?"

"No—you are not. But we're *not* back home. This is America, and they have different rules and different ideas about the game. This is also strange to me, but we have to play their way or we'll be sent away. They're paying us good money, much more than we can make in Cuba, to do things like they want, so we should. This is also why Mr. Dressen doesn't much want us around and doesn't play us much. Because our baseball is different, I think he thinks we're lazy."

"Lazy?" Carlos practically shouted. "How could he think that? We're good players. We run fast, and we play with *style*. Most of our teammates are afraid to do that. I'm not. *We're* not."

Jose leaned forward and lowered his voice. "That has nothing to do with it. Well, maybe a little. Do you remember last week when you hit a ground ball to shortstop and didn't run hard to first? You didn't see it, and he didn't say anything to you at the time, but I thought Mr. Dressen was going to explode right in front of me. I'm not sure of some of the words he used, but his eyes were crazy and wild. That much I could tell."

"Then why didn't he tell me? I knew I'd be thrown out. I just thought I'd save my energy for later in the game when it could matter."

"But what if that shortstop had thrown the ball away or pulled the first baseman off the bag? You could have been safe. *That's* why he was mad. That's one of the reasons he thinks we're lazy."

"Only *our* shortstop—*you*—would throw bad to first," Carlos teased, tapping Jose's chest. "He does that a lot."

Both laughed, but Jose quickly turned serious again. "One more thing. You've got to stop pretending you don't understand what Mr. Dressen says to us. I know English hasn't been easy for you. English hasn't been easy for me, either, but I'm trying. I also know you understand more than you let on when he and the other coaches talk to you. When you play dumb, it makes you look dumb and sound even worse. Same when you talk to the newspapermen. Have you seen what they write about you in the sports pages lately? They make your words sound like what a little child would say. They're making fun of you. When others read the stories, they think the same thing—that you're a child—and not a man."

Jose could tell his words stung. After a few quiet moments, he said, "I'll help you. We'll go over English words and sentences every day, especially the baseball ones."

Carlos suddenly became defensive. "Who are you to teach me? Your English isn't the best."

"At least I try, and they see that. They don't make fun of *me*, do they? Just you. And, sometimes I don't blame them. You ask for it by not trying your best to learn the language."

Carlos downed the last of his Coca Cola, set down the bottle, and turned again to his friend. "I thought you knew . . .." His voice trailed off. "Sometimes I pretend I don't understand because I don't agree with what they're saying. Other times, there's just too much talking. I'm here to play baseball—not give speeches. If they think I'm not too smart, then I don't have to answer the same questions over and over and over every day. The reporters in Cuba ask a simple question, get an answer, and leave us alone. The ones here are like a pack of dogs that follow us everywhere. They never stop their barking. One followed me to the shower last week!

"And, I don't like talking to them because if I make a mistake out there, they write it like I just spit on a child or something. They're mean. I know they make fun of me. They don't do that to Mickey Vernon or Pete Runnels or Roy Sievers when they make errors or do bad things. They don't say anything about them, only when I do it. So I don't talk to them."

Jose shook his head in frustration. "Have you been listening to me? You bring much of that to yourself—for all the reasons I just told you. But you can change things, my friend, if you try. I know you can. If you don't, they'll send you away, and I'll be alone. I don't want that. I don't think you do, either."

Carlos exhaled loudly. "Then what do I do? Where do I start?"

Relieved that Carlos was at least willing to listen, Jose jumped right in. "We'll start by having English lessons after games. I ask Ted Abernathy to help me learn five new words or sentences every day. He's good about it and doesn't make fun of me. I write them down and keep them in a little notebook so I can practice them later. I'll get one for you, too. We need to learn how to speak English to show we are trying. Next, both of us—me *and* you—need to remember this isn't Cuba. We have to play like Americans."

"But they don't play with soul and passion. This isn't a game here. This is *work*. A *job*!"

"I agree, but, again, we can't make this money at home or live like we do here. I'm sending as much as I can back to my parents to help take care of the family and our relatives. I *need* to be here for that reason alone. It makes me feel good to help, to make their lives better. Besides, we can have the best of both. We can go back home and play in the winter in the Cuban League. We can have more fun there and get good food and clothes we like because we will have money from here. I feel lucky to have both places. This changes everything for me."

"I miss home. I miss my family."

Sensing he needed to change the mood, and quickly, Jose leaned forward. "And your grandmother? Did she rise from the grave so you can miss her, too?"

"I'm telling you; it was my *other* grandmother!" Carlos protested but then smiled. "But I don't think Mr. Dressen will ever like us, no matter what we do. Ever."

"Now, *you're* missing the point," Jose countered. "Mr. Dressen doesn't have to *like* us. He probably never will. The reporters, too. But that won't matter if we play good and always look like we're trying. He'd play his worst enemy if that could help him win games. We're in seventh place right now, just two games from the bottom. How many games have we won? Not many. Less than half we've played. Manager Harris got fired at the end of last season because the team wasn't good. Mr. Dressen knows the same will happen to him if we don't do better."

Pointing first at Carlos, then back to himself repeatedly, he added, "If we hit, we field, we throw, we play like Americans, he may not like us, but he'll have to play us. I don't know about you, but I'm tired of not seeing my name on the lineup card. I'm tired of sitting on the bench. We need to show him we can do it—all of it. We need to show that even though we're not from here, we can still help win games. If we do that, I believe all will be good."

"You're dreaming. You have your head in the clouds. There are days I think we should just go home."

"Not me. But, if you don't start trying at least to get him to *respect* you, he'll be sending you home. Do you really want that?"

Carlos shook his head. "It's hard here."

"I don't disagree. But what we need to do *right now* is show what we can do. Look—we have a double-header today against the Yankees. I've seen the lineup card, and we're both playing. I hope in the second game, too. Let's show them who we are—and what we can do. We'll give everything we have, play our best, and let Mr. Dressen see why he should play us more. What do you say?"

Carlos stuck out his hand. "I'll try. Thank you. Thank you for what you've said." After shaking Jose's hand, he pounded his right fist into his left palm, and shouted, "Let's get ready for those Yankees!"

Just then Charlie Dressen stuck his head above the dugout and shouted, "Well, you boys going to come in for the pregame meeting—or are you just going to stuff your faces and take a nap?"

"We were going over the Yankees' hitters," Jose called back. "Want to make sure we think about where they hit the ball so we can play better."

Dressen looked surprised as he nearly lost his balance on the top dugout step. "Now, that's what I want. That's using your noggin'. Now get down here and join the rest of us." Specifically addressing Jose, he said, "And tell him, too. He's startin' today."

"Be right there—and we'll be ready!" Jose called out as Dressen disappeared from view.

He turned to Carlos, who had heard his manager perfectly and was already starting to stand. "Let's go!" Carlos said, reaching for Jose's arm. "We don't want to be late!"

Jose smiled broadly. "Maybe that skull of yours isn't that thick after all. I have the feeling this is going to be a good day for both of us.

….. ….. …..

At the start of the first game of the double-header, the New York Yankees' record stood at 55-29—with the team in first place by five games over the Cleveland Indians. In contrast, the Senators' 27-54 record reflected inconsistent pitching, poor hitting—especially with runners in scoring position—and a lack of confidence evident every time they took the field. It was no surprise, then, that the Yankees went about their batting practice and fielding drills with a swagger and bravado that had most members of the Washington club leaning on the railing of their dugout and watching. Hank Bauer, Mickey Mantle, Bill Skowron, and Elston Howard all easily lofted balls into the outfield stands while infielders Gil McDougald, Andy Carey, and Billy Hunter scooped up practice ground balls and fluidly tossed them to their coaches. On top of that, Whitey Ford, their ace who always dominated Washington, was to be their starter. As Chuck Dressen watched Whitey rolling off curveball after curveball during his warm-up session, he cursed under his breath. This, he thought, was going to be another *long* day.

It appeared he was right when the Yankees took a quick 2-0 lead in the first inning on a tremendous home run to deep center field by Mickey Mantle. They added another run in the second when Elston Howard scored from third on a groundout. The score remained that way until the fifth when Mantle clouted another home run, this one high into the left field stands, putting his club ahead 4-0 as Washington came to bat in their half of the inning.

Carlos and Jose had vowed before the game to show their manager and teammates that they deserved regular playing time. Carlos had rocketed a line drive to the shortstop in the second, and Jose had sacrificed a runner into scoring position in the third, but that was hardly the impression they had hoped to make. Now, as the home half of the fifth was about to begin, Jose walked over to Carlos and said, "Now. This inning. Now's the time. I *feel* it." Carlos, who was first up, grabbed his bat and nodded.

Unlike the rest of his teammates, Carlos wasn't intimidated by Whitey Ford's assortment of pitches. Ford constantly changed speeds, trying to keep hitters guessing and off-balance. However, Carlos had always hit left-handed pitching well, so it didn't matter to him who was on the mound. At the same time, he always saw the ball well when it came out of Ford's hand, allowing him to set the timing of his swing. He wasn't always successful, but Carlos went to the plate with great confidence and actually enjoyed the challenge against such a great opponent.

Before stepping into the batter's box, Carlos took a few extra practice swings and studied where the outfielders were playing him. They were shading him slightly toward left field, which typically indicated he was going to see softer pitches he could pull if he put wood on the ball. "Curveball," he thought to himself as he settled into the box.

Whitey looked in for the sign from his catcher, Yogi Berra. When he was ready, he went into his windup and snapped off a slow, looping curve that started toward the outside of the plate then dipped suddenly right at its center. Carlos, timing the pitch perfectly, caught it on the sweet spot of his bat. The crack that followed brought his teammates to their feet, and they rushed toward the rail of their dugout. The ball was hit hard and it lofted high as it sailed deep into the left-center field stands, ricocheted off an empty seat, and bounced a good dozen times down the steps before it disappeared. Just over fifteen thousand fans had shown up for the double header, so this section of the park was completely empty. However, those in attendance in other sections stood and marveled at just how far the ball had traveled. A smattering of applause could be heard from the sparse crowd as Carlos rounded third base and headed for home.

When Carlos reached the dugout, Dressen, his face expressionless, nodded to him and then turned his attention back to the field. In contrast to his manager's reaction, his teammates rushed over, each wanting to give his version of just how far the homer was hit and what the ball did when it finally touched down. Dressen finally turned and barked, "We've got a game going on! And, I don't see no reason to celebrate yet, do you?" His tone removed the smiles, and all became quiet again. That is, all but Jose, who came over, clapped softly, and winked. Carlos smiled back and urged his friend, who was three spots behind him in the lineup, to grab his bat and loosen up for his turn at the plate.

The next batter, Tom Umphlett, Washington's centerfielder, on the very first pitch, another curveball, laced a single to left. This brought a few of the Senators to their feet and toward the railing, where they could get a better view of the action in case a rare rally against Ford was about to take place. However, the next batter, Pete Runnels, drove a fastball high and deep to center, where Mickey Mantle gloved it just before the wall. It was an out, but it also indicated Whitey wasn't as sharp today as was usually the case when he took the mound.

Jose was next in the batting order and walked quickly from the on-deck circle to the plate. As with Carlos, Jose much preferred facing left-handers. However, this was his first at-bat against Ford, and even though he had been studying his motion from the dugout, he decided he'd take a pitch or two to set up his timing. The first pitch was a fastball, low and away. Ford then let loose a sharp biting curve that caught just the outside edge of the plate to even the count at a ball and a strike. Given the count, and the fact he didn't move a muscle on the last pitch, Jose figured another off-speed pitch of some type would follow. He was right. His timing right on the mark, Jose lined a shot over the leaping second baseman's glove and into right field.

The ball was hit hard and the right fielder got to it quickly and kept Umphlett from racing to third. Jose rounded the first base bag, stopped short when he saw the runner ahead of him hadn't taken off for third, and had to dive back into the bag to avoid being thrown out. His hustle wasn't unnoticed by his fans and his teammates, all of whom again stirred and clapped. Jose stood, brushed himself off, and looked in the dugout. Carlos first clapped, then went through the motion of swinging an imaginary bat and pointing to right field, and finally shouted to Jose—in perfect English, "That's the way to hit!" Several teammates standing next to Carlos gave a quick glance, shocked by his sudden proficiency with the language.

Charley Dressen knew his team seldom put up runs against Whitey Ford, so he didn't want to take the chance of missing an opportunity, especially because Whitey's command was off this day. So, he pulled his starter, Dean Stone, even though it was still very early in the game, and sent up Mickey Vernon to pinch-hit and, hopefully, keep the rally going.

After Vernon was announced as the pinch-hitter, Yogi Berra went out to confer with his pitcher, who he knew wasn't as sharp with his pitches as he usually was. Yogi wanted to stall and give Whitey time to gather himself and get ready for Vernon, who everyone knew was a tough out. They spoke so long that home plate umpire Nestor Chylak finally walked to the mound to hurry them up. When play finally resumed, Vernon dug in, took a couple of practice swings, held his bat high, and waited for the pitch, a curve that had very little movement. Vernon was a little off balance, but he still managed to poke the ball into left-center field. Umphlett scored easily.

Jose, off as soon as he saw the ball was going to fall in, never hesitated as he approached second base—rounding the bag and running as hard as he could toward third. He knew it was going to be a close play so, instead of sliding, he dove headfirst, stretching his arm out as far as he could. Andy Carey caught Mickey Mantle's throw about shoulder high and swiped down his tag. At first, Jose thought he would be called out. So did Carey. However, Bill McKinley, umpiring at third, roared, "Safe!"—and waved his arms back and forth to indicate the same. Casey Stengel, New York's manager, stormed out of the dugout and started protesting. Soon, the whole Yankee infield was there, all shouting at McKinley and pointing to the bag. McKinley held his ground, folding his arms across his chest and allowing them to vent their frustration.

A few moments later, Charlie Berry, umping at second, came over and separated everyone, warning them that any more discussion would lead to ejections. The Yankees weren't happy, but they had had their say. The whole time this was taking place, Jose jogged back and forth about fifteen feet along the third base line to keep his legs loose. His teammates, appreciating his daring run, shouted their approval. When Jose was finally back on the base, Carlos led his teammates in a long round of applause and tipped his cap. Chuck Dressen again chastised his players, this time not as gruffly, and reminded them they still had work to do.

As soon as Casey Stengel got back to his dugout, he emerged again and walked to the mound, signaling along the way he wanted right-hander Tom Morgan to come in and take over the pitching. Casey knew Ford had piled up a lot of innings recently, and, on top of that, this wasn't one of his better days. The decision wasn't a tough one.

However, changing pitchers didn't help the Yanks out of the trouble they found themselves in. Washington's next hitter, Juan Delis, ripped a single to left, scoring both Jose and Ramos, pinch running for Vernon. They had tied the score, 4-4. The fans rose to their feet, cheering wildly, and the Senators' dugout came alive again. This time Dressen smiled. The next batter was hit by a pitch. John Groth then reached on an error by the third baseman, which allowed another run to score and Washington to take the lead. Roy Sievers followed and grounded into a force-play at second for the second out of the inning. With runners on first and third, Carlos came up for the second time in the inning.

As Carlos took his practice swings and readied himself to dig in at the plate, Casey Stengel came out to talk to his pitcher and catcher. Their visit was brief, Casey walking back to the dugout before the home plate umpire got halfway to the mound.

Tom Morgan relied mostly on his fastball, which had good movement. Carlos knew this from the pre-game meeting Dressen had held about the opposing pitchers. When Chylak shouted, "Play ball!" Carlos dug in and stared out at Morgan, waiting for his delivery to begin. The first pitch was, as Carlos expected, a fastball, but it tailed low and outside. He had a good rip at the next pitch but fouled it straight back. With the count at 1-1, Morgan fired another fastball, this one catching too much of the plate. Carlos swung and drove the ball on a line into the left-center gap. Fitzgerald scored easily from second. Roy Sievers, not noted for his speed, ran through the third base coach's stop sign and headed home. The relay throw from the shortstop caught him just before his slide got his right foot to the plate. He was out, the inning over. Carlos was credited with a double, and as he trotted back to the dugout to grab his glove before taking the field again, Dressen patted him on the behind. Carlos turned to him, and said, "You're right. He throws fastballs." Dressen, taken aback, simply nodded.

As Carlos headed for the field, he looked back and could have sworn Dressen smiled just for a second. He turned and smiled himself, making sure it wasn't seen. He ran as fast as he could out to right field. His team had just scored six runs and gained a lead they'd never relinquish. Carlos added an exclamation mark to the victory during the Yankees' final at-bat. Joe Collins launched a fly ball deep to right field. A collective groan came from the stands as all believed the ball would end up in the seats. However, Carlos, tracking the ball, ran to the wall, timed his leap to the split second, reached high above the wall and caught the ball in the very tip of his glove's web. He crashed into the wall, tumbled to the ground, and rolled a few feet, finally holding up his glove to show he still had possession. Since Carlos was not noted for his defensive skills the crowd reacted by giving him a standing ovation. Final score: Senators 6, Yankees 4.

Between games, Dressen walked over to where Carlos and Jose were sitting tightening the laces on their gloves, and said, his tone as warm as they'd ever heard it, "Nice game—both of you." Each thanked him and continue working on their gloves. When he had gone, Jose slapped Carlos playfully on the knee. He didn't say anything.

Washington lost the second game 8-3, but Carlos and Jose still put on quite a show. Jose went two for three, scored a run, and drove in a run. Both of his hits were doubles. In the fifth inning, he made a mad dash for the plate on a single to short right by Ernie Oravetz. In a bang-bang play at the plate, he was declared safe, but the Yankees saw it differently, sparking a lively argument. Then, in the seventh, he made a full-extension dive to his right to snag a hot shot off the bat of Andy Carey, jumped back to his feet, and threw him out by a fraction of a second. The play saved a run and helped squash another rally. He followed that up by robbing Cary in the top of the ninth, this time making a spectacular leap to capture a line drive several feet above his head, saving yet another run.

Carlos went one for four and scored a run. He singled in the second. The next batter, Clint Courtney, hit a blooper to right field. Carlos instantly read the trajectory of the ball and knew it was going to fall in. Racing as fast as his legs would carry him, he rounded second base and tore for third. The throw in was a strong one, but Carlos made an exaggerated slide, his spikes catching the third baseman's left leg just enough he lost his balance and couldn't make the tag, falling to the dirt instead. Carlos' teammates shouted their approval, especially when they saw Yanks' third baseman, Andy Cary, who had been victimized by the Senators all day, call for the trainer to check his leg, which had been badly spiked. Even Dressen joined in and shouted, "That's the way to get 'em!"

After play resumed, on the next pitch Pete Runnels hit a flyball to short left-center field. As soon as the ball was caught, Carlos sped for the plate. Again, the play was close, but he clearly beat Berra's tag. He bounced back up from his slide and, head down, started jogging back to the dugout. In the past, he might have made the time to mock Berra for not blocking the plate better, but Jose's words were still ringing in his ears. He needed to play *American* baseball—not the flamboyant game he left behind in Cuba.

Carlos' final highlight of the day took place in the sixth when Yogi Berra lofted a high flyball deep and fair into the right field corner. Carlos had been playing Berra straightaway, so he had to run full-out and finally dive right toward the wall. The ball hit the webbing of his glove, and for an instant it popped back in the air. However, Carlos snagged it and again held his glove high to show the out had been made. The play saved a run and ended another threat.

After the game, Dressen, called his players together in the clubhouse. He was never comfortable giving speeches, so he kept his comments short. He told the team he was proud of the way they had played against the first-place Yankees. He mentioned a few highlights of the day: Mickey Vernon's double that sparked a rally, Johnny Groth's hustle to beat out a slow roller to third, Ernie Oravetz' punch-single to right field that drove in a run. The mood in the room was light, and cheers went up as each play was mentioned.

Dressen then motioned for quiet. "I also want to say something about Jose and Carlos and what they did today. We need more of that. That was as close to a compliment they were going to receive, and they knew it. Carlos stood, and said, quietly, "We will try very hard, Mr. Dressen. Very hard." Jose nodded. No one said anything in response, but almost immediately the rest of the team started clapping, lightly at first, then louder and louder until Dressen interrupted. "That's enough! After the All-Star break, we've got a tough double-header against the White Sox. So, get dressed, get out of here, rest up, and get ready. I want this same play next Thursday. Got it?"

Jose looked at Carlos and smiled broadly. Leaning closer so he could whisper, he said, "I told you. Maybe Jose is not so dumb. What do you think?"

"I think we'll have to wait and see," Carlos replied. "I still don't think he likes us."

"I'm telling you; it doesn't matter."

Carlos shook his head and headed for the shower. He hoped his friend was right.

....

Carlos Paula's all too brief Major League career consisted of one series of ups and downs after another—but it was always interesting.

He finished the 1955 season with a .299 batting average and was named to the "All-Rookie" team, an honor given to those thought to have an outstanding career ahead of them. He seemed on one level like a star in the making, but the "all-out" style of play he had learned in Cuba didn't transition well to the Major Leagues. He ended up leading the American League in errors, much to the dismay of his manager and the hometown fans, thus starting a love-hate relationship among all parties.

At the end of the '55 season, Carlos returned to Cuba to play Winter Ball, where he again hit for high average and became one of the more popular players in the league. There, the fans quickly forgave his mishaps in the field because they knew most were the result of his aggressiveness, which they respected and admired. That wasn't the case at all in the States. As soon as the regular season closed, the Washington sportswriters' "Year in Review" pieces mocked Carlos' play in the field, making him seem almost cartoonish and made him look like he had possibly the worst defensive skills in the history of the Washington ball club. Their words stung Carlos, hurting him deeply, but he kept playing the only way he knew how.

Washington's coaches had planned to work closely with Carlos on his defense when he reported to spring training in 1956. However, after just a few days in camp, he received word his mother had suffered a heart attack in Cuba. He requested, and was granted, permission to travel home to help with her recovery. However, through a serious miscommunication, likely on *both* sides, he stayed away longer than the club anticipated, missing almost all the remaining spring games. When he did return, that left precious little time for the coaches to work with him, which angered his manager and the front office. As a result, he was sent to the minors just before the team broke camp to start the season. In the minors, he tore the cover off the ball, earning him a call-up to the big club in May.

Again, because of another miscommunication, he showed up several days late, much to the consternation of everyone. Carlos was never forgiven and soon found himself relegated to the bench and

in the regular lineup only occasionally. Because of his lack of playing time, he lost the edge to his skills, and base running blunders,
errors, and inconsistent hitting followed. As his play deteriorated,
the sportswriters swooped in again, magnifying and criticizing his
every move. The fans followed suit, and the boos rang out regularly.
A little over a month later, he was back in the minors, where he
remained the rest of the season.

Carlos was invited back to spring training in 1957 but he showed
up late to camp, never explaining why. He hit well that spring but,
by this time Dressen, still not quite sure what to make of Carlos
and his erratic play in the field, shipped him out to the minors once
again. He hit over .400 and was leading the league in almost all
offensive categories, but the call back to the big club never came.

The Washington organization decided to give Carlos one last
chance to stick with the team and invited him to spring training in
1958. However, this time he showed up fifteen days late and his
manager and ownership had seen enough. They traded Carlos to
Sacrament of the Pacific Coast League, where he promptly led the
league in hitting. At the end of that '58 season, he returned to Cuba
to play in the Cuban Professional Baseball League and became a
star. He never played in the Majors again. His final career statistics
included a lifetime batting average of .271, 124 hits, 9 home runs,
60 RBI's, and 157 games played—not much to show for a career
that started with so much promise.

Carlos bounced around from there, playing in the Mexican
League and finally back to Cuba, where he played the rest of his
career. Much of what happened to Carlos after his playing days is
still shrouded in mystery. One report, which turned out to be untrue,
had him shot by a firing squad for rebelling against the revolutionary
government in Cuba. His name would also pop up from time to time
when Major League players would go to Cuba to play Winter Ball

and, while there, have brief visits with him. On June 15, 1983, Carlos passed away at age 55. The cause of death was never determined.

In the end, Carlos Paula is another "what might have been" story, a player whose full potential was never realized. Still, his debut with Washington on September 6, 1954 opened the door to possibilities for other players from Cuba who quickly followed him: such players as Pedro Ramos, Jose Valdivielso, Juan Delis, Julio Becquer, Evelio Hernandez, and Camilo Pasqual. Carlos' time in the Majors was short, but his pioneering influence lives to this day.

NOTE: *Carlos' teammate and dear friend Jose Valdivielso played in the Major Leagues for five seasons, four with Washington, and the last with the Minnesota Twins when the franchise was moved there. He played largely in a utility role, except for the 1960 season, when he won the starting job at shortstop. His Major League career ended after the 1961 season, but he eventually returned to Cuba to play in the Cuban Professional Baseball League until he hung up his spikes. He always credited his success in the Major Leagues to the support and friendship he received as a rookie from Carlos Paula.*

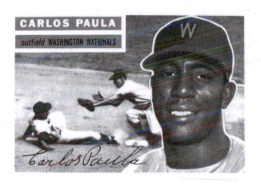

1956 Topps #4, Carlos Paula
Courtesy of The Topps Company, Inc.

12

Elston Howard

New York Yankees

Elston Howard with his 1955 New York Yankees teammates
(Elston top row, 2nd from right).

Elston "Ellie" Howard was born on February 23, 1929, in St. Louis, Missouri, where he spent a good deal of his early childhood playing "pick-up" baseball and football games every chance he had. He was a gifted student in the classroom, often achieving the highest grades of anyone in his class. He attended segregated Vashon High where he achieved All-State honors in basketball while also excelling in football and track and field. However, it was on the newly formed baseball team, created only after Jackie Robinson broke the color barrier in Major League Baseball, where his athletic prowess was most noted. As the best hitter on the team, he attracted the attention of a local semi-pro team manager, who convinced him to play for them whenever he could get away from his studies. He was the youngest player in the semi-pro league, but he held his own, hitting for high average and fielding almost flawlessly.

Although Elston was offered several full scholarships to play college football, he turned them all down after his semi-pro baseball coach sent him to a tryout with the Kansas City Monarchs of the Negro Leagues. He put on quite a show that day, and the Monarchs signed him to a contract that would pay him $500 per month. His professional career was underway. While there, he roomed with a skinny, but incredibly talented kid, by the name of Ernie Banks. The two challenged each other to improve their skills and constantly teased each other about who would be the first to make it to the Major Leagues.

In mid-summer of 1950, the New York Yankees purchased his contract from Kansas City and sent him to their minor league affiliate in the Central League, where he continued to play well, earning high praise from all his coaches. However, he was drafted into military service and served two years, from 1951 through 1952, in the Army, where he primarily played baseball in the Special Services branch. Once he was discharged, the Yankees assigned Elston to their AAA club in Kansas City, where his professional career had begun. Even at his young age of 21, Elston's on-field leadership skills were excellent, so the Yankees decided to switch him to the position of catcher. To help him make the transition, Hall of Fame catcher and Yankee great Bill Dickey was assigned to teach him how to maximize his skills behind the plate. New York still had Yogi Berra catching regularly for the big club, so they had Elston continue his work in the outfield.

The Yankees invited Elston to spring training in 1955, where he showed he was ready for Major League duty. When the season started, he made his debut in the second game, April 14, 1955, thus becoming the first person of color to play for the New York Yankees. He entered that game as a replacement for Irv Noren, who had been ejected for arguing with an umpire over a close call at the plate. Elston promptly singled and drove in a run, foreshadowing the outstanding career that was to follow.

….. ….. …..

April 1, 1961
West Point, New York

"It's just not right," Whitey Ford said to his dear friend and teammate Mickey Mantle. "And I don't like it."

"What's that?" Mickey asked, looking up from his scrambled eggs. The two, who had been out on the town late the night before, were eating a late breakfast in the small restaurant just off the lobby of the Ambassador Hotel where the team was staying so they could participate in the annual charity exhibition game with the West Point cadets. All proceeds from the gate and other items donated by the Yankees and auctioned off went to a special fund set up for veterans who were still dealing with wounds and injuries suffered during WWII and the Korean Conflict. The "game" was set for four innings, and the team had already been told to "take it easy" on the cadets, especially because the event with West Point went back to 1927, when Ruth and Gehrig took the field, and, thus far, the Cadets' record stood at 0-11. Many on the team would rather have been anywhere else, but Yanks manager Ralph Houk, who served in combat in WWII, had impressed upon everyone just how important this exhibition was and what an honor and privilege it was to participate.

"I'm talking about Coates," Whitey replied. "What he did again to Ellie in practice yesterday after we got here. Called him everything he could think of, but I think what got to Ellie the most was when he called him 'Whitey.' Then Coates started shaking off pitches—in a *practice* session, for Pete's sake. Practice! He was trying to show him up, make him look stupid. That's got to stop."

Ralph Houk was planning on Jim Coates to be a major part of the Yankees' pitching plans for 1961. The previous year, Jim had had a terrific season for the club, going 13-3 as a combined starter and reliever. His .813 winning percentage was the best in the American League, which bought him a lot of leash when he aggravated members of the team, and that seemed to be happening more and more.

Jim was born and raised in Farnham, Virginia, where segregation was a way of life. Even though he had been on the field with Black players before, he was now finding himself in a situation he'd never been in: the person catching his pitches, Elston Howard, was not white. Jim was still sorting through and digesting what that meant to him.

"Coates calls *everyone* something," Mickey shot back. "I don't mind it when people call me Country or Rube or Oakie or things like that. One time he called me White Trash. I called him out on it and let him know that was the last time he'd ever say that, but you know him. He said he was kidding and backed off. Every time he causes trouble, he says he's kidding. I don't know about him, but the S.O.B. can sure pitch when he's on. That's puttin' money in our pockets."

Whitey nibbled on his toast and said, "You remember a couple years back what Hank Bauer did when a fan behind our dugout started screaming all that stuff at Ellie? Hank went crazy. Climbed on top of the dugout and threatened to pinch that guy's head off if he didn't shut up. That poor jerk took off like a scared rabbit."

"I remember that!" Mickey shouted loud enough the few others in the restaurant turned and stared at him. "But I'd run, too, if Bauer was after me. He's one tough son of a gun."

A wide smile spread across Whitey's lips as he put down his coffee cup, slapped the table, and said, excitedly, "I've got it! This is going to be great!"

"Oh, this ought to be good," Mickey said as he leaned forward. "But remember—we're already in the doghouse with Houk for staying out after curfew. He said he wasn't going to put up with us anymore, and I believe him."

"Don't worry—if anybody gets in trouble, it won't be us. We can just shrug our shoulders and say we're innocent."

"Houk will *never* believe we're innocent of anything," Mickey laughed just as Elston Howard entered the room and walked over to their table.

"Speak of the devil," Mickey said, pulling out a chair. "Go ahead—sit down. Whitey's just got another one of his brainstorms, and this has you in it. Take a look at that smile of his, and you just might want to go sit somewhere else."

Elston looked at Whitey, who was also laughing, and asked, "OK, Ford—what is it now? How much is it going to cost me this time?"

"Won't cost you *anything*," Whitey replied. "But, I think you are going to *gain* something that'll make your life a lot, lot better."

Whitey ignored the skeptical look Elston gave him as he went on. "I know Coates has always given you a really rough time, and yesterday I thought you were going to explode when he was calling off pitches during warm-up. Well, how would you like to get even with him? Better than that, how would you like to show him up for a change and shut him up for good?"

"Don't think that could happen. Don't think he'll ever change. Nobody will ever be able to knock anything into that thick skull of his."

"But, what if you could?" Whitey said, leaning forward, lowering his voice. "I know a way."

"We'll get caught if we use a hit-man," Mickey interrupted, laughing again.

"No, I'm serious," Whitey said. "I've got the solution. We won't have to kill him, but he might wish he was dead if what I *think* will happen really does."

"Let's have it," Elston said. "I've tried ignoring him, but I'm about up to here." He raised his right hand just under his nose.

"I want to ask you something," Whitey said, turning serious. "Didn't you tell me once that you were one heck of a boxer when you were growing up? That you took lessons and were in some type of boxing league?"

"Yes, but what does that have to do with—"

"It has everything to do with what we're—*you're* going to do. Now both of you, listen up. Mick, you're going to have a big part here, so pay attention."

For the next several minutes, Whitey laid out the plan. The team was scheduled to play the exhibition against the cadets at 1:30. Whitey guessed the game and all the ceremonies would take about two hours. After signing autographs and posing for pictures with the fans and dignitaries, everyone would still have plenty of time to get cleaned up, dressed, and ready for the "Honor Banquet" that always followed these games. The banquet was part of the fundraising effort, and donors would be there from all across the region to hear Ralph Houk, Whitey, Mickey, and several of the other members of the team talk about the team's chances for the upcoming season, all the while encouraging everyone to open their wallets and purses to help support the funds for the veterans. It was the time *before* the banquet Whitey focused upon.

"Look," Whitey said, getting to the heart of his plan, "Coates thinks he's a real tough cookie. Talks big, like he could take out the whole room with an arm behind his back. The best way to deal with a guy like that is to give him a dose of his own medicine—and that's what we're going to do."

"First of all, Mickey, since Coates thinks he's so tough, and it doesn't take a genius to figure out he'd like to smash Ellie's face in, you're going to convince him you know a way he can do exactly that."

"What?" Elson cut in. He didn't like where the discussion was moving. "Wait a minute—"

"Let me finish," Whitey insisted. "Listen to the rest of this." He turned back to Mickey. "Yesterday after practice I went over to that big gymnasium they have here and shot a few baskets on the court to cool down and relax. Well, while I was there, I noticed off in the corner was this boxing ring—a professional one."

Mickey's eyes lit up. "And . . . and—I'm liking this. Go on!"

Elston started to speak, but Whitey didn't give him a chance. "Mick, you tell Coates that after the game the whole team is going to go play some basketball at the gym. He'll go for that. He always brags about how good he was in school." Here Whitey paused, leaned closer, and lowered his voice further. "Tell him about the boxing ring. Tell him we're going to have a couple guys get in and play around. Now, here's the best part. Tell him you know how much he'd like to pound Ellie, and you're going to help him do it."

"But he knows Ellie's my pal," Mickey said, reaching over and patting him on the back.

"I know—and I know Jim knows it. So, you're going to have to convince him that Ellie did you wrong somehow. Tell him Ellie owes you money from our card games and won't pay it back. Tell him you think he stole something out of your locker last year, and it has been eating at you. I don't care what you tell him, but make him think you have a grudge to settle. Then, tell him you'll arrange it so that he can get in the ring with Ellie and beat the tar out of him."

"He'll never do it," Mickey and Elston said at the same time, then looking at each other and laughing.

"Oh, yes, he will," Whitey said. "And, here's why. Tell Jim that Ellie's scared to death of boxing and that he has a glass jaw. Say you saw him get beat up last year when we were out on the town—and the team covered it up. Tell him Ellie just got a shot from the trainer in his right arm this morning and it's really weak. He'll believe that because, Ellie, here's you do."

Turning toward Elston, he continued. "This is just an exhibition, so tell Ralph you're not feeling well—that maybe your breakfast was bad, which wouldn't be too much of a stretch based on what I just gagged down here. Say you're going to be OK, but ask him if you can sit this one out unless he really wants you in there. Say you don't want to embarrass everyone by getting sick on the field."

"I don't know if I can do that," Elston said, easing back in his chair. "I don't lie like that. I don't like it."

"OK, then figure out something else to get out of the game. Or, start the game, and then ask to be taken out. Tell him the truth about something that he'll agree is a reason for you to ride the bench. Just get out of the game early."

Turning back to Mickey, Whitey said, "You have to lay it on thick. Convince Jim he can step in that ring and pound the stuffin' out of Ellie—that Ellie won't be able to block his punches because his arm's hurt. A guy like him will go for that. I know it. And, I know *you*. You, Mister, could talk a man dying of thirst to give you his last sip of water. You egg people on in a way I've never seen before. You should be ashamed of yourself, but you never are."

"Who? Me? I can't believe you said that," Mickey said.

Elston interrupted, "I'm still not sure I see where this is going."

"You're kidding, right?" Whitey said, turning to his friend. "All we have to do is get him in the ring with you, and then you can play patta-cake on his face. What part of that aren't you getting?"

"But I might hurt him! I really *can* box."

"So . . ." Whitey and Mickey replied together.

They all laughed, until Whitey jumped in again. "You don't have to murder him, but a good taste of the canvas will do him good—and be even better for you. I'll bet money he'll leave you alone after that."

"I don't know . . ." Elston said, looking back and forth between them. "Do you really think we should do this? I don't like the guy, but we're going to need him his year. I don't want to hurt him. That'd be hurting us."

"Just hit him in the head," Mickey jumped in. "Can't hurt him if you hit him there. It's empty, right?"

"Well?" Whitey asked. "Let's do this. I'll talk to the rest of the team about playing basketball after the game. I'll tell them we'll make teams and play for beer and a few bucks—maybe have a contest. That'll get 'em there. After we get there, Mick will take over and say something like, 'Geez—look at that ring over there. Why, we ought to have a few bouts. Hey, I know—let's get Ellie and Jim in there. You know, a pitcher and catcher. Those positions always think they're smarter than the other guy.' We won't have to do anything else after that. The rest of the team will shame both of them to get in the ring. There's a whole rack of boxing gloves on the wall right there. Mickey, you get Jim into his gloves before he has a chance to back out. I'll be in Ellie's corner and get him laced up. This is going to be *great*! I can't wait!"

Elston shook his head. "You two are always getting me in trouble. I don't know why I ever get around you."

"Because we're your friends," Mickey said, smiling broadly.

"Then I'd sure as heck hate to see what would happen to me if you were my enemies."

Whitey and Mickey just laughed and said at exactly the same time, "Who, *us*?"

Elston rolled his eyes. "Heaven, help me."

….. ….. …..

Over four thousand jammed into Doubleday Field to see their cadets facing the reigning American League champion New York Yankees. It was a beautiful, late spring afternoon, the sun shining, the temperature just above seventy. The game started right on time, and the cadets, acting as home team, gave up four quick runs in the bottom of the first, two of them scoring on a towering home run by Mickey Mantle that left the stadium and bounced across the road running behind it. As Mickey crossed home plate, Ralph Houk signaled to his bench he didn't want a blowout. He at least hoped to make the game interesting for those who had paid handsome sums to sit in the stands.

The cadets scored a run in the second inning when Bob Cerv, playing right field, lost a fly ball in the sun, allowing a runner to score from second. That ended up their only run, and the Yankees went on to win the game 6-1. However, for the West Pointers, it was a moral victory of sorts because they played a good game, one they could be proud of and talk about in future years.

As soon as the game was over and autographs were signed and photos taken, all started leaving the field. Whitey and Mickey had done their jobs well, so most of the Yankees headed to the school gymnasium to engage in a little recreational basketball. Mickey had each person put up five dollars, and the one who could sink the farthest shot would take the pot. Each man shot the ball first from the free throw line. Over half the group missed the shot and were immediately eliminated. Whitey and Elston missed their shots on purpose, with Elston clutching his arm and grimacing as soon as he let go of the ball. Mickey nudged Jim in the side, then pointed to Elston, who was putting on quite a show of pain. Those who remained had to move three feet back and shoot again. About half of the group missed, reducing the final group to five players: Coates, Roger Maris, Clete Boyer, John Blanchard, and Mickey who, as it turned out, was also a natural with a basketball. From there, the group backed up five feet and shot again. Only Coates and Mickey made their shots, and it appeared there would be a showdown between the two. However, Whitey and Elston, who had set themselves up as judges after being ousted from the completion, both jumped in and shouted, "Foul!" after Coates let his ball fly. Both declared Jim had stepped a foot forward before making his shot, thus disqualifying himself, which made Mickey the winner.

Jim immediately rushed the two and lit into them, saying they were as blind as umpires and had no clue what they were talking about—and he had definitely *not* cheated. The rest of the team joined in, suggesting playfully that Jim had, indeed, committed a "foot foul." However, Mickey came to Jim's defense and offered a solution: each would take one more shot, and the winner would be awarded all the money. Jim was still upset about the call, but he agreed to the challenge. Shooting first, his shot bounced off the backboard and right into the net. He raised his hands and shouted "Yes!" as Mickey took his stance and prepared to shoot. Mickey knew if he sunk his shot, the contest would continue, taking time away from the main event he hoped would follow. So, he purposely hit the rim, and the ball bounced away, giving Jim the victory. Jim immediately started bragging about how he could have kept backing up all the way across the room and still made his shots.

"I've had enough of basketball," Whitey finally interrupted. Then, acting as if the idea had just come to him, his face lit up. "I've got it! Look at that ring—and all those gloves on the wall. Let's do some friendly boxing!"

The group came alive and headed straight across the room. That is, all but Yogi Berra, who said, "Nothin' ever came from boxin' except leather." No one had a clue what he meant, but that wasn't all that unusual when Yogi gave his thoughts on a subject. He headed for the door, but everyone else congregated around the gloves, many trying them on right away.

Mickey climbed into the ring and said, "OK—everybody listen up. I think it's only fair that Jim gets to climb in first because he won the shootout fair and square. He's our champ today, so come on up, Jim, soon as you get your gloves laced right. I'll help you." Several members of the team urged him forward, and Bill Skowron waved off Mickey and quickly tied Jim's gloves.

As soon as Jim climbed into the ring, Mickey continued. "Let's see. We need someone to mix it up with him. I know! Let's have a 'pitcher and catcher' match! Ellie—get some gloves and get in here. You two can fight over *signs* in here."

All laughed at Mickey's last remark because they had seen Jim shaking off Ellie's signs in practice two days before. Elston immediately protested, saying his arm was too sore to do any punching. However, before he could back away, the others egged him on, especially Clete Boyer who yelled "Chicken!" and started making loud clucking sounds as he moved forward and urged Ellie toward the ring.

After a minute of taking all the razzing, Elston finally said, "OK—I'll do it. But my arm hurts so much I don't think I can—"

Whitey, who was lacing up Elston's gloves, interrupted him and said, loudly, "Jim, go easy on him. He's playing with only one wing. Doesn't seem all that fair to me. Don't you hurt him."

A few others echoed Whitey's words as Elston, keeping his right arm close to his side, started under the bottom rope and slowly entered the ring. Mickey immediately stepped between the two and said, "I'll do the refereeing. There'll be no low blows. And no nose twisting!"

All laughed as the group stepped forward, right to the edge of the ring, where they'd have a clear view of the action. "You get him, Ellie!" Skowron shouted. Other shouts of encouragement followed—but none directed at Jim.

"Gentlemen," Mickey said, turning to both, "I want a clean round. You ready?" Elston, still rubbing his arm, nodded. Then Jim nodded and started stepping toward Elston. Mickey jumped between them one last time and said, "OK—both of you get set. Gloves up. Here we go!"

As soon as Mickey stepped to the side, Jim charged ahead, jabbing repeatedly toward Elston with his left hand. Elston easily blocked all the shots, then hurriedly backed up, rubbing his arm. "I don't know about this," he said loudly enough all could hear. "Don't know if this is a good idea."

The group urged him on. Bobby Richardson suggested he "turn southpaw" so he could use his bad arm to block shots and take a few swings with his left. All the while, Jim moved in again; this time his jabs were not so playful. As the force of his punches increased, Elston had to keep moving to his left to deflect them and soften their impact.

"What's the matter, Boy?" Jim shouted in Elston's face as he finally landed a decent punch to his cheek. "Don't you know how to box? Thought surely you, of all people, would know how. Let me show you how it's done."

Whitey, standing on the other side of the ring, waved to catch Elston's attention, then mouthed the word, "Now—!"

Elston dropped his gloves slightly to lure Jim in close, and when Jim went for a right roundhouse, Elston quickly stepped to his left and drove his right glove as hard as he could, catching Jim squarely on the chin. The force of his punch added to Jim's forward motion produced a loud thud that could be heard by all. As soon as he was hit, Jim's head snapped back, and his knees started buckling. He tried regaining his balance, but before he could move, Elston followed up with a powerful, driving left hook, catching Jim flush on the side of his head. As the onlookers let out a collective gasp, Jim went down, hard, face-first onto the canvas. When he didn't move, Roger Maris screamed, "Jeez—he's killed him!"

Whitey and Mickey, who had both been laughing just seconds before, turned pale and rushed toward Jim, worried that he really had been hurt badly. When Mickey rolled Jim over, he was relieved to see him blinking rapidly, as if trying to shake away dizziness. "Quick—somebody get some water!" Whitey shouted.

While Bob Cerv ran to the drinking fountain and filled a paper cup, Elston looked down at Jim to make sure he was breathing. Then, as Mickey started raising Jim up to a sitting position, Elston used his teeth to undo the laces of his gloves. Once he had both off, he casually dropped them at Jim's feet, brushed his hands together, and without saying a word, stepped from the ring and headed toward the exit.

He didn't look back.

The others, stunned by what they had just seen, started climbing into the ring to make sure their teammate really was going to be fine. Whitey urged Jim to drink the water Bob had brought from the drinking fountain. After he had taken a couple of gulps, he handed the cup to Whitey and finally spoke. "What the heck was that!" he shouted. A roar of laughter from all followed.

"*That*," Mickey jumped in, "is what happens when you shake off your catcher's signs." Laughter erupted again.

Whitey said, "You know, Ellie's a good guy. A great teammate. Some of us know that better than others. He was a professional

boxer for a time when he was younger. He *could* have really mu
dered you. You're lucky he just knocked you down. Remember tha
the next time you're around him. Give him a chance, Jim, an honest
chance."

Jim, the cobwebs finally clearing, looked up at Mickey, who
nodded his agreement with Whitey. At that moment, Jim knew he'd
been had, that all this had been orchestrated for his benefit, and his
alone. As his teammates helped him to his feet and playfully brushed
him off, Jim didn't say a word. It was the first time any of them had
seen him speechless.

As he was helped from the ring, the exit door opened, and
Elston stuck his head in. "Just checking," he said. Then, louder, he
added, "Jim—you OK?"

Still woozy, Jim said, "I'll survive"

When everyone saw he wasn't going to light into Elston, as
he'd done every chance he got, they started patting Jim on the back.

Elston just smiled and closed the door.

….. ….. …..

November 7, 1963
Teaneck, New Jersey

"Arlene—answer the phone!" Elston shouted to his wife as he carried another box from their basement up the steps and toward their
kitchen. Four straight days of steady rain had turned the basement
of their new home into what looked like a small lake. They had
been in the home only a week so many of their belongings were still
in cardboard boxes, many of which were now floating around the
basement.

"I'm all wet!" Elston said when he got to the top step. "I
shouldn't run into the living room like this. I'll ruin the rugs."

"OK, OK—I'll get it!" Arlene called back. "Probably my sister again. Ellie, you need to settle down. I've never seen you so jumpy. Take it easy. If it happens, it happens. If it's supposed to be, it will."

Right after she answered the phone, he heard her say, "Oh, hi, Roger. Thanks for calling. No, we haven't heard a thing yet. We were told they were going to announce it this morning. At least that's what Dick Young at the *New York Daily News* told us yesterday. And ever since, Ellie's been driving me crazy. We don't know for sure he's going to win it, but Young's got him all convinced and practically jumping up and down." After a brief pause, she continued. "Roger, I just have one question for you. You won this in 1960 and 1961, right? So, my question is this: how in the world did Pat stand to be around you while you were waiting for the calls? The woman must be a saint."

Elston could hear Roger laughing all the way from where he was still standing in the kitchen. Finally, Arlene said, "Thanks again for calling. Yes, I'll tell him. Say hi to Pat for me. Goodbye."

She walked into the kitchen, put her hands on her hips, and said, "Well, you going to stand there and drip all over my floor?"

"What'd he say?" Elston asked, setting down the box and retreating to the top step, which was already full of water from all the trips he'd made up and down that morning.

"Just wishing you luck is all. That was sweet of him."

The phone rang again, startling Elston so much he nearly fell backward. He grabbed hold of the rail to steady himself before urging Arlene back toward the phone.

This time, after she answered it, all she said was "Hello" and then fell silent. After a few moments, she finally said, "Hang on. I'll go get him."

As she reentered the kitchen, she smiled and said, "I think you better take this one yourself." When Elston looked down at his wet shoes, she said, "Oh, go on! Don't worry about it."

His shoes squished and left tracks as he walked tow. phone, but he was so nervous he barely noticed. "Hello," he s. he put the receiver to his ear. "This is Elston."

"Dick Young here," the voice on the other end responded. just wanted to be one of the first to congratulate you, Ellie. I know I can be a royal pain in the arse at times, but I want to say in all sincerity I'm very happy for you, and I believe you were the most deserving candidate—by miles and miles. So, how does it feel? What was your reaction when you got the call?"

Stunned, Elston replied, "Mr. Young, I haven't heard anything from anybody yet." His voice quivered. "You sure about this?"

The silence that followed was awkward for both men. Dick finally spoke. "Yes, I'm sure. I just heard it. Nobody's called you yet?"

"Just you."

"Well, I'm sorry I wrecked the surprise. Truly. I am. I just thought . . . .. "Geez—I feel bad now. I'm really sorry."

"That's OK," Elston said. "Really. As long as you're not trying to pull a joke on me."

"I swear to goodness I'm not. It's for real. We better get off the phone so the line is free—so they can call you. But, quick, if you don't mind, I'd like a quote for my column tomorrow. What do you think about the award? What first comes to your mind?"

Elston didn't hesitate. "You know, Mr. Young, I've been fighting one thing or another all my life just so I could play ball. It's what I love—more than anything. Well, I better say except for my wife, right?" He laughed softly. "Baseball has been everything for me, and I know that. I don't take it for granted. Ever. So, to me, the Most Valuable Player award means everything. I'm just one player on a really, really good team. I feel like all my teammates are MVP's because we win, and lose, together —and everybody plays a part. Singling me out this way, well . . .."

، Elston's voice started cracking, Dick interrupted and asked,
put it in plain English. Ellie, how are you feeling now?"

"Like this is the happiest day of my life. But, right now I'd
ather be the most valuable plumber. Mr. Young, I've got water
everywhere. You should see this place. What a mess! That's what
I'm thinking."

Dick laughed long and hard, finally gathering enough compo-
sure to say, "OK—I've got my quotes. Now hang up the phone and
act surprised when you get called. Again, congratulations. Richly
deserved—and that's what I'll write tomorrow.

"Thank you, Mr. Young. I really appreciate it."

As soon as he hung up the phone, Arlene hugged him tightly
from behind. "Well, what'd he say? You got it, right?"

Elston, still in her grip, turned toward her, grinned, and said,
"You be careful. You're squeezing the 1963 MVP!"

He wrapped his arms around her, pulled her closer, and said,
"Let's just enjoy this a minute. Mr. Young wasn't supposed to tell
me until the official call came, but I'm glad I know now. I feel so
lucky, so blessed. I'll never forget this. Ever."

They held each other close for several minutes, neither speaking. Finally, the ringing of the phone startled them both, and they
quickly backed away from each other. "This has got to be it," he
said, staring at the phone. "You know, I could get used to people
calling to tell me how good I am."

Arlene just rolled her eyes and started for the kitchen. Elston
laughed and finally picked up the phone.

....

Elston Howard's professional career spanned twenty years, six in the
Negro Leagues and fourteen in Major League Baseball. Wherever
he played, he demonstrated he was one of the best, and most

respected, players in the game. He was chosen for the All-Star team twelve times, was awarded two Gold Gloves for his work behind the plate, helped lead the New York Yankees to nine World Series—and Boston to another. At the time of his retirement, he had one of the best catching defensive fielding averages in Major League history (.993). On top of all this, he was named the American League Most Valuable Player in 1963. His final career statistics included a .274 batting average, 167 home runs, 762 runs batted in, and 1,471 hits in 1,605 games played.

His time in baseball was also dotted with "firsts and "innovations." Elston was the first person of color to take the field for the Yankees. In his very first season, 1955, the Yankees decided on a "first" for the organization when they decided they would no longer stay in hotels where Ellie wasn't also welcome to stay, which was a step noted by teams all across the game. He was credited with being the first catcher to hold up his index and little finger, and wiggle them, to indicate more clearly to outfielders there were two outs in an inning, a practice that other catchers around the league copied immediately. Elston was also the first Black player to be awarded MVP honors in the American League (1963). When he retired from active play, he became the first African American coach for the Yankees; he then served as their first base coach from 1969-1978.

Elston is credited with making two significant "equipment" innovations in the game. He was the first to develop a "hinged" baseball glove, one that allowed him to catch the ball one-handed. This revolutionized the defensive side of catching duties across baseball. He also designed and created what was immediately called the "baseball donut," a weighted ring that slipped over the baseball bat so that batters waiting to hit could warm up more quickly and efficiently. Until his "donut," players typically would swing multiple bats to stretch their arms and ready themselves for the plate. He received a patent for his revolutionary device, and it soon became a staple in the world of baseball at all levels.

In 1968, the Yankees were contacted by the Boston Red Sox, who were in the thick of the American League pennant race and badly needed another catcher. Elston was traded to them in early August, and even though he didn't hit for high average with Boston, his leadership, both on and off the field, helped them to the World Series against the St. Louis Cardinals. He became an unofficial coach for the pitchers, and his experience in tight pennant races helped settle the team down the stretch. His contributions were so highly regarded he was invited back with the team the following year. However, Elston suffered a series of injuries both in spring training and at the start of the season, so his contributions that season were limited. At the end of the year, he decided to call it a career, but he didn't have much of a chance to relax. The Yankees immediately called him and offered him their first base coaching job, which he accepted. He remained in that role until 1978, when a heart ailment kept him away from the game all the way through the 1979 season. When it was finally decided his medical situation would not allow him back on the field, he was shifted to serving as a Special Administrative Assistant for the organization. He served in that role only a short time. A few months later, Elston passed away on December 14, 1980, at age 51. The Yankees retired his uniform number four years later—in honor of a great player and true pioneer, not just for their own organization, but also for the game itself.

NOTE: *After their boxing match and for the remaining time they formed a pitching-catching battery for the Yankees, Jim Coates never again shook off Elston's signs. As unlikely as it had seemed early on, both men eventually became good friends. When Elston won the American League Most Valuable Player award in 1963, one of the first congratulatory calls made to him was from Jim, who wanted Elston to know how proud he was of him.*

Elston Howard

1956 Topps #208, Elston Howard
Courtesy of The Topps Company, Inc.

John Kennedy

Philadelphia Phillies

John Kennedy with his 1957 Philadelphia Phillies teammates
(John bottom row, 3rd from right).

John Kennedy was born October 26, 1926 in Jacksonville, Florida, and spent most of his early life there. As a youngster, John loved basketball, and he practiced and played the game every chance he got. He was interested in football by the time he entered high school. He never played baseball—never had the *opportunity* to play the game—because persons of color were not allowed on the high school team.

Shortly after John graduated, a scout saw him playing softball and noticed his skills on the diamond. At the scout's urging, John

...ed working out with local semi-pro baseball teams, and he soon ...veloped a reputation as a slick fielding, line-drive hitter with great ...otential. Another scout, this one from the Canadian League, offered him a contract, and John's professional career initially started in Winnipeg. From there, he was assigned to the New York Giants minor league system but was dropped after one season. Not wanting to give up on the game he had come to love, he had stints in the Negro Leagues with the Birmingham Black Barons and the Kansas City Monarchs. He hit close to .400 his last year with the Monarchs, which drew the attention of the Philadelphia organization.

At the time, the Phillies were the last team in the National League without a person of color on their Major League roster, and groups around the city were pressuring the organization to address this concern. John's performance in his initial tryout with the team went poorly, but the team's representatives saw enough potential they decided to give him a chance to show his true skills. He seized on this opportunity and was soon demonstrating their decision had been a good one.

....

March 1, 1957
Clearwater, Florida

"*One day,*" John Kennedy said, drawing out the words so slowly his roommate, Eddie Logan, turned and looked at him, quizzically. John's voice grew louder. "Just *one* day on a Major League baseball diamond. That's all I want."

"What in the world are you talking about?" Eddie asked.

John smiled. "It's all I've thought about for the last ten years, ever since Jackie did it. He showed he could play up here—that we could *all* play here—and I want to do it so bad I can taste it. I've played so long, in so many places, I want this for *me*. I *need* this."

"I don't know if you can pull it off," Eddie laughed. "Y
you're good. No doubt about that. But, you're no spring chicke
you know. If they find out how old you really are, you're cooked
They think you're twenty-two or three. What fibs you can tell!"

"My age don't matter," John said, glaring at him. "I've got a
few swings left, and I can still cover a lot of ground around short.
And I want to clear something up. *I* never said one word about my
age. *I* didn't tell any fibs. It was the *Monarchs* who put my age on a
piece of paper. They probably thought they could get more money
for my contract if people thought I was younger. Nobody here ever
asked me my age, and I don't think it's my business to bring it up."

"But what if they do bring it up? What are you going to tell
them?"

"I'll worry about that when and if the time comes. Not worried
about that now. What we need to be thinkin' about is they wouldn't
have invited us to this 'instructional camp' if they didn't think we
had something. They invited only a few of us. *This* is our big chance.
I hope they'll keep us and send us to one of their top minor league
teams. From there, who knows what can happen. Just might get to
the Majors one of these days."

"Well, they say every dog has his day. I guess this camp might
be ours. At least we'll give it our best. But if they ever find out about
you—"

"I'm not old! I've been conservin' my strength for this stretch
is all. I can still show them a thing or two. You, too. And they must
believe it because, well, here we are. And you're not just ripe off the
vine yourself. You aren't twenty-three. Who you kiddin'? If they
find out about me, you'd be on the fire, too. We best not talk about
this. Lots of ears around here. Besides, a man's only as old as he
feels, right? I feel fine right now. Ready to go."

John and Eddie sat quietly in their room at the Blue Cat Hotel, ...ch waiting for Rich Jackson, one of the minor league coaches for ...he Philadelphia Phillies, to come get them and three white players who were staying across town and take them all by bus to the team's spring training complex in Clearwater, Florida. There, they would receive a week of intense hitting and fielding instruction. This was the second year of what the Phillies's coaches called "Rookie School," a time when top prospects were gathered a week before members of the big club reported for Spring Training. John and Eddie both had excellent seasons with their teams the previous year and had recently been signed to minor league contracts by the Phillies. The organization hoped the invitation to Rookie School would show just what type of players they had signed.

While they waited for Coach Jackson, Eddie tossed a *Life* magazine to John, but neither was in a mood to read. "Thanks, but no thanks," John said, placing the magazine on the bed. "I want to ask you something. I've been hearing about some ministers in Philadelphia who might be the reason we're here."

"I heard that, too," Eddie said, reaching again for the magazine. "Supposedly, a bunch of ministers got together and said they'd get Negroes to boycott the games if Philly didn't start signing some of us. That would hit 'em where it hurts—right in the wallet. This team's been pretty bad these last years, and not many people been going to games. If they lose any more, they'll be in trouble. At least that's what I heard."

Thumbing through the magazine, Eddie went on. "Doubt it will be you or me, but they're going to have to put somebody in the Majors soon. They're the only team left in the National League that hasn't brought up any Negroes. I guess those ministers are really pushin' for this. Bless 'em all."

"Last team? Then maybe it *will* be one of us. You never know.

I'd hate to get in the dugout that way, but I'll take anything I can g
I just want to play."

Eddie just shook his head as someone knocked loudly on their door. "I'll get it," John said. When he opened the door, a short, stocky man with horned-rimmed glasses and wearing a well-worn Phillies uniform stuck out his hand and said, "I'm Jackson. Supposed to take you to the park. Can I come in?"

John shook his hand, motioned him inside, and offered him a chair.

"No, thanks," Jackson said, folding his arms across his chest. "Just have a few things to say before we get going. Just want to make sure you understand what's going to happen."

He continued, "Me and the other coaches will be working with you this week on fundamentals. Fielding, throwin', hitting, bunting—*everything*. You may think you know how to play ball, but we're going to show you *our* way—the way this organization does it. We expect all our players to learn it. If they don't, they're out. That plain enough?"

John and Eddie nodded as he went on. "We do drills in the morning and games in the afternoon. Other clubs in the area do the same thing, so you'll play against their top boys. That way, you'll get a chance to show us what you've got *and* what you're learnin' from us. Don't worry—we'll keep you hoppin'. Got all that?"

"I've been wondering," John asked. "Does this mean you'll keep us here for the spring training, too? Will we get to work with the regulars when they get here?"

"Not so fast," Jackson cut in, unfolding his arms and putting his hands on his hips. "Let's see what everybody's got before we even think about that. Some might, and some might not. Too early to tell."

"Thanks," John said. "Just wanted to know if there was a chance is all. Nice to know."

"You just worry about today, and tomorrow, and the day after. That's all you need to think about." Turning to Eddie, Jackson asked, "Any questions from you?"

"No, Sir. I'm just here to play ball."

"Good. Grab your gear and follow me. The bus is outside. You're the first stop. We'll pick up the others on the way to the park. Hurry up now."

Once outside, Jackson opened the bus door, climbed in, and slid into the driver's seat. Looking out at John and Eddie, who were still standing at the edge of the curb, he asked, "Well, what are you waiting for?"

John turned to Eddie and said, "Just for a chance. That's all. Just a chance."

"Let's go," Eddie said, urging John ahead of him and up the bus's steps. "Like you said, this could be *our* chance."

John smiled. "I'm prayin' it's so."

....

Coach Jackson had been right: they *were* kept "hoppin'"—and the week passed quickly because the long days seemed to blend one into the other. Every day Jackson picked up John and Eddie at 6:00 a.m. and they weren't back to their room until almost 7:00 p.m. Jackson had given them an accurate description of what their daily schedule would be, but he left out a few important pieces. In addition to learning the "Philly way of baseball fundamentals," they spent hours watching instructional films about hitting and fielding that had been put together by the organization. Other coaches were also brought in to teach everything from sliding into bases to how best to manage "run-down" plays in the infield. One afternoon they were even given a talk about how to take care of their equipment over the course of a season, which included the importance of keeping gloves well-oiled and their strings tightened.

Twenty-five of the organization's top prospects were invite to the camp, representing all levels of experience from just ou. of high school ball to those with college baseball backgrounds to those signed off semi-pro teams. The first day the coaches grouped everyone so that outfielders, infielders, and pitchers and catchers were kept together for special sessions. All met together in the early morning to hear the main talks, but as soon as those were finished, the groups went off for their special instruction. John stayed with the infielders and Eddie joined the outfielders, so they didn't have much practice time together.

In the afternoons, either prospects for other teams were bussed in for games, or they made the trip to other camps for "away" games. The contests always started out normally enough, but in the middle innings onward, player substitutions happened whenever the coaches wanted to see one of the individuals in a particular situation. One afternoon, in the sixth inning, John was asked to switch spots in the batting order with another player so the coaches could see how he would fare against a tough sidearm pitcher. On the second pitch, he drilled a single to left. However, once at first base, a pinch runner was sent in, and he hit again three batters later when his assigned spot in the order came up, which gave him two at-bats in the same inning. In another game, he was put in the game as a pinch runner— *three times*—and told to steal on each occasion. He was thrown out only once while showing off his good speed on the base paths.

John was seeing the ball well in the bright Florida sunshine, and his batting average showed it. He had batted seventeen times in the first five games, getting nine hits: two home runs, two doubles, a triple, and four sharply hit singles. His bat was singing, but his work around shortstop also had the coaches watching him closely every time he took the field. He made no errors, and his range was excellent. The only negative brought up by the coaches was his throwing

:emed only average, so they started working with him on getting rid of the ball quicker to compensate.

All was going well, except for one area that John and Eddie discussed at length every night when they were returned to their room at the Blue Cat. While all the players were together for morning sessions and met in their individual groups for specialized coaching, at all other times John and Eddie found themselves alone. The other players played cards and visited together during the lunch breaks and before and after games, but John and Eddie were never invited to join them. Compounding the situation, their hotel was five minutes away from everyone else, so even that opportunity to get together was taken away. The situation reminded both men of the times they barnstormed with white players while still in the Negro Leagues. They played on the field together, but as soon as the games were over, they went their separate ways. That was still happening to them now.

It was late afternoon Friday when, after lining a single to right off one of the St. Louis Cardinals top pitching prospects, John looked back toward the dugout to see the reaction of one of the coaches when he saw him—an old nemesis from his days in the Negro Leagues. James Spangler had bounced around as a sports reporter from paper to paper in the early '50s, developing a reputation as someone more interested in controversy and gossip than recording the action in games. John's first year with the Kansas City Monarchs started off rough because of a shoulder injury, which kept him in a prolonged slump. Spangler was covering games for a small Kansas City daily at the time and, for reasons no one ever really understood, took a disliking for John. Every time John made an error or struck out a couple of times, James blasted him in the paper.

The last straw finally came when he hinted in two columns that John's batting woes could be the result of long nights on the

town in the company of alcohol and women—and lots of be
John shrugged off the first piece, but the second came after a gam
in which he struck out three times and made a throwing error. He
became furious, mostly at himself for his continued poor play, but
he also waited outside the stadium the next night to confront James
and let him know, in no uncertain terms, that if more writing along
that line showed up, he'd be waiting for him every night thereafter—with his fists at the ready. James backed off, and the two had
not spoken since. However, John received word later that season
that James had been overheard to say he'd find a way, no matter how
long it took, to "fix" him.

The game against the Cardinal prospects was still tied 4-4
after nine innings, and both skippers decided their athletes had had
enough. All were instructed to shower, get a good supper and some
rest, and then be ready to go even earlier the next morning when
special coaches were going to be brought in to teach them better
base running skills.

As soon as John had showered and started walking back to his
locker to get dressed, he saw James was waiting for him, sitting in a
chair just to the right of the locker.

James stood, extended his hand and said, a little too loudly,
"Well, Johnny, so good to see you. Been a long time. How in the
world have you been?"

John pulled up short of his locker and did not reach out to shake
his hand. "What do you want? I thought we agreed—"

"Now, Johnny," James cut in, shaking his head, his voice full
of mock surprise. "That's all behind us now. Long time ago. A *long*
time."

John finished toweling off and started getting dressed. "What
are you doing here? What do you want?"

James sat down and crossed his legs. "Why, haven't you heard?
I'm working for a new sports magazine. I'm going to be putting

_ether stories of the Black players who'll be here for spring train-
_ng with all the teams this year. So, let me ask you—do you think
they'll keep you for the spring games? Seems like you're a top
prospect—"

John interrupted sharply. "Nobody's talked about it, and I hav-
en't asked. Don't know, and that's all I'm going to say. Every time I
say anything, you twist it, or have you forgotten that? I sure haven't."

"Johnny, those were in the old days. We've all changed, right?
I need a story from you—just in case you stick around. Won't take
long. Just have a few questions. Now, let's start with this one."

John cut him off, glared at him, and said, "I don't think we have
much to talk about. I think you should go. I'm not in the mood to
talk. I'm tired, and I want to get out of here."

James leaned back in his chair, took off his hat, wiped his fore-
head, and said, "Well, if you don't want to talk to me, I guess there's
nothing to do about it." He started to stand. "Guess I'll just have
to go with the story of how I covered you when you were with the
Kansas City Monarchs. Let's see—back in 1955—when you were
leading the league in batting average most of the year? Seems I
recall you were about, what, twenty-seven or twenty-eight then?
Now I'm confused."

He reached into a thin satchel he had strapped around his neck
and withdrew a piece of paper. "It says here in the Philadelphia press
sheet that you're now twenty-two. Hmm. How does this work? I'm
not good at math, but it seems like the numbers don't match up here."
He paused one last time, staring this time right at John. "Wonder if
the team knows about this? Wonder if it would make a difference to
them when they decide who to keep here?"

John turned, made fists with both hands, and moved toward him
as James backed against the wall. "But I'd never write about that,"
he stammered. "No reason to. Not when I could write instead about

how you started out in the game and how much you love it. Tha[t's] the story everybody back home wants to hear. That's what I'll writ[e] about—if you'll just answer a couple of my questions. Shall we?"

"You're really something," John replied, stopping inches from James' face. "Don't you have any conscience at all? Don't you care at all about other people? What is it with you?"

"Conscience doesn't sell magazines. Just looking for a good story is all. Got to keep the readers happy and entertained, you know." He flipped open a small notebook, readied his pencil, and said, "Now, if you're ready, tell me about how you feel here in this special camp. What does it mean to you? I bet readers will love this story."

John backed up, continued dressing, and said without looking back at James, "Let's make this fast. I want to get out of here. It's starting to *stink* here."

"Well, it's a locker room. Always some smell here. Comes with the territory. You should know that."

John glared at him again. "What I know is *some things* make it worse."

For the next five minutes, John sat for the interview, cracking his knuckles and staring blankly ahead the whole time, not deviating from the usual platitudes about just being happy to be there and how willing he was to help the organization any way he could. When James said he had enough for his story, John turned without looking back, and walked out of the clubhouse.

....

On Saturday afternoon of that week, the players were brought in one at a time for a meeting with the coaches. The sessions were mostly devoted to evaluation of their skills and play from the previous week. They were also told which of their affiliate teams they'd be assigned at the start of the season. The assignments ranged from low A-ball up to high Triple-A, just one rung below the Majors. Eddie Logan was thrilled he'd shown enough promise to be sent to High Point-Thomasville in the Carolina League, a Class B team always stocked with players the organization had high hopes for. John was happy for his friend and hoped he might get a chance to play there as well because he knew that would be one step closer to his dream of one day playing in the Big Leagues. As he sat in the clubhouse waiting his turn, he grew more and more anxious. Finally, after all the other players were gone, Coach Jackson opened the office door and called over, "Kennedy—get in here!"

All the coaches were seated at a round table when he entered the room. Each nodded to him as he was instructed to take a chair off to the side. Coach Jackson took charge of the session immediately. "John, we won't beat around the bush. We like your play."

"Thank you, Coach. I'm trying—"

Jackson interrupted him. "Hold on, young man. Hear me out." Several of the other coaches laughed softly as he continued. "I'm looking at your chart here. Want to know what it says?"

When John nodded, he continued, "Good bat. Line drive, gap power. Hits to all fields. Doesn't waste at-bats. As to the fielding, solid glove. Makes the routine play. Keeps head in the game. Range only average now but should improve with instruction. Throwing arm above average but will likely also improve over time. Good speed on the base paths and good instinct for taking the extra base. Could steal more bases if learns to read pitchers better. Good attitude. Listens well. Willing to take advice."

He looked up from the sheet and said, "You get the idea. We're high on you—and your potential. We think you can help us and maybe soon. That's why we've decided to have you stick around for spring training. We want you to work out with the big club. I think you're ready for that."

"I . . . I don't know what to say," John said when Jackson pause
waiting for his reaction. "I thought I'd be sent to the minors."

Jackson finally broke into a smile as John continued, "I didn't
even think about this happening. I thought . . .." His heart was racing. "I don't know what to say except thank you for this. I'll do my
best. I promise you that. I'll work hard every day. I'll—"

"I know you will. So, take a deep breath. Sit back. I've just a
little more to say now. I'm sure you've seen some of our regulars,
the early birds, over on the other fields the last two days. You'll start
working out with them tomorrow. The Major League coaches will
get here tonight. I'll introduce you to them tomorrow, and they'll
get you organized and ready to go." He opened a folder. "We're also
moving you to a hotel closer to here. You'll be able to walk to the
park. Get here on time every day. Don't you ever be late. You'll be
on your own for that. The rest will be explained to you tomorrow.
You ready for all this?"

"Yes, Sir, I am," John replied. "Thank you so much. I still can't
believe it. Somebody better pinch me."

They laughed as Jackson reached out and pinched John lightly
on the elbow. "It's no dream, Kennedy."

"It is for me," John replied. "A dream coming true."

….. ….. …..

March 30, 1957
Jack Russell Stadium, Clearwater, Florida

Mayo Smith, Philadelphia's manager, looked grim as he instructed
his coaches—Wally Moses, Andy Seminick, and Whit Wyatt—to
take seats in his office.

"What's up, Mayo?" Moses asked as he settled in. "You look
like you've seen a ghost."

"Don't know, but it's never good when Hamey calls a meeting on the fly like this. Something's up."

At that moment, Philadelphia's General Manager, Roy Hamey, walked through the door, closing it slowly and quietly behind him, as if he didn't want others to know the meeting was taking place. They started to stand, but he motioned for everyone to stay seated. Before anyone could speak, he said, "Gentlemen, I'd like your advice. What's your impression of Kennedy's skills?"

When no one spoke up, he said, "I know the reports from the instructional camp were good, but what's he done the last couple weeks against Big League pitching?"

Before anyone could respond, he looked directly at Wally Moses, the Phillies' hitting coach, and asked, "Wally, your judgment, your evaluation? Don't mince any words. Give it to me straight."

Wally looked first at Mayo Smith, who nodded and urged him to speak up. "Well, Sir, he tore the cover off the ball through Rookie School, and he's hit pretty good through most of the regular spring games. He's slipped off some in the last week, but not terrible."

"Judge his swing for me. Strengths? Weaknesses?" Hamey asked.

"Still too loopy, but we're working on that. Eats up fastballs over and on the outside part of the plate. Pitches more inside are a problem because of that big swing. We'll work on it. He's never going to hit a lot of homers. He's a line drive hitter with decent gap power. But he's young and listens to advice. We might be able to squeeze more pop out of him eventually."

Hamey didn't comment about Wally's report. Instead, he turned immediately to Andy Seminick, the team's fielding coach, and asked, "Coach Seminick, you've worked with the infielders more than anyone else, and I know you're good at what you do. So, I want to ask you about Kennedy's glove. Tell me about it—in plain English."

Andy looked at his manager, who once again nodded. "M[r.] Hamey, I wasn't here when the Rookie School started up, so I haven't worked with him that long."

"That's OK," Hamey interrupted. "Just tell me what you've seen so far. Your impressions."

"Well, at shortstop, he's average at best on a good day. Can't say yet about other positions. Haven't seen him at all at second. His arm is average, which I can live with, but his footwork when he catches the ball isn't consistent, so some of his throws are off. Not like they should be. But, like Wally said, he's young. We can work on a few things."

Hamey took off his glasses, cleaned the lenses with his handkerchief, put them back on, and asked, this time addressing both coaches at once. "Let me ask you this. If he stayed the same, if he never improved any, would he be good enough to be our regular shortstop over the long haul? Again, I'm asking you to judge him right now—not what he *could* be doing down the road."

Mayo Smith, who had been listening intently to what his coaches had been saying, finally spoke up. "Fred, what's this all about? What's goin' on here?"

Hamey held up his hand and said, "Just a minute. I want to hear their answers first. Hold on." He pointed to Wally.

"That's tough to say, Sir. As you know, spring games can make a hitter look like he's ready for the Hall of Fame. Pitchers are still working on their stuff and getting in shape, so it's hard to get a good read on a new player. But, if you're asking me if I think he'll keep hitting during the regular season, I'd have to be honest and say we won't know that until he faces Major League pitching on a daily basis. I just haven't seen him enough to tell you what you want to know right now. Right now, we don't have a lot of other options I can see. Nobody else who can play short can hit worth a lick. That's also true."

Hamey reached over, picked up a pencil from Mayo's desk and started drumming it against his leg. "And what do you have to say?" he asked Andy.

"We can work on the footwork and maybe speed up his throws, but—"

"Go on," Hamey urged, moving closer to him.

"His range isn't the best but, like I said before, if I had more time with him that could also get better. Can't do much now, though. He took a tumble in drills the other day and hurt his shoulder pretty bad. Going to take a while, I think, to get him up to speed again."

Hamey looked down at the floor and said, "You seem pretty much on the fence here. I was hoping you'd give me a better picture."

Mayo interrupted again. "Fred, they just haven't seen him that long. Neither have I, but I'm curious about something else now. Why haven't you asked me what I think?"

"No offense intended, Mayo. I just wanted it straight from the horse's mouth, from those who have worked closest with him so far."

All were quiet for a few moments while waiting for Hamey's next words. After drumming the pencil again on his leg, he finally spoke. "What I'm going to say will stay right here in this room." When all nodded, he said, "We're still checking on it, but we got a tip yesterday his contract from the Kansas City Monarchs might have had some things a little off."

"Off?" Mayo asked. "How? What do you mean?"

"We're looking into it, but we think Kennedy's really thirty— and *not* the twenty-two-year-old we thought we had. In fairness, nobody ever asked him his age. All we had to go by when we signed him was on the K.C. documents. If this is true, it isn't the first time I've been snookered, and it won't be the last, but it sure would be a new one, wouldn't it?"

Mayo and his coaches sat there, stunned, speechless, as Hamey continued. "*Now* you know why I asked those questions, why I wanted to know if he never got any better would it be enough. If he's an old dog and not a young pup, is our effort worth it with him? That's what I was trying to get at."

"I don't believe it," Mayo said, his voice rising quickly.

"I don't, either," Wally joined in. "He *looks* young enough to me. If he's not, I sure have had the wool pulled over my eyes."

"Looks like we all did," Hamey replied, matter-of-factly. "Wally said something to the effect that we didn't have many options at short. Well, what if we did? I already knew about Kennedy's injury and how bad it could be, so yesterday I made some phone calls to see about insurance. I've got something in the works that might help us out—a lot. Again, this stays inside this room, but we have a chance to pick up that Fernandez kid from Brooklyn. Well, who really knows if he's a kid? I'm going to start asking for birth certificates."

All laughed as he continued. "All the scouting reports I've seen rate him really high, in all areas. But he's stuck behind Pee Wee Reese, so they've got no place to play him in that infield. That's why they're willing to let him go, and we might be able to get him. Any of you know anything about Fernandez you can add for me?"

"I've seen him some," Andy replied. "And, Jim Taylor, one of our Winter League scouts has seen him enough he mentioned him to me and was high on him. Said the same thing about the other scouting reports that you did."

"Sounds like he could be a good addition," Hamey said. "Mayo, your thoughts?"

"I've heard the name. Don't know much about him, but I'm feeling mighty dumb right now. Thirty?"

The laughter came again until Hamey spoke. "We can't cry over spilled milk. Season's less than two weeks away. Here's what

I think we should do. Keep working with Kennedy when you can. I'm inclined to keep him with the team when we go north no matter how this turns out. We could let him and Fernandez fight it out, and we'd have insurance either way when the games start for real. Sound like a good plan?"

When all agreed, he said, "Good. I'll keep working on the trade. I'd like to talk to you about that, Mayo. The rest of you can go. Thank you for your input. Appreciate it."

As soon as the coaches had gone, Hamey turned to Mayo and said, "I've got our roster here. Let me run some things by you."

Mayo just shook his head, "Thirty?"

Hamey laughed. "Let it go. We've work to do."

....

April 22, 1957
Roosevelt Stadium, Jersey City, New Jersey

The first week of the season had been agony for John Kennedy, both literally and figuratively. The pain in his shoulder caused by a fall during running drills in late spring training continued to plague him, his arm swelling and aching terribly each night. As a result, newly acquired Chico Fernandez had started every game at shortstop, hitting well and fielding steadily, if not bordering on spectacularly at times. Meanwhile, John had been relegated to the bench, watching Fernandez impress teammates and the fans while still waiting for his Major League debut. However, he had been kept with the big club, an accomplishment that still surprised and filled him with joy. John had expected to be sent to the high minors after the spring games, but found himself poised to fulfill his greatest dream: to play in a Major League baseball game.

The Phillies had started the season winning two and losing three. The sportswriters' projection for their season wasn't all that positive. They did have mound stalwart Robin Roberts to anchor the rotation, but the rest of the pitching was thin. The team also lacked power and had only a few regulars who were expected to hit for high average. At best, the writers said, they would settle in the middle of the pack. However, a team looking to move up in the standings was always striving to improve the roster, especially among the regulars, so John felt he might have a legitimate shot at breaking through if his health improved.

The day's game was against the Brooklyn Dodgers, who were off to a fast start to the season, their record standing at 4-1. Fernandez again got the start at short. A pitcher's duel between Brooklyn's Roger Craig and the Phil's' Jim Hearn kept the score close, and at the beginning of the top of the eighth, the score was Dodgers 3 and Philadelphia 1. As they came to bat, Mayo Smith urged his team to find a way—any way—to get a runner aboard to bring the tying run to the plate.

Frank Baumholtz, the first batter up, grounded weakly to first, making the first out. However, Richie Ashburn, Philadelphia's best hitter, especially in clutch situations, drilled a single to center. Solly Hemus followed with a double into deep right center, but Ashburn had to stop at third when the relay thrown was right on the mark. The Dodger faithful became restless as the lead suddenly seemed in jeopardy, the tying run now at second base. Knowing that a single would likely tie the score if a swift runner were on second, Manager Smith went to his bench to replace the aging legs of Hemus out at second. He looked around the dugout a second before barking, "Kennedy—stretch out as fast as you can. You're running for Solly. Get to the top of the steps and wait for my signal."

Mayo exited the dugout, walked slowly over to the home plate umpire, and indicated on his lineup card he was sending in Kennedy to pinch-run and removing Hemus from the game. Once the move was acknowledged, Mayo turned toward the dugout and shouted to John, "Get going! Watch for the signs—and keep alert."

As soon as John reached the second base bag, he stood there, smiling broadly and looked around at the eleven thousand in attendance and then at his teammates, all urging him on. He realized at that moment his dream had come true. He was now fully a Major League baseball player. His smile grew even wider.

….. ….. …..

John Kennedy's dream did come to fruition on the afternoon of April 22, 1957 but, primarily because of the injury to his shoulder, his Major League career was over almost as soon as it started. He appeared in just four more games. In two of them, he again served as a pinch runner. He also played at short in two others, but he never started a game at the position. While in the field, he committed one error as the result of a wide throw to first after a grounder had been hit to him. Over the course of those five games, he had two at-bats— with no hits and striking out once. His last appearance was on May 3, 1957, as a pinch runner in the seventh inning. He never played in the Majors again.

John was sent to the minor leagues, where the Phillies hoped he'd regain his health and, therefore, his hitting and fielding forms. However, Chico Fernandez continued to play so well there wasn't a need to bring John back to the roster. He continued playing baseball the rest of his life everywhere from the minors to semi-pro leagues and eventually in "Senior" leagues back in his hometown of Jacksonville. His love and passion for the game never dwindled. John Kennedy passed away on April 27, 1998, at age seventy-one.

Records found after his passing indicated he was just shy of his thirtieth birthday when he made his major league debut with Philadelphia. He may have been older than the typical rookie of the time, but his heart was young—and remained so all the rest of his days.

NOTE: *While it is true John Kennedy was the first African American to play for the Philadelphia Phillies, the first player of color to take the field at the major league level for the organization was Chico Fernandez of Puerto Rico, who stepped into the lineup on April 16, 1957—a week before Kennedy made his debut. Both men were true pioneers not just for this organization, but the game itself.*

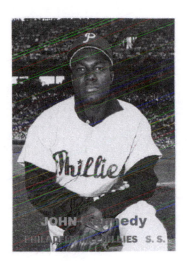

John Kennedy baseball card
Courtesy of Max Sullivan Collection

14

Ozzie Virgil

Detroit Tigers

Ozzie Virgil with his 1959 Detroit Tigers teammates
(Ozzie middle row, 8th from left).

Ozzie Virgil was born May 17, 1932, in Monte Cristi, Dominican Republic. When he was a young teen, his parents moved the family to the Bronx in New York City, where he attended high school and became a standout on local semi-pro baseball teams. By the end of his senior year, scouts from several organizations were knocking on his door. However, his first obligation was a stint in the U.S. Marines. While he was in the service he played, and exceptionally well, for the Marine Corps baseball team at the base where he was stationed in North Carolina. Word of his fine play reached Major League scouts, who followed his play there and took note of his keen batting eye and slick fielding.

As a result, the New York Giants invited Ozzie to a tryout as ɔon as his military service was completed. He impressed the coaches and was signed to a minor league contract. They sent him to their affiliate in the Northern League for his introduction to professional baseball. The next year, 1954, the Giants sent him to their ballclub in the Piedmont League, where he hit right at .300 and flashed a gifted glove in the field. That earned him another promotion, this time to one of their top farm clubs in the Texas League. There, he led all third basemen in fielding and continued his steady hitting. He was also selected for the league's All-Star team, which gained him status as one of the organization's top talents.

The following season he continued his improvement in all facets of his game, and on September 23, 1956, he was called up to the Giants and made his Major League debut. In doing so, he became the first person from the Dominican Republic to play in a Major League game, opening the door for others who followed from that country. While with the Giants, who already had a strong lineup, Ozzie was used mostly as a utility player. After the season was over, in January of 1958, he was acquired by the Detroit Tigers, who were trying to improve their infield defense, especially at third base. To get him ready for the rigors of the season, they sent him to play regularly on their AAA team in Charleston, West Virginia. There, he once again excelled both at the plate and on the field, which earned him a call-up to the big club. When Ozzie took the field on June 6, 1958, he became the first player of color to appear in the Majors for the Detroit Tigers.

....

May 31, 1958
Briggs Stadium, Detroit, Michigan

John McHale, General Manager of the Detroit Tigers, had planned the meeting very carefully. He and his Assistant General Manager,

Andy Carrington, had met beforehand with team owners and their lawyers. Now, finally, they had the go-ahead to bring Ozzie Virgil up from their minor-league system and make him the first Black player on the team. Appeals from church groups, civic organizations, and the Detroit Negro community had certainly influenced their decision. Threats of boycotts made this new direction the team was taking even more necessary. Perhaps the tipping point was not wanting to be known as the last team in Major League Baseball to integrate. That dubious *honor* would go to the Boston Red Sox.

All that was left to do was to get the backing of the larger Detroit community, so McHale had invited to the meeting the individuals he badly needed to help with his plan—a plan highly controversial and not popular with many in his city. This group consisted of Leonard Stubbs, Executive Assistant for the Mayor of Detroit; Bill Velarde, one of the lead writers of the *Detroit Free Press*; Mary Beck, a prominent member of the Detroit City Council; Charles Sadler, the team's chief attorney; Emily Stanton, the Tiger's publicist; and Buck James, Assistant Chief of Police for Greater Detroit.

John closed the door of his office on the lower level of Briggs Stadium and addressed the group, all of whom were seated around the large, oblong meeting table in the center of the room. "I suppose many of you are wondering why you're here at this *very* short-notice meeting—and on a Saturday at that. I won't waste your time. I'm going to get right at it and make my introductory comments as brief as I can before I ask for your advice and counsel. I want to make sure everyone knows exactly what's going on—and what we have at stake—before we leave this room. In short, we're going to try to kill *a lot* of birds with one stone—and that stone is Ozzie Virgil."

There were plenty of confused looks around the table as he continued. "I'm afraid the team hasn't done as well as we'd all hoped so far this season. Right now, we're in sixth place and not far from the cellar. We need to do something to give us a spark, a jolt of some kind to get the boys playing at a higher level. The logical thing to do sometimes is make a change or two here and there—and hope these set things rolling."

Bill Velarde spoke up. "Forgive me, but I don't see how we can help with that. That is, unless you want to sign me up!"

A few nervous laughs followed, but all became quiet again when they saw the stern look on John's face. "Believe me," he said, "there are days I'm sure you might hit better than some we've got, but the change I'm talking about isn't going to be easy, and it won't be popular in some quarters.

"I'm sure some of you have followed this in the papers, in the editorials in particular, but there has been a groundswell of pressure for us to add a Negro to our team from groups and organizations all across the city, and even threats of boycotts . . . and worse. I don't know how many of you know this, but only the Boston Red Sox and we haven't yet integrated our teams. We're the last two. I think now is the time here, especially because if they do it first, would we really want to be known as the last team and city to do this? I think not. I also want you to know up front I'm not doing this to give in to pressure. The team needs help, and it just so happens this young man, this Ozzie Virgil, is better than anyone else we've got in our minor-league system right now. He just might be the spark we're looking for."

Buck James groaned loudly and shook his head. He started to speak, but before he could, John kept going, this time his voice louder, hoping to indicate he wasn't yet ready to yield the floor. "In a couple of days, we're going to call up Mr. Virgil, who will be our first Black player. I wanted to call all of you together because I'd like your help to make this go as smoothly as possible. Well, that's it. Now I'll shut up a minute because I want to know what you have to say about this—your advice, suggestions, thoughts. We don't have time to play around here, so let's hear it."

Bill Velarde from *The Detroit Free Press* spoke first. Addressing the whole group, he said, "I agree it's time to integrate the team. This is *long* overdue. If Emily can give me information on Ozzie's background—like where he grew up, where he's played before—I'll write some pieces about him before his arrival. That should help at least some of the Tiger fans get ready for him, so it isn't so much of a bombshell when he finally does show up."

John thanked Bill for his show of support as those around the table, except Buck, nodded approvingly. Having the support of the press was a good beginning, but John knew he still had to address the big issue—the major reason behind the meeting. John again addressed the group, but, this time, directed his comments right at Buck.

"Thanks again, Bill. That early publicity will really help, and I appreciate it. I've got to be honest with all of you. Getting the word out isn't the main reason you're here. I'm afraid there is potential for violence once we make this move, and I think we all better face that fact now and have a unified front and plan in place just in case that happens. I've had letters you can't believe from people who do *not* want us to integrate the team. Some of these have been threats that we have to take seriously. That's also part of the reason we're planning on calling Mr. Virgil up when the team's on the road—*before* we play games here in our home park."

"John, I know what you're saying because we've received dozens of the same sorts of letters at the Mayor's office," Leonard Stubbs, Executive Assistant for the Mayor, said, glancing around at the group. "There are just a lot of folks who don't think this should happen. I'm not one of them. Frankly, I think this is a good idea, especially because I don't want us to be the *last* team on the list.

That would *not* be good for Detroit. Still, I understand your concerns about safety. That could jump up and bite us."

City Council member Mary Beck spoke up in agreement. "I'm sorry to be so blunt, John, but the City Council has heard from a lot of people who tell us they're not happy with this whole integration thing—that if our Tigers go there, they'll stop coming to games and stop supporting the team. You and the Mayor's office know how much tourist revenue the city gets from people coming here for the games every summer. If people stop coming to games because of this, the team—and the city—are going to suffer. We better be very careful here in how we proceed. That's why I really want to hear what Buck has to say about all this. Buck, what do you think is going to happen?"

John had hoped someone else would draw Buck into the discussion, so he hid his excitement as he pointed to him and urged him to respond to the question.

Buck had done little throughout the meeting to hide his distaste of the whole proposal, often groaning softly but audibly and shaking his head. Now that he finally had a chance to speak, he didn't mince his words. Pounding his fist on the table, he said, "I think it's all a mistake. We *don't* need this right now. There are race problems brewing, and this can't help at all. I think you're asking for trouble, and I'm sure I speak for most of the boys in the precincts all around the city. You asked me what I think, and that's it. I'm saying *don't do it*."

John saw the concern on the faces around the table after Buck's response and knew he had to jump in quickly to support his case even more or risk losing their much-needed support. "Buck, I respect what you're saying. We *all* know there will be some opposition. And, yes, there have been racial issues here and everywhere across the country lately—a lot more than we're used to—but it's time to move forward. I appreciate your forthrightness and your honesty, even if it wasn't what I was hoping I'd hear. So, here's what I'm going to ask from you, and I know it won't be easy.

"*Safety* always has to be the first priority. I know where you stand, Buck, but I'm asking you to forget about your own beliefs a minute and tell me what we can do to minimize the risk of violence and danger here at the ballpark and surrounding areas where the fans will be in bars and restaurants when this unfolds. What's our best strategy? You're the expert in this area. I'd really like your suggestions."

All eyes were now on Buck, who sat back in his chair, exhaled loudly, and finally said, "If you've made up your mind, and I really do think that's a mistake, there are a few things that *could* be done. First off, your idea of bringing him up while you're out of town is a good one. That'll buy us time to get things ready here. I'll talk to the Chief about doubling security around the stadium when he has his first game here. Have you figured out when that will be?"

"The next home stand starts June 17. That's the target."

"Then we'll get the security in place, but we don't want to overload the stands with men in uniform. It's hard for most civilians to believe, but having a lot of cops around can go both ways. Sometimes it keeps people in line. Other times it's like a call to fight. So, what we'll do is keep a lot in street clothes—and keep 'em walking through the stands to look for any trouble breaking out.

"If it were my man, I'd sneak him into town and hide him out until it's time to get to the stadium on the 17th. I don't know how he's coming—train, plane, car—but whatever you do, I'd keep that a secret. And, I wouldn't put him in a hotel just yet. We'd probably have to assign guards if you did, and that wouldn't help, either. Mr. McHale, take my advice on this. Hide him out best you can until the . . . *unveiling*."

"Good points," John said. "Exactly the type of advice I was looking for. Since Mr. Virgil will already be with the team when they fly in, we'll change the time the plane touches down. There's always a pretty large group of fans there to meet them as they get off the plane. I hate to trick them like this, but I'll see to it the team gets here a couple hours before the scheduled time and won't tell anyone else about that. Then I'll take Buck's advice and not place him in a hotel just now. We've got a team booster I know would be glad to help out. Name's Dave Boston. He's a local businessman and sort of an unofficial historian for us. We'll put Virgil up at his house, at least for this home stand. We'll get him into the stadium quietly that night. We'll organize it so two plain-clothes officers can escort him in without drawing attention.

"Yes, no doubt there will be some rough spots because, well, this is new territory for us all. But this is a big moment for the team, the city, the community—everyone. Let's try to do this right. Let's try to do this as smoothly as we can. And let me finish this meeting by saying one more thing. We've checked him out, and this Mr. Virgil is a good man. I believe he is also the *right* man for this. He's soft spoken. By all accounts he's a great teammate and doesn't cause trouble, on or off the field. He's a man of faith, which I'd like to see in print soon. I think that would also help.

"And this son-of-a-gun can hit. I saw him a couple weeks back at Charleston, our AAA club, and in the game I was watching he hit *three* home runs in a row against the best team in that league. Three. He's not seen as a home run hitter, but he's got some pop in his bat, and we need that right now. I think he'll fit in just fine. That is, if he's given a chance. Let's all work together to give him one. Are you all with me?"

"Count on the Mayor's office to do everything possible," Leonard said. "Personally, I also think a lot of good can come of this—if we don't mess it up."

"Exactly," Buck cut in. "There also could be one heck of a

mess. I still don't agree with this, but if it has to be done, let's stay out of the mud as much as we can."

With the rest of those present in agreement, John brought the meeting to a close. "I want to thank you all again for coming this morning. I want you to know how much I appreciate this."

Surprising everyone, Buck stood, walked over to John and extended his hand. The two men shook hands, firmly. "Mr. McHale, I don't always agree with things like this, but I do respect people who talk right up and take a stand—and that's what you've done. I've said my piece, but now I'll do all I can to help with this. That's my job, and that's what I'll do. I just wish you luck. You're going to need it."

"I think we all will," John replied, shaking his hand again. "Probably more than we realize right now."

....

June 17, 1958
Briggs Stadium

"Yes, Mr. McHale!" Al Kaline, the Tiger's slugging outfielder shouted into the telephone in the locker room. His voice was loud enough that all could hear every word he was saying. "Gee—that's rough news! And, what a time to deliver it. That's too bad. I know he's going to be upset. Let me see if I can get him to the phone."

Covering the receiver, he shouted, "Anyone seen Virgil? Is he here—or out warming up?"

"He's over here!" Harvey Kuenn called back. "Right here at his locker."

"Virgil!" Al Kaline shouted, frantically motioning him to get to the telephone. "You've got to take this call. It's McHale—the General Manager! I'm afraid this is bad news. Awful news."

Ozzie, who had been sitting at his locker and putting on his uniform socks, quickly stood and asked, "McHale? What emergency? It's not my wife, is it? Oh, no!"

In his haste, his foot caught on the edge of the stool, and down he went, hitting his head on the locker next to his. His new teammate Billy Martin reached down and helped him up, brushed him off, and asked, "You OK? How's the noggin'?"

Ozzie didn't answer him. Instead, he rushed as fast as he could toward the phone as his teammates stepped to the side to let him pass. However, when he got there, Kaline held the receiver behind his back and gently pushed his other hand against Ozzie's chest. "Wait a minute, Virg. I hate it, but it looks like I'm the one who is going to have to prepare you for this. When I answered the phone, I could hear McHale talking to someone while he was waiting for someone to respond to him. I'm really sorry, but it looks like you were just traded to Washington, and you're going to have to get across the field to their locker room before the game starts. Here. Mr. McHale is waiting."

But instead of handing Ozzie the phone, Al tucked it behind his back again and addressed the rest of his teammates, all of whom were now staring his direction. "Well, first they fired the manager. Now they are getting rid of more and more of us. I know we aren't off to the best start, but this is getting ridiculous. This just isn't fair."

Ozzie appeared at least partially relieved when he heard that his family wasn't involved in the bad news. Seeing this, Al finally handed him the phone while saying, "I'm sorry but, by league rules, now that you've been traded, we have to get you and your belongings out of here as fast as we can because we are playing the Senators today." He yelled to his teammates, "Boys, get one of those new laundry carts on rollers. Start putting Virg's equipment and other items in there. When you finish, we'll roll it across to the other locker room. It's the least we can do."

A collective groan and shouts of "We're sorry!" and "Tough break!" were shouted toward Ozzie, who now appeared completely stunned. The situation seemed so unreal, so shocking, he barely understood the words he heard when he finally took the phone and put the receiver to his ear. "I'm truly sorry, Ozzie," the voice said, solemnly. "This was just a business decision. I want you to know that."

Ozzie looked up from the floor and saw that nearly everyone had converged on his locker and was roughly pulling out his belongings and throwing them into a laundry cart. He couldn't see who it was, but someone asked, quite loudly, "Think he'll mind if I keep some of these ties?"

The voice on the phone continued, "Ozzie, the truth is we received a great offer for you. In exchange for you, we're getting their assistant trainer, two whirlpool tubs, their bullpen catcher, and thirty-six dollars."

"What?" Ozzie asked, his attention still focused on everyone rummaging through his locker and Billy Martin handing out the ties. "What do you mean? I don't understand—"

"Look, it's like this. We didn't think we'd ever get more for you than now, so we pulled the trigger on this deal. I think we just improved our club a great deal. "

Ozzie started to ask more questions, but his attention was drawn back to the locker room, where everyone suddenly backed up against the wall, leaving a direct view across the length of the room to the door of the training room. There, with cigar in his mouth and phone in hand, stood Gail Harris, the Tigers' first baseman, who said loudly enough into the phone everyone could hear him, "Frankly, Virgil, I think a change of scene will do you good. What do you think?"

As Ozzie's mouth dropped open, his teammates burst into laughter and started clapping. He'd been had. Completely.

His teammates gathered around as Al Kaline reached over, slapped Ozzie on the back, hugged him tightly, and said, "*Now you're part of this team! Welcome to the Detroit Tigers!*"

Cheers erupted as Harris shouted, "Speech! Speech!"

Ozzie hung up the phone, a relieved smile spreading across his face. "You had me believing it!"

More applause followed as he continued, "You should all be ashamed of yourselves. I really thought I now belonged to Washington!" Ozzie rubbed his eyes. "Thanks. Thanks—*I think*—for welcoming me. I guess this means I have to play good now, right? That's pressure!"

All laughed until Bill Norman, the Tigers' recently appointed manager, walked into the room. Suddenly everyone became quiet. "Sounds like a circus in here," he said. "OK—you've had your fun. We've got a game in a few minutes. I want everyone out to the dugout!" Walking over and shaking Ozzie's hand, he said, "Welcome, son. Appears they like you. Wouldn't have done it otherwise."

"Thanks, Coach," Ozzie replied. "I meant what I said. I'll play good—and starting tonight! Just you wait and see."

"You're starting at third base. Get your glove, and get out there. Show us what you've got."

"Yes, Sir! I'm ready. Those Senators better watch out!"

….. ….. …..

The sweetest sounds in baseball are the crack of the bat, the roar of the crowd, and the cheers of your teammates. Ozzie heard all three five times during his first game as a Detroit Tiger.

His manager had penciled him in at third base and batting second. His first time up, against Senators' starter Pedro Ramos, he doubled to deep left center field. Next, leading off the bottom of the third inning, he ignited a rally with a leadoff single. The Tigers batted around the order, and in Ozzie's second at-bat of the inning he singled again, this time off reliever Al Cicotte, as they scored seven runs on seven hits. That put him at three for three, a nice exclamation mark on his pregame declaration. Now, after his fourth hit in a row—a rocket off the shortstop's glove—he was positively giddy and proud as he stood on first base. Tiger fans erupted in applause while his teammates stood in the dugout and clapped and cheered. He had made a bold declaration before the game that he was going to give the Senators fits, but as he stood there, brushing the infield dirt off his uniform pants, not even he could believe what was unfolding.

Ozzie came up one last time in the seventh, with the Tigers ahead of the Senators 8-2. Frank Bolling, the Tigers' second baseman, had just knocked his fourth hit of the game, a single to center. As Ozzie strolled to the plate, Frank yelled to him, "That puts us even! I caught you, Virg. Think you can do it again?"

Ozzie smiled as he dug into the batter's box and took four quick practice swings. Al Cicotte was still on the mound for the Senators. He looked in for the sign, went into his windup, and tossed up a sharp-breaking curve that caught the inside corner for strike one. Ozzie stepped out of the box, took two more practice swings, and then before he could resume his stance, the crowd started cheering louder and louder, chanting his name, "Ozzie! Ozzie!" He stepped out again and looked around the stadium at the fans who were urging him on. Many had needed to check their programs at the start of the game to see who their new third baseman was, but now they were shouting his name in chorus. The sound made him shiver.

Home plate umpire, Eddie Rommel, called out above the roar of the crowd, "Well, you going to hit—or just stand there?" Ozzie didn't reply. Instead, he dug in again and tried to shift his attention to the pitcher, who was looking in for the sign. Cicotte nodded and started into his windup. Ozzie gripped the bat tighter as he focused on the delivery. The pitch was a fastball that caught too much of the inside part of the plate. Ozzie put a good swing on it and lined the ball to left, just out of the reach of the diving third baseman.

When he reached first base, the fans erupted again, this time coming to their feet—a standing ovation that lasted a full two minutes. Frank Bolling yelled over from second base, "OK—you win!" He then called time and walked over to first to shake Ozzie's hand. The crowd roared again, saluting Ozzie by calling out his name louder and louder. Some teammates in the dugout waved towels as many also whistled. Proud, but also somewhat embarrassed by all the attention, Ozzie tipped his cap to the fans, then nodded toward his teammates. Even his manager prolonged the celebration by motioning for Harvey Kuenn, the next batter in the order, to stay a few moments longer in the on-deck circle so the Tiger faithful could continue their applause.

With his heart pounding and adrenaline pumping, Ozzie took a long lead off first as Kuenn stepped into the batter's box. All sat down again as Kuenn, one of the better hitters in the league, dug in. On a 1-1 count, Harvey rocketed a double off the left field wall. Frank Bolling scored easily from second but, as Ozzie blazed toward third, his coach wildly waved him toward home. Ozzie rounded the bag as fast as he could. He knew it was going to be a close play, so on instinct slid toward the outside part of home plate. However, halfway into his slide, Steve Korchek, the Senators catcher, moved to his left to block the plate just as the ball hit his glove. Ozzie's foot never touched the plate. He was out—by inches and a split-second.

As the umpire stood over Ozzie and raised his thumb, the stadium became eerily quiet—until Ozzie stood and started brushing himself off. The applause started slowly from the box seats behind the Tigers' dugout, but it quickly spread all through the stadium. Before Ozzie was halfway to the dugout, the fans were standing again, cheering even louder than they had only moments before when he delivered his fifth hit of the game. Tears welled up in his eyes as he started down the dugout steps. His manager patted him on the back, and his teammates gathered around him, all wanting to shake his hand and offer their congratulations.

Frank Bolling was the last to walk over. "So, you outhit me today. That's good news—bad news for you."

"What do you mean?" Ozzie asked. "Why *bad* news?"

"Because you just went five for five in your first game here. The fans are going to expect that every game now for a while. You know that, right?"

"I don't care," Ozzie replied. "All I want to do is play. That's it. Just play. I'll do my best for them—every day."

"I believe you will," Frank replied, smiling and shaking his hand again. "I've got only one more thing to say. Welcome to the club."

....

Ozzie Virgil's Major League career spanned nine years, mostly as a utility player, and included stints with the New York Giants, Detroit Tigers, Kansas City Athletics, Baltimore Orioles, Pittsburgh Pirates, and San Francisco Giants. When his playing days ended, in 1969, his career statistics included a lifetime .231 batting average, four-teen home runs, and seventy-three RBI's. Everywhere he played he was known as a great teammate and positive influence in the dugout. It was no wonder, then, that as soon as his playing days were over, he was offered coaching jobs that would keep him active in the game for over nineteen more years.

Ozzie is considered one of the more important pioneers in modern baseball history. Baseball historians most often talk about his role in breaking the color barrier for the Detroit organization, a significant and historic accomplishment, indeed. However, that wasn't the only door he opened. When he debuted with the New York Giants on September 23, 1956, he also became the first person from the Dominican Republic to play in a Major League game. His groundbreaking appearance soon paved the way for other players from his home country, among them through the years outstanding players such as Juan Marichal, Felipe Alou, Pedro Martinez, David Ortiz, and Alex Rodriguez. Today, he is known by many in the Dominican Republic as "their Jackie Robinson" for his role in creating opportunities for so many—and is seen as a national hero and role model.

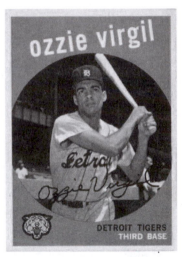

1959 Topps #203, Ozzie Virgil
Courtesy of The Topps Company, Inc.

15

Pumpsie Green

Boston Red Sox

Pumpsie Green with his 1960 Boston Red Sox teammates
(Pumpsie bottom row, 3rd from left).

Elijah "Pumpsie" Green was born October 27, 1933, in the small, central Oklahoma town of Boley, a pioneer town established mostly by and for African Americans just after 1900, but he spent most of his childhood in Richmond, California. Pumpsie was a natural athlete who later competed in football, basketball, and baseball while attending El Cerrito High School. The basketball court was where he excelled the most, but baseball scholarships came pouring in after scouts saw his skills on the diamond: soft hands, strong arm, excellent batting stroke, ability to switch-hit, and respected team

263

leadership. After sorting through his options, he decided to attend Contra Costa College where his high school coach had taken a position. There Pumpsie blossomed as the team's starting shortstop.

Just as Pumpsie was nearing graduation, he was invited to a tryout for the Oakland Oaks, the team he grew up following as a youngster and one of the top teams in the Pacific Coast League. Seeing his strong performance in their drills, the team signed him to his first professional contract. At that time, teams in the Pacific Coast League had their own version of a farm system. Believing Pumpsie's future was bright, they sent him right to their top affiliate, the Stockton Ports. There, with guidance from their top coaches, he improved his batting and fielding skills even more. Scouts from the Boston Red Sox saw him play and were so impressed they purchased his contract in late 1955 and sent him to their minor league team in Montgomery, Alabama, where his skills continued to develop. The next year he was promoted once again, this time to the Sox' club at Albany, New York, where he had a fine year on both offense and defense. As that season ended, he was assigned to the Minneapolis Millers, a relatively new Boston AAA affiliate. While with the Millers, Pumpsie was schooled in playing several different infield positions, which added an important measure of versatility to his baseball resume.

When the 1959 season rolled around, nearly everyone in the Boston system believed Pumpsie was ready for promotion to the big club. Invited to spring training that year, he played exceptionally well, initially drawing high praise from both Pinkie Higgins, the Sox's manager, and his coaching staff, especially Jack Burns, the team's fielding coach. However, Pumpsie slumped badly both at the plate and in the field right before camp ended. In a move that surprised many, management decided a little more development in the minors would prepare him for games at the Major League level. This caused an uproar in Boston's fan base and in civic groups in and around the city. Pumpsie was, of course, also upset he didn't make the team, but he quickly resolved he'd play so well back in the minors they'd have to call him up before the season ended. After just a couple months, Boston couldn't ignore the fact he was bashing the ball at a .320 clip and fielding flawlessly, so they finally promoted him to the Major League club.

Pumpsie made his debut on July 21, 1959, in a game against the Chicago White Sox, becoming the first person of color to play for the Boston Red Sox. That night was a *first* for both Pumpsie and Boston, but it was also a *last* for Major League Baseball. When Pumpsie entered the game as a pinch-runner for Vic Wertz in the eighth inning of their game against Chicago at Comiskey Park, the Red Sox became the last of the sixteen teams in the Major Leagues to drop the color barrier—*twelve* long years after Jackie Robinson made his debut for the Brooklyn Dodgers. From the milestone moment when Pumpsie stepped onto the field, he, Boston, and Major League Baseball were forever changed.

....

August 4, 1959
Fenway Park, Boston, Massachusetts

Pumpsie Green had been riding in the back seat of the Checker Cab about six blocks when he noticed the driver, an older Black man he estimated near sixty, looking at him in the mirror instead of paying attention to the thick early morning traffic. As the cab slowly swerved into the other lane, nearly hitting a tow truck, the piercing honks of horns startled both Pumpsie and his driver, who let out a loud whistle and shook his head. "Sorry! That was a close one," he said, craning his neck around to face Pumpsie.

When the cab started swerving out of its lane again, Pumpsie shouted, "Look out!"

The driver jerked the wheel back to the left, just avoiding a collision with another cab, and this time said, "Guess I better pay attention. Sorry, again." He paused a few seconds, glancing in the mirror one more time. "I know I know you from somewhere. You famous or something?"

Pumpsie, still shook up from the last narrow escape, did his best to smile. "No—not in the least."

"But you said Fenway Park, right? Don't look like you work there. Don't look like you're going to the double-header. What's your line, Mister?"

"But I do work there," Pumpsie said relaxing a bit in the seat. "Today's my first day. You'll have to help me find the entrance when we—"

"That's it!" the driver shouted, honking the horn repeatedly. "You're him! You're *Green*. Big as life! Saw you in the papers. I can't believe my luck. Wait until my wife hears about this."

Embarrassed, Pumpsie just nodded. Then, a few moments later, he asked, "Sir, do you know where the player's entrance is? That's where I'm supposed to go, but I've never been there before."

"Don't you worry, Mr. Green. I'll see to it. And, I'll mash the pedal—get you there in a flash."

The cab sped up as the driver zipped in and out of traffic, honking nearly the whole time. "Just get me there in one piece!" Pumpsie shouted over all the commotion. "You can slow down. We have plenty of time."

"Nah," the driver replied. "Always good to be early your first day. Watch this!" Picking up even more speed while weaving around cars, he turned one last time and said, "Mr. Green, welcome to Boston! We're so glad you're here!"

A good half dozen near accidents later and after one of the scariest rides of his life, Pumpsie quickly reached for the door handle as the cab screeched to a halt in the player's parking lot just outside the ballpark. But, before he could get out, the driver reached back around, grabbed his arm, and said, "You knock 'em dead. We've been waiting for you. I'll be rootin'."

Pumpsie finally pulled himself free, stepped out as fast as he could, and asked, "What do I owe you, Sir?"

The driver waved both hands in front of his face. "Not a thing. Just do your best, which I know you will." He pointed to a door off to the left. "That's where you go in. Good luck, Mr. Green. It's been a pleasure. Wait until my wife—"

"No, thank *you*—I think. You *did* get me here fast."

"Knew you'd be nervous today, so I took it easy. Smooth as silk ride, wasn't it?"

Both men laughed as Pumpsie started toward the door. He hadn't gotten ten feet when he heard someone call out, "Hey, California! You get yourself over here!"

Standing just inside the player's entrance was Bill Russell, the star Center for the Boston Celtics basketball team. Both were from near the San Francisco area and had known each other from their high school days when they played basketball for teams in the Oakland area. "Bill!" Pumpsie shouted, rushing over to shake his hand. "What in the world are you doing here?"

Bill shook his hand firmly. "Us California guys have to stick together. Just wanted to be one of the first to welcome you to Boston. It's a long way from home, isn't it? Actually, I thought maybe I could help a little today—block for you and play a little defense before the reporters swooped in. It wasn't much of a big deal when I got here because the Celtics had guys like us almost ten years ago. But this baseball outfit has been fighting this the whole way."

"I know. I know. I've been asked almost constantly how I feel about being some kind of pioneer. I keep telling them all I want to do is play baseball, but they won't leave me alone."

"That's also why I'm here," his friend said. "I don't know how much you've been following the Boston papers, but when you didn't stay with the team after spring training, groups all over town had a fit, and rightly so. One story after another popped up, and a whole bunch of groups threatened not to come to games at all if you weren't put on the club. I even talked to some reporters about it myself. You're supposed to be some champion coming to drive the team to the pennant. At least that's the impression I get from the papers. No pressure on you there, right?"

Pumpsie rolled his eyes. "I just want to play ball."

"Well, good luck with that. Whether you know it or not, there are a lot of people counting on you, so you better get used to it." Bill paused and looked around the parking lot before laughing. "Guess I was wrong. Where are the reporters? I thought there'd be a flock of them. Can't believe nobody was here to jump you right off the bat. I just don't understand—"

Bill stopped in mid-thought when he saw Ted Williams approaching from his right. Ted immediately squatted down and started pretending he was dribbling a basketball. He stopped, sprang up, and made the motion of taking a jump shot. Bill played along, reaching his left arm high as if to block the shot. Both men laughed. "What in the world are you doing here?" Ted said, shaking Bill's hand. "Come to play for us? We could use another hitter or two."

"Just came to see my old buddy and wish him luck," he replied, pointing to Pumpsie. "And to make sure the reporters didn't carve him up too bad today."

Ted's eyes lit up. "Those lousy vultures." He turned to Pumpsie. "You just stick to me. They hate me like nobody's business. They'll completely ignore you if I'm around to pick apart." Turning back to Bill, he asked, "Really, what are you doing here? You really know each other?"

"Played basketball together when we were just kids." Bill smiled. "He never got a shot off when I was defending him. Not once!"

"Wait a minute!" Pumpsie interrupted. "That's not true. You kept fouling me all the time. Cheap shots if I remember right."

"Cheap shots!" Bill protested. "Didn't have to resort to that for a scrawny kid like you."

Ted laughed, but brought the banter to a quick end. "Uh, oh—newspaper men at ten o'clock. We better get inside, and Bill—you better get moving the other way, fast, or you're stuck with 'em. Then again, it might be good for you, might give you more practice with the ink-stained devils."

"No, thanks!" Bill reached out to shake Pumpsie's hand again. "Listen, I'll get in touch with you in a couple of days. I'll take you around the city and give you the grand tour. OK with you?"

"That would be great. I'd really appreciate it. Thanks, Bill, for coming today. It means a lot to me."

Ted jerked on his arm and said, "Enough of the old home week. We've got to get out of here and into the locker room. See you, Bill. Take care and keep your head down 'till you get out of here."

As Bill headed across the other side of the lot, Ted ushered Pumpsie ahead of him. "Good thing you got here early. I do every day. Only way to keep ahead of those news rats."

Pumpsie motioned for Ted to lead the way. After they walked down a long hallway and a short set of steps, they entered Boston's locker room. Ted turned to Pumpsie and said, "I'm back over there, in the corner. I like to be by myself before games. My guess is you'll be over there, on the other side. And, listen—one more thing. You're warming up with me when we go out to the field. Remember that."

Pumpsie walked down the long row of lockers and finally found his at the end, directly across from Ted's. "Looks like we're neighbors, sort of, Mr. Williams. I'm right here."

Ted squinted at him. "What's this *Mr. Williams* business? We're teammates now. You call me Ted. Or something really flattering. I don't mind that, either."

Pumpsie nodded as several of his teammates entered the room. Pete Runnels, the Sox's regular second baseman; Jackie Jensen, right fielder; and Frank Malzone, shortstop—all were in the middle of a lively conversation but suddenly stopped when they saw Pumpsie rearranging the items in his locker. Runnels walked over, slapped Pumpsie on the back, and said, "Pump, welcome to Fenway. I'm—we're—really glad you're here. This is our home, and now it's yours, too." Frank Malzone joined in. "Seriously, let us know if we can help you get yourself situated today. This old place is held up with glue and toothpicks and seems like a maze 'till you get used to it. So, if we can do anything, just let us know."

"Same here," Jackie Jensen added, stepping forward to shake Pumpsie's hand.

"Thanks—I appreciate it." Embarrassed and not sure what to say next, Pumpsie turned the subject. Pointing around the room, he said, "I thought this would be bigger. This isn't as big as what we had at Minneapolis."

All laughed, especially Jensen, who said, "*This* is the price of history—and a lot of sentiment. They'll *never* tear this place down. The locals love it too much. I think it's creepy. I got bit by a spider down here last year. Thought I was going to lose a finger!"

Pete cut in and said to Pumpsie, "Don't listen to a thing he says. He's always complaining about something. But I wouldn't stick your hand in your glove until you mash the finger holes just in case some spiders really are in there."

"OK, you guys," Williams said. "That's enough. Leave the poor guy alone. Give him some time to get ready. We've got a double-header today, you know." Ted headed out to the field, calling behind him, "I'll be back later."

"Where's he going?" Pumpsie asked.

"It's his ritual," Pete replied. "He goes out before every game here at Fenway to check the sky, the wind, and the temperature. Says he studies all that to know how to hit that day. He's the best there is, so I can't make fun of him for doing all that." Moving over to Pumpsie, Pete motioned for him to lean close so he could speak quietly to him. "Pump, I don't want you to get off on the wrong foot with Ted, so I'm going to fill you in on something." Jackie and Frank, nodding seriously, came over and sat right in front of Pumpsie's locker. "You see, it's like this," Pete continued. "Every new rookie has to do something special for Ted on the first day he gets to this park."

Pumpsie leaned closer as Pete went on, "Besides checking outside, he also does something else before the games here. He has *five* cups of black coffee and reads the sports pages to see what the writers are saying about him. He says the coffee makes him concentrate better when he hits, and the writers make him mad, so he's fired up when he gets to the plate. It works for him. Now, I don't know exactly when this all started, but *I* had to do it—and so did Jackie and Frank when they were new. *Every* new rookie has to get the coffee and papers for him on the first day they're in here. You better do this. If you do, you'll be on his good side the rest of the season."

Jackie and Frank supported the idea and urged Pumpsie to go into the trainer's room, where there was always a coffee pot boiling away. "And, while you're at it, you can get the newspapers from Manager Higgins' office. He won't mind."

"You better hurry," Pete urged. "Ted never stays outside too long."

"I want him to like me," Pumpsie said to his new teammates. "I don't mind doing this at all. I'll hurry."

"He'll be impressed. He'll like you all the more," Pete added, pointing again to the trainer's room. "You better get going."

It took several trips, but Pumpsie, working as fast as he could, finally had five steaming cups of black coffee and a stack of four papers on the stool in front of Ted's locker. Just as he was heading back to his own locker, Ted stepped back into the room.

"What the heck is this?" Ted asked, staring at the treats waiting for him. Pumpsie turned and replied, "Just the way you like it—I was told. Hope the coffee isn't too hot, Mr. Williams."

"What are you talkin' about?" Ted asked, shaking his head.

The others burst into laughter as Pumpsie looked from one to another. Ted put his hand on Pumpsie's shoulder. "They put you up to this?"

"I can't believe it!" Pumpsie shouted. "All of you are horrible. Horrible!"

They walked over, surrounding Pumpsie. One at a time, they shook his hand again and wished him well. Pete finally spoke up. "Pump, we really are glad you're here. Welcome to the club."

Ted started handing each a cup of *his* coffee and sections of the papers. While doing so, he shook his head.

It wasn't long before Manager Higgins and the rest of the team arrived, each going through his personal preparations for the game. A few others acknowledged Pumpsie and wished him well, but most were focused solely on getting ready to take the field. Manager Higgins finally came out of his office, and shouted, "Five minutes to batting practice and fielding warm-ups. Get a move on!"

Pumpsie, dressed and unsure of what to do next, decided he'd wait until others started outside before he left his locker. Just about a minute later, Jackie Jensen started for the steps but, before Pumpsie could follow, he heard his name called out from the trainer's room. Charlie Neubold, the team's trainer of ten years, stuck his head out and called again, "Green—phone call. Important. You can take it in my room. Get yourself over here. Quick!"

All eyes were on Pumpsie as he started across the room. He wasn't sure who it was, but someone said just loud enough that he could hear, "Players *don't* take calls in the locker room. Just isn't done." It was instantly clear to Pumpsie he was violating some unwritten rule, so he quickened his pace and closed the door behind him as soon as he was inside. Charlie handed him the phone, adding, "Better make it quick—and don't let Higgins catch you."

As soon as Pumpsie picked up the phone and asked who was calling, the voice on the other end replied, "This is Jackie Robinson. Just wanted to wish you good luck today. I'm really proud of you, Pumpsie."

"OK—who is this!" Pumpsie demanded, sure that his team-mates were joking with him again. "Runnels—is that you? I fell for your gags once, but—"

Jackie Robinson cut him off. "No, Pumpsie, this really *is* me. This *isn't* a joke. I swear it." Jackie started laughing. "You're prob-ably going to be given a lot of grief today, but it won't be from me. Rachel and I just wanted to let you know how excited we are for you—and how proud we are of what you are doing today. Boston's an *interesting* place, so we thought you should hear a friendly voice before you run out in front of the fans."

Pumpsie, suddenly realizing it really was Jackie, was over-whelmed by his kindness, his thoughtfulness, and didn't know what to say. Jackie finally had to ask if he was still on the line. "Yes, Mr. Robinson," he finally said. "I'm just so grateful you called. This is . . .. This is . . .." He paused a few seconds, and finally stammered, "Mr. Robinson, when I was a kid, I saw you come through where I lived on one of your barnstorming teams. You were my hero. I watched every move you made that game and—"

Jackie laughed again. "Please—don't remind me of how old I am now! You just focus on what you need to do today. This is a big game for you, and it's a big game for baseball. I'm going to give you one piece of advice, and then I know I need to let you go. Whatever happens today, you play *your* game and you be yourself. You're a fine player. Let your bat and your glove do your talking. Do your best to ignore everything else. That's my advice. That's what I wanted to say. Now, you better get going. I see you play two today. Good luck, Pumpsie. Know that Rachel and I will be with you all day."

Pumpsie wiped his eyes and, with his voice starting to crack, finally replied. "I'll never forget this, Mr. Robinson. Not as long as I live. Thank you."

"No, thank *you*. Now, get out there and show them who you are, you hear me?"

"Yes, Sir," was all Pumpsie could say before the trainer grabbed the phone from his hand and hung up the receiver. "Knew you should have this call," Charlie said, smiling broadly. "Get out of here before Higgins finds out!"

Pumpsie, his heart full, thanked him and headed out to the field with the rest of his teammates.

....

Boston had always drawn well for double-headers, but the senior sportswriters in the Press Box were buzzing before the game started that they hadn't seen this many fans in Fenway Park since Game 5 of the 1946 World Series. Team ownership had badly misjudged the effect one man would have on the turnstiles. The stadium was absolutely packed, and extra space had to be created in center field to accommodate an overflow crowd that had come just to see Pumpsie Green play for their beloved Red Sox.

As Boston took the field and Pumpsie headed toward second base, where he'd been assigned to play in the first game of the

double-header, the normal, welcoming applause greeted the team—
only this time, something was different. Many in the stands rose to
their feet, cheering wildly, stomping their feet, and wildly waving
their hands. One reporter after another looked back and forth at the
others and smiled as they knew something special was unfolding
right before their eyes.

On the mound for the Red Sox was Tom Brewer, a stalwart of
their pitching rotation since 1954. He had the reputation as a hurler
who liked a fast game and didn't take much time between his pitches.
This held true as he mowed down the Athletics in the first frame on
six pitches that resulted in two groundouts and a strikeout. It happened so quickly many fans were just settling into their seats while
the Sox were already heading off the field for their first at-bats.

As soon as the Red Sox players entered their dugout, a low rumble started spreading through the stands. In anticipation of what was
coming next, everyone in the press box, writers and photographers
alike, stood and jockeyed for position along the railing, squeezing in
as tightly as they could. As soon as Pumpsie Green, Boston's lead-
off hitter, was announced and climbed out of the dugout and walked
toward home plate, the fans started standing. By the time he reached
home plate, he received a standing ovation, which went on for a full
minute. Pumpsie hadn't expected anything like it and didn't know
what to do, so he backed away from the plate and took several extra
practice swings as the applause and shouts of encouragement became
even louder. Eddie Rommel, the home plate umpire, leaned forward
and said loudly to Pumpsie, "Welcome to the Major Leagues. Good
luck!" Athletics' catcher, Harry Chiti, who had been in his catching
crouch, stood and, over the still increasing cheers of the crowd, nodded and said, "Same for me. Good luck, Buddy."

Rommel finally called out to Pumpsie, "If we had just one
game, I'd let this go on, but we've got two today. Time for you to
get in the box."

Pumpsie stepped in, digging his back cleats into the soft dirt. He looked toward the mound and was relieved to see the Athletics' tough right-handed pitcher, John Tsitouris, whom he'd faced many times in the minor leagues. He had always hit him well, and that thought was a badly needed boost of confidence as he settled in and readied himself for the first pitch.

As the crowd continued to stand and applaud, Tsitouris nodded after receiving the sign from his catcher and immediately went into his windup. His first pitch, a fastball, darted down and in toward Pumpsie's feet, and he had to quickly jump back to avoid being hit. Boos and catcalls rang down at Tsitouris, who just smiled and waited for a new ball to be thrown out to him.

Pumpsie dug in again, this time taking a long, looping practice swing before he settled himself in the batter's box. Tsitouris snapped off a sharp-breaking curve that just missed hitting the outside part of the plate. Chiti then called for another fastball. This time, Pumpsie jumped on it, catching it squarely on the barrel of his bat. As cheers erupted all throughout the stadium, the ball rocketed toward deep left, finally bouncing off the thirty-seven-foot-high wall known across baseball as the Green Monster. Running as fast as he could, Pumpsie rounded first, then second, and sped with all the strength he could muster toward third. A's left fielder, Russ Snyder, had trouble corralling the ball as it took an odd bounce after smacking the wall, so Pumpsie was already past second when he finally retrieved it. He grabbed the ball with his bare hand, whirled, and fired a strike to third base. However, Pumpsie timed his slide perfectly, catching the bag with his right shoe a fraction of a second before third baseman Dick Williams could swipe down his tag. While everyone in the stadium held their collective breath, third base umpire John Rice furiously swiped his arms back and forth across his chest and shouted, "Safe! Safe! Safe!"

As soon as Pumpsie called time and stood up to brush off his uniform, he was given another standing ovation, this one even louder and longer than the first. Reporters in the press box immediately ran to their typewriters and starting clicking out the lead for their stories. One fan behind the third base dugout called out so loudly Pumpsie could hear him above all the rest. "Green, it's about time! Way to go!"

The umpires, while still marveling at the jubilant reaction to Pumpsie's at-bat, finally had to motion for play to resume. Pumpsie took a long lead off third as the next batter, Pete Runnels, dug in for his turn at the plate. The first pitch to him was a ball, high and outside. Many in the stands finally sat down again, but they weren't there long. On the next pitch, Runnels lined a two-hopper to the right of the first baseman, who dove and was able to get his glove on the ball. However, Pumpsie, off at the crack of the bat, streaked home, sliding safely across home plate. For the third time in the inning, the fans stood and cheered, continuing to do so long after Pumpsie ducked into the dugout. Runnels, who had just barely been thrown out, lingered along the first base line so the crowd could devote full attention to Pumpsie. Pete stopped about fifteen feet from the dugout and started applauding. He then urged the rest of his teammates to do the same. Soon, everyone in the dugout mobbed Pumpsie, shaking his hand and offering their congratulations. Ted Williams was the last to come over. He extended his hand, shook Pumpsie's firmly, and said, laughing, "Enjoy it while you can. In a week, the writers will be calling you, like the rest of us, dog meat."

"I don't care," Pumpsie said, as tears welled in his eyes. "This has already been the greatest day of my life."

"Yeah, but what I want to know," Ted barked back, "is what in the heck are you going to do tomorrow for an encore?"

Pumpsie just grinned and said, "You'll just have to wait and watch!"

Both laughed as Higgins yelled at them to settle down and get back in the game. However, even he was smiling.

....

Pumpsie played in fifty more games during the 1959 season. He ended the year with a .233 batting average, far below his minor league numbers, but his defensive skills made him a valuable player in the Red Sox infield. He had a fine spring training again in 1960, this time breaking camp right along with the big club. Over the course of the '60 season, he appeared in 133 games, split between second base and shortstop, and again proved himself a defensive strength for the team. His batting average improved to a respectable .242, and Boston was convinced his development at the plate would continue in future seasons.

However, the 1961 campaign offered both the highlight, and the low point, of Pumpsie's Major League career. In spring training, he flirted with a .500 average, earning him the starting shortstop job as the team began the season. Coaches in the organization had been right: his offense continued to improve as the year progressed, and his batting average rose to .260. He also slugged 12 doubles, knocked in 27 runs, hit six round-trippers and even stole four bases. All was going well until Pumpsie started having pains and cramps in his side as May rolled around. Doctors soon discovered he needed an operation to have his appendix removed. Because of complications, he missed nearly a month and a half of playing time while recovering, costing him games during the best season of his life.

The 1962 season was a disaster right from the start. In later years, Pumpsie often suggested that he was likely still suffering the lingering effects of the previous year's surgery, which had caused him to lose quite a lot of weight—and his stamina and strength. He started the year slowly at the plate and soon found himself on the bench. The club had signed veteran shortstop Eddie Bressoud before the start of the season as infield insurance, so when Pumpsie's difficulties continued, he lost his starting role. He ended the year getting into just 56 games and, when he did play, he was used was primarily as a pinch hitter and late-inning defensive replacement.

After limited play during that season, and with Bressoud playing well in his place, Boston decided to trade Pumpsie that winter to the New York Mets. He did not play well in spring training before the '63 season, largely the result of injuries and not being in shape, so he wasn't asked to start the season with the club. Instead, he was sent to the minors, where he ended up spending most of the season. He was finally promoted to New York after the September call-ups but was played sparingly, getting into just seventeen games. Finally, on September 26, 1963, he was penciled into the lineup for a game against Los Angeles Dodgers. He went 1-4 that night and made two spectacular plays in the field while playing third base. It was his last contest in the Major Leagues. Pumpsie did play two more years in the minors but called it a career before the 1966 season. His Major League record included a .246 batting average, 13 home runs, 12 stolen bases, and 344 games played.

After retiring from baseball, Pumpsie worked for the Berkeley, California, school district. There, he became a very popular math teacher, adored by his students and admired by his colleagues. He wasn't sure he wanted to do it at first, but he was also finally talked into coaching the Berkeley High School baseball team. He was a natural in that role and remained as the coach for twenty-five years. At the same time, he spoke as often as he could to youth groups in the area and served as mentor and counselor for troubled youth.

On April 17, 2009, the Boston Red Sox invited Pumpsie back to Fenway Park to honor him and to have him throw out the ceremonial first pitch to help commemorate the 50th anniversary of his helping tear down the color barrier for the franchise. As it was during his first trip to the plate at Fenway in 1959, Pumpsie was greeted by a rousing standing ovation.

Pumpsie Green passed away on July 17, 2019, leaving behind a legacy of admiration and respect.

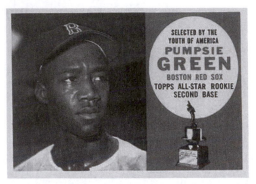

1960 Topps #317, Pumpsie Green
Courtesy of The Topps Company, Inc.

Epilogue

THE LIVES AND ACCOMPLISHMENTS of the "other fifteen" after their playing careers were over were detailed at the end of each chapter included here. Therefore, instead of recounting that information, I will note a few other areas in the saga of these pioneers.

This book was a labor of love to write but also, at times, incredibly challenging to put together. First of all, no book about these individuals would be complete without at least some discussion of a question that pops up often in the historical record. It seems just about everyone, and not just fans of baseball, know that when Jackie Robinson took the field for the Brooklyn Dodgers in April of 1947, he was the first person of color to participate in a Major League game in the modern era. But, while so many know Jackie was the groundbreaker, what immediately becomes fuzzy right after that knowledge is this question: *Who* really were the "other fifteen" men?

During my research, I discovered that there were many different lists of what players were first for the different organizations. Organizations from Major League Baseball itself to the National Baseball Hall of Fame to the Library of Congress to prominent sports networks and organizations had slightly different versions, complete with all manner of explanations and justifications. The deeper I dug, the more I discovered different definitions for "person of color" were used by the various groups when deciding which player broke the barrier for each individual team. Some lists focused primarily on the first African American players to appear in a regular season game for the teams. Other lists included players of Latin ancestry. Some focused simply on the first non-Caucasian players to take the field. Still other lists made use of a blend of all these.

On top of that, some lists ignored completely the actual *chronology* involved. Confusing? Very much so.

A number of organizations declare that on April 13, 1954, Curt Roberts, an African American, broke the color barrier for the Pittsburgh Pirates. However, Carlos Bernier, who was from Puerto Rico and whose family was of African ancestry, debuted for the Pirates almost a full year before on April 22, 1953. So, why isn't Mr. Bernier listed as the Pirates' pioneer on many lists? Complicating the Bernier case, almost every organization generally accepts that Carlos Paula, also from the same region of Cuba and also of African ancestry, broke the color barrier for the Washington Senators in 1954. Why accept Paula as the first for his team and not Bernier for his?

Much of the disagreement in the lists seems to stem from how individuals of Latin ancestry and heritage were viewed. For instance, Chico Fernandez, who also grew up in Cuba, stated repeatedly in interviews that he did not consider himself Black, as the media most certainly did—many reporters of the time describing him as a "Negro" player—because his family traced their heritage back to Spain. Fernandez played as a regular for the Philadelphia Phillies almost two weeks before John Kennedy, an African American, got into a game. Because of how Fernandez chose to self-identify, Kennedy is generally credited as the individual who knocked aside the color barrier for the Phillies—but Fernandez still does show up first on several lists. And, what about Nino Escalera? He appeared one batter before Chuck Harmon on April 17, 1954 in Cincinnati's game against Milwaukee. Mr. Escalera, from Puerto Rico, was of African ancestry, yet Harmon is most often recognized as the groundbreaker for Cincinnati, adding confusion for fans and baseball historians.

Then, consider the case of Hank Thompson. Most groups list Mr. Thompson as the groundbreaker for the St. Louis Browns when he appeared in a game for them on July 17, 1947. However, Hank also appeared in a game for the New York Giants on July 8, 1949, starting the game at third base. Monte Irvin got into that same game as a pinch hitter in the 8th inning, and it is Monte, *not* Thompson, who now shows up most often as breaking the color barrier for the Giants, which is simply not accurate if order of appearance is used. If strict *chronology* is followed when dissecting the baseball history, then Hank Thompson should be listed as the groundbreaking individual for *two* Major League Baseball teams, the Browns *and* the Giants. However, and curiously, that is seldom the case.

It finally became apparent to me that having *one* list everyone could agree upon wasn't going to happen, so I decided to respect the lists "collectively." That is, to me, what was most important here wasn't about who appeared first. The greatest importance is that the other fifteen teams eventually—a long, drawn-out road for many of them—joined in ending a terrible, restrictive practice. For some teams, this involved putting multiple players on the field either at the same time or in very close order. Therefore, I decided to use the "generally accepted" list of the "other 15" individuals but would reserve the right to make note of and recognize the contributions of those who also participated in initiating this dramatic change. *All* of these individuals are important in their own way. *All* had courage, determination, and the inner-strength that allowed them to take their place in history.

The next challenge was choosing from so many stories that could have been told about each of these pioneers. Early in my research, I discovered the historical records for these men often consist of multiple, *and quite different*, accounts of their accomplishments, both on and off the field. Separating fact from fiction—and even, at times, *legend*—was difficult. There are multiple reasons for this. First, the reporting related to contests in the Negro Leagues, where many began their professional careers, was often spotty at best in the newspapers of the era. Many of the game records were simply not preserved. Although oral history accounts of many of those games have been collected through the years and are invaluable resources, *time* can sometimes do strange things to the memories of those who later spoke of the games.

Also, when many of these pioneers finally did reach the Major Leagues, bias in reporting often led to their accomplishments being ignored or downplayed, or even their individual character being attacked. Two quick examples are how sportswriters repeatedly mocked Carlos Paula's lack of proficiency in English, which overshadowed what he did on the field. Newspaper accounts often described Hank Thompson as "lazy" in every facet of his life. Information about Thompson also differs so much from piece to piece it is often difficult to believe they cover the same individual. Sadly, descriptions such as these were common. They were also grossly inaccurate—and often replaced chronicles of these players' on-field performance, leaving a gaping hole in their records. In addition, when their actual accomplishments *were* reported, they were often buried in the back pages of sports sections.

The challenges here were significant but, while some discrepancies and debates existed at times in the historical record, what was common and at the forefront throughout was just how important the contributions of these men were. Issues of race, color, and national origin formed the backdrop for many of their stories—on both sides of that long and irregular fence—because they were at times welcomed, despised, or a combination of both when they joined their respective teams. However, while facing these challenges, they provided a spark so desperately needed during this time of change.

Change came slowly, but consider the most recent diversity report prepared by Major League Baseball. This report (2018-19) states that 42% of today's Major League players are persons of color, quite a change from when Jackie stepped on the field by himself. The fifteen who followed him continued building upon the legacy started by Jackie Robinson and helped pave the way for even greater opportunities for those who followed. The foundation built by these men will continue to provide inspiration and lessons for all time.

….. ….. …..

Acknowledgments

This book could not have been written without the generous assistance provided by many organizations and individuals, all of whom gave freely of their time and knowledge.

First and foremost, I'd like to give my warmest thanks to Cassidy Lent, Reference Librarian, Emily Wilson, Reference Librarian, and John W. Horne, Jr., all of the National Baseball Hall of Fame and Museum, for allowing me to ask endless questions—and for allowing me into their special collections and archival material. It was like entering holy ground. My days there at the Hall of Fame were invaluable—and some of the best days of my writing life.

The many Research Librarians at the Library of Congress who helped source historical documents and records—and helped me gain digital access during the time of the pandemic. They went above and beyond to help with this research at a time of great distress for everyone in the country, and their contributions can't be acknowledged enough.

Jason Stratman, Librarian and Research Specialist, Missouri Historical Society Library and Research Center, for helping secure everything from baseball box scores to ballpark histories to newspaper accounts of games and players, and biographical information about the players, managers, and owners described in the pages of this book. This book could not have been written without his wonderful assistance.

All the individuals, everyone from researchers, historians, and clerks, at the individual baseball organization museums, archives, and records centers. Everything—from our phone conversations to Zoom and FaceTime meetings to our general mail correspondence—made it possible for this book to be written at a time when face-to-face meetings were impossible because of issues related to the pandemic. Your assistance was invaluable, and your kindness and support will never be forgotten.

Douglas Hartley, for his wonderful photography and image collection.

Brock Swarbrick, graphic designer, for assistance with manuscript preparation and layout/design consultation.

Hadley Barrett, Senior Executive Assistant, and Valerie Fabbro, Associate General Councel, at Topps Incorporated for help sourcing historical images and player biographical information.

Mrs. Maria Green, wife of Pumpsie Green, for historical and biographical information related to her husband's life and baseball career. Her "clarifications" of the historical record were extremely helpful and appreciated.

Tazena Kennedy, daughter of John Kennedy, for allowing me to interview her about the life and career of her father.

Raymond Doswell, Curator of the Negro Leagues Baseball Museum (Kansas City), for his expertise, advice, and suggestions in the initial stages of this project.

Todd A. Davidovits, Anheuser-Busch, Inc., for his assistance in tracking down team photographs.

Michael Anderson, Public Relations Manager, Cincinnati Reds Baseball Club, for information related to Chuck Harmon and Nino Escalera (and historical photographs).

Bill Christensen, writer and baseball historian, for sharing his knowledge of the Pacific Coast League and the players in this book who played there.

Dr. Jennifer Cooley, Latin American culture and history specialist at the University of Northern Iowa, for providing valuable background related to the careers of Minnie Minoso, Carlos Paula, Chico Fernandez, Nino Escalera, and Carlos Bernier.

Richard Noffke, for historical photos and baseball history accounts.

Dave Dowling, baseball historian, for sharing his vast knowledge of the Negro Leagues and its history and players.

Ronald Britt, baseball historian and sports memorabilia expert, for background information related to the lives and careers of the players.

Ben Gassaway, Mile High Auctions, for his advice and encouragement of the project—and for providing historical photos and documents.

Max Sullivan, graphic artist, for assistance with photo sourcing and image consultation. In addition, my gratitude is extended for providing the custom baseball card image of John Kennedy.

Larry Fritch Cards, Inc. (FritchCards.com), for providing the custom baseball card image of Nino Escalera.

Gordon Anderson, publisher, for his inspiration, encouragement, and support of my writing career.

I would also like to thank Rosemary Yokoi, the best editor I've ever known, for her guidance and friendship through the years.

Finally, I'd like to thank my wife, Linda, for providing editorial assistance and help gathering research materials—and for putting up with and supporting all the time and travel required to complete this project.

Sources Consulted

This section must begin with a special acknowledgment to the National Baseball Hall of Fame and Museum in Cooperstown, N.Y., who allowed me special access to their collections of archival documents, biographies, oral histories, photographs, and team and player statistics and histories. Their resources were used for every section of this book.

All player statistics, game box scores, and team histories were checked with the records of the National Baseball Hall of Fame and the Society for American Baseball Research (SABR).

In addition, a special thank you to the Library of Congress, which allowed online access to its vast holdings of audio recordings, books, films and videos, newspaper and periodical archives, and personal narratives related to baseball and its history.

Books Consulted:

Appel, Marty. *Pinstripe Empire: The New York Yankees from Before the Babe to After The Boss*. London, England/New York: Bloomsbury, 2014.

Borst, Bill, Bill Rogers, and Ed Wheatley. *St. Louis Browns: The Story of a Beloved Team*. St. Louis, MO: Reedy Press, 2017.

Branson, Douglas M. *Greatness in the Shadows: Larry Doby and the Integration of the American League*. Lincoln, NE: University of Nebraska Press, 2016.

Broeg, Bob. *The St. Louis Cardinals Encyclopedia*. Carrolton, TX: Masters Press, 1998.

Bruce, Janet. *The Kansas City Monarchs: Champions of Black Baseball*. Lawrence, KS: University Press of Kansas, 1985.

Craig, William J. *A History of the Boston Braves: A Time Gone By*. Charleston, SC: The History Press, 2012.

Deveaux, Tom. *The Washington Senators, 1901-1971*. Jefferson, NC: McFarland, 2001.

Eig, Jonathan. *Opening day: The Story of Jackie Robinson's First Season*. New York: Simon & Schuster, 2008.

Freedman, Lou. *Ernie Banks: The Life and Career of "Mr. Cub."* Jefferson, NC: McFarland, 2019.

Frommer, Frederic J. *You Gotta Have Heart: A History of Washington Baseball from 1859 to the 2012 National League East Champions*. Dallas, TX: Taylor Trade Publishing, 2013.

Golenbock, Peter. *The Spirit of St. Louis: A History of the St. Louis Cardinals and Browns*. New York: William Morrow, 2000.

Gummer, Scott, ed. *The Philadelphia Phillies: An Extraordinary Tradition*. New York: Insight Editions, 2010.

Heaphy, Leslie, A. *Black Ball 9: New Research in African American Baseball History*. Jefferson, SC: McFarland, 2017.

Heaphy, Leslie A. *Satchel Paige and Company: Essays on the Kansas City Monarchs, Their   Greatest Star, and the Negro Leagues*. Jefferson, SC: McFarland, 2007.

Hogan, Lawrence D. *Shades of Glory: The Negro Leagues and the Story of African-American Baseball*. Washington, D.C.: National Geographic: 2006.

Holway, John B. *The Complete Book of Baseball's Negro Leagues*. New York: Hastings House, 1998.

Howard, Arlene, and Ralph Winbish. *Elston: The Story of the First African-American Yankee*. Guilford, CT: Lyons Press, 2018.

Howard, Arlene, and Ralph Winbish. *Elston and Me: The Story of the First Black Yankee*. Columbia, MO: University of Missouri Press, 2001.

Impemba, Mario, and Mike Isenberg. *If These Walls Could Talk: Stories from the Detroit Tigers' Dugout, Locker Room, and Press Box*. Chicago, IL: Triumph Books, 2014.

Johnson, Richard A. *Boston Braves*. Mount Pleasant, SC: Arcadia Publishing, 2001.

Kaese, Harold. *The Boston Braves, 1871-1953* (Sportsman Series). Lebanon, NH: Northeastern University Press, 2004.

Kepner, Tyler. *The Phillies Experience: A Year-By-Year Chronicle of the Philadelphia Phillies*. London, England: MVP Books, 2013.

Kubek, Tony. *Sixty-One: The Team, the Record, the Men*. New York: Fireside, 1989.

Lanctot, Neil. *Negro League Baseball: The Rise and Ruin of a Black Institution*. Philadelphia, PA: University of Pennsylvania Press, 2008.

Leptich, John, and Dave Baranowski. *This Date in Cardinals History*. New York : Stein and Day, 1983.

McCollister, John. *The Bucs! The Story of the Pittsburgh Pirates*. Guilford, CT:

Lyons Press, 2016.

Minoso, Minnie, with Herb Fagan. *Just Call Me Minnie: My Six Decades in Baseball*. New York: Sports Publishing, LLC, 1994.

Minoso, Minnie, with Fernando Fernandez and Robert Kleinfelder. *Extra Innings: My Life in Baseball*. New York: Gateway Books, 1983.

Moore, Joseph Thomas. *Larry Doby: The Struggle of the American League's First Black Player*. New York: Dover Publications, 2012.

Nowlin, Bill. *Pumpsie and Progress: The Red Sox, Race, and Redemption*. Boston, MA: Rounder Books, 2010.

Peterson, Richard. *The Pirates Reader*. Pittsburgh, PA: University of Pittsburg Press, 2003.

Peterson, Robert. *Only the Ball Was White: A History of Legendary Black Players and All-Black Professional Teams*. New York: Oxford University Press, 1992.

Pieratt, Marty Ford. *First Black Red: The Story of Chuck Harmon, the First African American To Play for the Cincinnati Reds*. Bloomington, IN: AuthorHouse, 2010.

Rains, Rob. *The St. Louis Cardinals: The Official 100th Anniversary History*. New York: St. Martin's Press, 1992.

Rampersand, Arnold. *Jackie Robinson: A Biography*. New York: Ballantine Books, 1997.

Rampoport, Ron. *Let's Play Two: The Legend of Mr. Cub, the Life of Ernie Banks*. New York: Hachette Books, 2019.

Ranier, Bill, and David Finoli. *The Pittsburgh Pirates Encyclopedia, 2nd ed*. New York: Sports Publishing, 2015.

Ribowsky, Mark. *A Complete History of the Negro Leagues: 1884 to 1955*. New York: Kensington Publishing Corporation, 2000.

Riley, James A. *The Biographical Encyclopedia of the Negro Baseball Leagues*. New York: Carroll & Graf, 2002.

Robinson, Jackie: *I Never Had It Made: An Autobiography*. New York: Putnam, 1972.

Rogers, Phil. *Ernie Banks: Mr. Cub and the Summer of '69*. Chicago, IL: Triumph Books, 2011.

Rogosin, Donn. *Invisible Men: Life in Baseball's Negro Leagues*. Lincoln: University of Nebraska Press, 2020.

Schwanke, Douglas C. *Washington Senators: History and Biographies*. Charleston, SC: BookSurge, 2008.

Stanton, Tom. *The Detroit Tigers Reader*. Ann Arbor, MI: University of Michigan Press, 2005.

Stewart, Wayne. *The History of the Cincinnati Reds* (Baseball Series). Mankato, MN: Creative Company, 2002.

Stone, Robert W. *Pumpsie Green and Boston's Struggle to Integrate the Red Sox.* Scotts Valley, CA: Creative Space Independent Publishing, 2016.

Taylor, Ted. *The Ultimate Philadelphia Athletics Reference Book 1901-1954.* Bloomington, IN: Xlibris Corporation, 2010.

Vanderberg, Bob. *Minnie and the Mick: The Go-Go White Sox Challenge the Fabled Yankee Dynasty, 1954-1964.* Lanham, MD: Rowman & Littlefield-Diamond Communications,1996.

Virtue, John. *South of the Color Barrier: How Jorge Pasquel and the Mexican League Pushed Baseball Toward Racial Integration.* Jefferson, NC: McFarland,2007.

Museums and Baseball Organizations consulted:

The resources of the following museums and organizations affiliated with specific professional baseball teams and baseball leagues were also consulted regularly for baseball statistics, game descriptions, and player information:

Baseball Heritage Museum—Note: for Cleveland Indians history (Cleveland, OH)

Boston Braves Historical Association (website and database)

Chicago Baseball Museum—Note: records for both Chicago White Sox and Chicago Cubs (Chicago, IL)

Cincinnati Reds Hall of Fame and Museum (Cincinnati, OH)

The Clemente Museum (Pittsburgh, PA)

Detroit Historical Society and Museum (Detroit, MI)

Hispanic Heritage Baseball Museum (website and database)

National Ballpark Museum (Denver, CO)

The National Baseball Hall of Fame "Starting Nine" special exhibits prepared for each team and highlighting players and team histories.

Negro Leagues Baseball Museum (Kansas City, MO)

New York Giants Preservation Society (website and database)

New York Yankees Museum (Yankee Stadium, New York, NY)

Philadelphia Athletics Museum and Library (Hatboro, PA)

Philadelphia Historical Society (website and database)

Philadelphia History Museum (Philadelphia, PA)

St. Louis Browns Historical Society (St. Louis, MO)
St. Louis Cardinals Hall of Fame and Museum (St. Louis, MO)
The Sports Museum (also called New England Sports Museum)—Note: for
          Boston   Red Sox history (Boston, MA)
Western Pennsylvania Sports Museum—Note: for records for Pittsburgh Pirates
          (Pittsburgh, PA)

Additional Online Resources and Databases Consulted:

Baseball Federation of Cuba archives and database
International League Hall of Fame
Mexican Baseball League archives and database
The Missouri History Museum Library and Research Center, St. Louis, Missouri
Pacific Coast League Special Collections and Hall of Fame
Society for American Baseball Research (SABR.org) player biographies and sta-
          tistics (all baseball fans are welcome to join).
South Atlantic League Hall of Fame
Southern League Hall of Fame
Texas League Hall of Fame
Topps Inc. archives and database

Online/Digital Newspaper Archives
(for box scores and game accounts):

Boston Globe
Chicago Tribune
Chicago Defender
Cincinnati Enquirer
Cincinnati Herald
Cleveland Plain Dealer
Cleveland Call and Post
Detroit Informer
Detroit Free Press
New York Post
New York Herald Tribune
Philadelphia Inquirer
Philadelphia Tribune

Pittsburgh Post-Gazette
Pittsburgh Courier
Richmond Afro American
St. Louis American
St. Louis Globe-Democrat
Washington Afro American
Washington Post

Personal Interviews:

Personal interview with Maria Green (wife of Pumpsie Green)
Personal interview with Tazena Kennedy (daughter of John Kennedy)

Oral Histories Consulted:

Louie B. Nunn Center for Oral History (Baseball Collection), University of
     Kentucky
National Baseball Hall of Fame Digital Collection (oral histories)
PBS Learning Media Oral History Interviews (Negro Leagues)
Society for American Baseball Research Oral History Collection
University of Baltimore Oral History Collection (Negro Leagues)

Archival Film Footage:

MLB "Digital Video Archive"
MLB "Film Room" Collection
National Archives "America's Favorite Pastime" Collection

Photo Credits

Cover Photo:

Jackie Robinson cover photo used courtesy of Mile High Auction Company and Ben Gassaway, Auction Coordinator.

Baseball Card Images:

Topps® trading cards used courtesy of The Topps Company, Inc., and they include the following images:

1951 Bowman #242, Sam Jethro
1953 Topps #20, Hank Thompson
1955 Topps #50, Jackie Robinson
1955 Topps #82, Chuck Harmon
1955 Topps #100, Monte Irvin
1955 Topps #107, Curt Roberts
1955 Topps #132, Bob Trice
1955 Bowman #257, Tom Alston
1956 Topps #4, Carlos Paula
1956 Topps #125, Minnie Minoso
1956 Topps #208, Elston Howard
1958 Topps #424, Larry Doby
1959 Topps #203, Ossie Virgil
1960 Topps #10, Ernie Banks
1960 Topps #317, Pumpsie Green

John Kennedy baseball card used courtesy of Max Sullivan Collection
Nino Escalera baseball card used courtesy of Larry Fritsch Cards (FritchCards. com)

Team Photos:

1957 St. Louis Cardinals Team Photo used courtesy Anheuser-Busch, St. Louis, Missouri
All other team photos from the Copeland Collection

Player Photos:

The following player photos used courtesy of the National Baseball Hall of Fame and Museum: Ernie Banks, Larry Doby, Elston Howard, Sam Jethro, John Kennedy, Minnie Minoso, Carlos Paula, Curt Roberts.

The following player photos are from the Copeland Collection: Hank Thompson, Monte Irvin, Bob Trice, Chuck Harmon, Ossie Virgil.

Tom Alston photo, and photo of Hank Thompson and Williard Brown, used courtesy of the Richard Noffke Collection.

Pumpsie Green photo from the Jay Publishing Collection.

Additional Photos:

Photo of the Tom Alston memorial plaque used courtesy of Douglas Hartley, St. Louis, Missouri.

About the Author

Jeffrey S. Copeland is a lifelong St. Louis Cardinals baseball fan and former member of the ownership groups of the Waterloo Indians (Cleveland Indians Class A affiliate in the Midwest League) and Waterloo Diamonds (San Diego Padres affiliate in the Midwest League). Jeffrey has also written for numerous sports publications, including *Sports Collectors Digest*.

He has also authored and edited over thirty books, including *Plague in Paradise: The Black Death in Los Angeles, 1924*; *Inman's War: A Soldier's Story of Life in a Colored Battalion in WWII*; *Olivia's Story: The Conspiracy of Heroes Behind Shelley v. Kraemer*; *Shell Games: The Life and Times of Pearl McGill, Industrial Spy and Pioneer Labor Activist*; *Ain't No Harm to Kill the Devil: The Life and Legend of John Fairfield, Abolitionist for Hire*; *Lt. Elsie Ott's Top Secret Mission: The WWII Flight Nurse Pioneer of Aeromedical Evacuation* (MEDEVAC); and *Finding Fairfield*. He is also a member of the Society for American Baseball Research (SABR).

When not writing or attending baseball games, he is a professor at the University of Northern Iowa. He lives in Cedar Falls, Iowa and St. Louis, Missouri.